Implementing the SIOP® Model through Effective Professional Development and Coaching

Jana Echevarría

California State University, Long Beach

Deborah J. Short

Center for Applied Linguistics, Washington, DC

Academic Language Research & Training, Arlington, VA

MaryEllen Vogt

California State University, Long Beach

Keep SIOP ing, Susan
Deborah Short

PEARSON

Boston   New York   San Francisco

Mexico City   Montreal   Toronto   London   Madrid   Munich   Paris

Hong Kong   Singapore   Tokyo   Cape Town   Sydney

> *To all the English learners in our schools who deserve the high-quality teaching that the educators in this book provide.*

Executive Editor: Aurora Martínez Ramos
Editorial Assistant: Lynda Giles
Marketing Manager: Danae April
Production Editor: Gregory Erb
Editorial Production Service: Nesbitt Graphics, Inc.
Composition Buyer: Linda Cox
Manufacturing Buyer: Linda Morris
Electronic Composition: Nesbitt Graphics, Inc.
Interior Design: Nesbitt Graphics, Inc.
Cover Designer: Kristina Mose-Libon

For related titles and support materials, visit our online catalog at www.ablongman.com.

Between the time website information is gathered and then published, it is not unusual for some sites to have closed. Also, the transcription of URLs can result in typographical errors. The publisher would appreciate notification where these errors occur so that they may be corrected in subsequent editions.

ISBN 10: 0-205-53333-7
ISBN 13: 978-0-205-53333-6

Library of Congress Cataloging-in-Publication Data was not available at press time.

Printed in the United States of America

10 9 8 7 6 5 4 3 2 CIN 11 10 09 08 07

Photo Credits: pages 1, 25, 41, 65, 119, 165, 183: © Bob Daemmrich Photography; pp. 11, 31, 50, 67, 87, 116, 121, 167: Courtesy of the authors.

contents

5 Coaching with the SIOP® Model 64

6 Enhancing and Sustaining SIOP® Implementation 86

7 Classroom Implementation of the SIOP® Model   118

8 The Impact of the SIOP® Model on Students and Teachers   164

What makes the difference between wishing and realizing our wishes? Lots of things, of course, but the main one, I think, is whether we link our wishes to our active work. It may take months or years, but it's far more likely to happen when we care so much that we'll work as hard as we can to make it happen. And when we're working toward the realization of our wishes, some of our greatest strengths come from the encouragement of people who care about us.

—Fred Rogers

In his book *The World According to Mister Rogers: Important Things to Remember* (2004; Hyperion of New York), Fred Rogers suggests how to turn our wishes into reality through hard work—with the support of those who care about us. What are your wishes about providing appropriate, effective educational experiences for all of the students in your school and district? If you are like the majority of teachers and administrators who care deeply for their students, the quotation above by a famous, caring educator may be especially relevant for one particular group of students with whom you work. These children and youth are English learners (ELs; also known as English language learners or ELLs), those youngsters who enter our schools with diverse personal, educational, cultural, and language differences.

What these students have in common is a wish to be educated, and through hard work and capable teachers, their wishes can be realized. This book describes how teachers and administrators have learned to provide appropriate language and content instruction for English learners in elementary, middle, and high schools throughout the country. In the pages that follow, and in their own words, you will "hear" the voices of educators who are learning how to make content comprehensible for English learners through the effective implementation of the SIOP® Model.

If you have selected this book, you are most likely a classroom teacher, ESL or bilingual teacher, special educator, curriculum specialist, professional developer, and/or administrator responsible for the academic achievement of students who are acquiring English as a second or multiple language. We hope this book increases your knowledge of the SIOP® Model while improving the effectiveness of the work you are doing on behalf of the English learners in your charge. We also hope this book will help you realize wishes for students, and that through some hard work and collaboration with those who care, the academic achievement of your English learners will be enhanced.

What is the SIOP® Model?

The Sheltered Instruction Observation Protocol (SIOP®) Model was developed to provide teachers with a well-articulated, practical model of sheltered instruction. The intent of the model is to facilitate high-quality instruction for English learners in the content areas. The model, based on current knowledge and research-based instructional practices, embeds critical features of high-quality instruction for English learners. The SIOP® Model was first published in *Making Content Comprehensible for English Learners: The SIOP® Model* (Echevarria, Vogt, & Short, 2000, 2004, 2008).

Administrators and teachers alike are frequently bombarded with new approaches, reform efforts, and initiatives that sometimes seem to be in competition with one another.

Often what is lacking in schools is coherence, or a plan for pulling together sound practices (Goldenberg, 2004). The SIOP® Model meets this issue head-on because it is viewed as an umbrella under which other instructional programs and reform efforts reside. The SIOP® Model is not another "add-on," but rather a framework that brings together a school's instructional programs by organizing teaching methods and techniques that ensure effective practices are implemented in a quantifiable manner by teachers, across grade levels and subject areas.

The eight components and a description of the thirty features of the SIOP® Model follow (see Echevarria, Vogt, & Short, 2008, for the Sheltered Instruction Observation Protocol):

1. **Preparation.** Teachers plan their lessons carefully, including attention to language and content objectives, appropriate content concepts, the use of supplemental materials, adaptation of content, and meaningful activities.

2. **Building Background.** Teachers make explicit links to their students' background experiences and knowledge and past learning, teaching and emphasizing key vocabulary.

3. **Comprehensible Input.** Teachers use a variety of techniques to make instruction understandable, including speech appropriate to students' English proficiency; clear academic tasks; and modeling, the use of visuals, hands-on activities, demonstrations, gestures, and body language.

4. **Strategies.** Teachers provide students with instruction in and practice with a variety of learning strategies, scaffolding their teaching with techniques such as think-alouds, and they promote higher-order thinking through a variety of question types and levels.

5. **Interaction.** Teachers provide students with frequent opportunities for interaction and discussion, group students to support the content and language objectives, provide sufficient wait time for student responses, and appropriately clarify concepts in the students' first language, if possible and necessary.

6. **Practice and Application.** Teachers provide hands-on materials and/or manipulatives and include activities for students to apply their content and language knowledge through all language skills (reading, writing, listening, speaking).

7. **Lesson Delivery.** Teachers implement lessons that clearly support content and language objectives with appropriate pacing, while students are engaged 90 to 100 percent of the instructional period.

8. **Review and Assessment.** Teachers provide a comprehensive review of key vocabulary and concepts; regularly give specific, academic feedback to students; and assess student comprehension and learning throughout the lesson.

What began as an observation protocol has now evolved into an empirically validated model of instruction for English learners, where the focus is on the concurrent teaching and learning of both language and content. While the SIOP® Model was originally substantiated with middle school students, it is now being implemented in pre-K through grade 12 throughout the United States. Our research has shown that given sustained professional development (from one to three years), teachers can learn to implement the thirty features consistently and systematically, from lesson to lesson (see Echevarria,

Vogt, & Short, 2008; Echevarria, Short, & Powers, 2006; and Chapter 8). Current longitudinal research studies are investigating the efficacy of the SIOP® Model with varied student populations over time.

Overview of SIOP® Implementation

Why This Book?

The SIOP® Model has been embraced throughout the United States and numerous other countries as an effective way to teach English learners. There are many issues regarding the implementation of the model, and this book is intended to assist teachers, schools, school districts, and universities in using the SIOP® Model effectively. Lessons have been learned along the way by personnel in schools, districts, and universities who have worked with the SIOP® Model in classrooms throughout the country. After receiving many questions about how to use the model effectively, we decided to ask the experts, those educators who have experienced success with it, both in terms of improvement of academic achievement for ELs and in teacher change.

The information in this book comes from a two-year study conducted with school districts in the United States (descriptions of the districts are found in Chapter 1). The purpose of the study was to learn how these districts and schools designed professional development in the SIOP® Model. During the many interviews of those who have been implementing the SIOP® Model, some similarities emerged from their suggestions and advice.

First, individuals learning the model need to have some background in second language acquisition and issues of English learners. Many of the features of the SIOP® Model reflect good instruction for all students. However, several of these same features take on a different level of complexity when teaching ELs. For example, differentiating instruction becomes more complex when teachers understand the levels of language proficiency and the stages of second language acquisition. Scaffolding is multifaceted when teachers support a student's learning of English because the teacher must consider the student's previous learning (in a different language, culture, and educational system); find a way to make the message understandable in English; and consider the student's need for assistance in completing tasks. Flexible grouping configurations to increase student-to-student interaction are essential for ELs because they provide students with necessary practice in English and reinforce academic English. While the features of the SIOP® Model are consistent with high-quality instruction for all students, certain instructional practices are critical for English learners. These can be implemented well only when teachers have an understanding of second language issues.

Second, in order to understand the model and implement it well, effective teachers must have a deep understanding of the core text, *Making Content Comprehensible,* so appropriate instructional strategies and techniques can be implemented to a high degree. Knowing the SIOP® Model well ensures fidelity to the model and promotes student achievement. Teachers and administrators who have seen positive results with the SIOP® Model have frequently reported that they spent time in book study discussions of the core text.

Third, there must be ongoing support and professional development for teachers to gain a deep understanding of the model and to implement it consistently and to a high degree (see Chapter 2: What the Research Says about Professional Development). The support has been provided in a number of ways, such as coaching, peer observations, mentoring, demonstration lessons, structured discussions, and so forth. These and other approaches are detailed in Chapter 3 (Getting Started and Building Capacity with SIOP® Professional Development), Chapter 4 (Models of SIOP® Implementation and Professional Development), Chapter 5 (Coaching with the SIOP® Model), and Chapter 6 (Enhancing and Sustaining SIOP® Implementation).

Finally, there is not one exclusive way to implement the SIOP® Model effectively. Some successful professional development efforts have focused on the belief that even with teachers who are committed to the SIOP® Model, administrative leadership at the school or district level is the first step in the process. Other equally successful programs have been grassroots efforts with the training of teachers preceding the acquisition of administrative support. There are reports of teachers learning together, teaching each other, observing, and providing constructive and supportive assistance—while at the same time working to bring the administration along (see Chapter 7: Classroom Implementation of the SIOP® Model, for a variety of examples). You will also notice throughout the book that interviewees refer to SIOP Institutes® where they received initial and ongoing professional development. A brief history of the SIOP® Model and descriptions of SIOP Institutes® are included in Appendix A.

Chapter 8 (The Impact of the SIOP® Model on Students and Teachers) entails how those involved in SIOP® implementation describe the influence of the model on their teachers and students. As always, we emphatically endorse data collection—as a field, we need more than anecdotes to support effective instruction for English learners. The book concludes with an Epilogue of lessons learned where we present some of the issues faced when implementing an innovative instructional approach such as the SIOP® Model and some advice from those who have experienced these issues.

Throughout this book, we work from the assumption that you are already familiar with the SIOP® Model, including having read the core text (Echevarria, Vogt, & Short, 2008). If you have come upon this book without the requisite background, please back up and read in detail about the SIOP® Model. It will make this text much more relevant to your current educational context.

We would like to express sincere and heartfelt appreciation to the many individuals who participated in the study described in this book. They are to be commended for providing the field with their valuable insights, and without them our work would not have such rich dimensions and grounded insights. It is important to point out that implementing the SIOP® Model is an ongoing process, and what you will read about in this book are true accounts with successes, challenges, and occasional warts. Our purpose is not to endorse one approach over another, but rather to report what is happening throughout the country at the time of this publication. Further, the individuals interviewed are not the only educators with whom we've worked who are implementing the SIOP® Model successfully in schools. However, these interviewees were selected to provide readers with a variety of experiences, from rural and urban schools, from large districts to small ones, from elementary and secondary settings, and from different regions of the country. We welcome hearing from any reader who has successfully implemented the SIOP® Model as well as those who have seen gains in student achievement. We invite you to share your experiences with us—as we all continue to improve and refine our content and language instruction for English learners.

The SIOP® pioneers and superb educators who have shared their work in this book include the following:

Tammy Becker, Laurie Beebe, Melissa Castillo, Mark Crossman, Charlotte Daniel, Susan Dean, Stefan DeVries, Amy Ditton, Dalis Dominguez, Elizabeth Fralicks, Wendy Fraño, Susan Hanson, Alvaro Hernandez, Socorro Herrera, Wanda Holbrook, Debbie Hutson, Magdieh Jawad, Denise Johnson, Shabina Kavimandan, Wilfredo Laboy, Suzanne Meador, Alicia Miguel, Kendra Moreno, Rebecca Peronteaux, Gail Rosengard, Marilyn Sanchez, Rosie Santana, Maura Sedgeman, John Seidlitz, Nicole Teyechea, Ivanna Mann Thrower, Martha Trejo, Leellyn Tuel, and Liz Warner. A very special thank you to Rebecca Dennis Canges, whose invaluable assistance made completion of this book possible.

Finally, our wish is that your wishes regarding the success of your English learners are realized through what Mr. Rogers advocated—hard work with the SIOP® Model, and the support of those who care about us.

je, ds, mev

Where Is the SIOP® Model Being Implemented?

It touches my heart that so many districts are reaching out to find ways to help English learners, and SIOP® is the way to do it. Five years ago I wouldn't have imagined I would be working with so many districts across the country. It is really incredible!

Melissa Castillo, SIOP® National Faculty

Since the first edition of the book *Making Content Comprehensible for English Language Learners: The SIOP® Model* was published in 2000, the authors have had the opportunity to meet with hundreds of educators who tell us their stories of success using the SIOP® Model. We have been impressed with the creativity we have seen and heard about as the SIOP® Model is implemented in classrooms across the United States and abroad. While it would be impossible to include all of those experiences in this book, in the following chapters we feature school and district reform efforts for English learners that represent a variety of geographic areas, settings, and demographics. Some schools and districts have only a handful of English learners, whereas ELs represent a majority of students in other regions. Similarly, the issues facing rural schools may not be the same as those found in urban settings. By no means are the stories included here the only examples of successful SIOP® Model implementation, but they provide a range of models, ideas, and approaches for you to consider. We hope that within this variety of situations, contexts, and professional development models, there will be at least one that is similar to yours.

Demographics of Profiled Schools and Districts

Over a two-year period, district and school-site personnel from throughout the United States were interviewed about how they implemented the SIOP® Model. From hours of interviews, there emerged stories of implementation from school districts large and small. You will find throughout this book descriptions of district, school, and classroom implementation of the SIOP® Model with minimal editing for clarification. Educators' comments, insights, and suggestions from the following districts are sprinkled throughout the book. They do not necessarily represent the "ideal" or our endorsement of the way "things should be." Rather, they serve as examples that we hope will be useful to you as you assume and/or continue the important work of educating English learners in your own schools and districts through the SIOP® Model.

What follows are brief demographic descriptions of each of the school districts, including a few schools that are profiled in the following chapters. Information in the descriptions was accurate at the time of this writing and was gathered via district Web sites and selected interviews.

American Falls Joint School District, American Falls, Idaho

American Falls Joint School District in American Falls, Idaho, serves 1,619 students from preschool to twelfth grade within six schools. This rural school district enrolls students from ethnically diverse backgrounds, including Native American/Alaskan Native, African American, Asian/Pacific Islander, White, and Hispanic. The school district is composed of thirty-three percent English learners. Fifty-seven percent of the students within this district participate in the free and reduced lunch program.

Beaverton School District, Beaverton, Oregon

Beaverton School District, located in Beaverton, Oregon, is an urban school district located in the Pacific Northwest region of the United States. The district serves approximately 35,333 students from preschool to twelfth grade in forty-nine schools. Ethnicities represented within this district include White, African American, Hispanic, Asian/Pacific Islander, and Native American/Alaskan Native. More than eighty different languages are spoken within the homes of the students attending this school district. Fourteen percent of the total student population is identified as English language learners. Thirty percent of the students in this district are enrolled in the free and reduced lunch program.

Charlotte-Mecklenburg School District, Charlotte, North Carolina

Charlotte-Mecklenburg School (CMS) District in Charlotte, North Carolina, is the largest district in the state. Located in the Southeast region of the United States, it is one of the fastest-growing districts in terms of ELL enrollment. An urban district, it houses 161 schools and serves more than 132,000 students, pre-K through grade 12. More than 10,800 students were identified as English learners in the 2005–2006 school year. These students came from more than 152 different countries, and they speak 97 different native languages. Forty-five percent of the student body qualifies for the free or reduced lunch program.

Creighton School District, Phoenix, Arizona

The Creighton School District is located in an urban community in Phoenix, Arizona. The school district has nine schools and serves students from kindergarten to the eighth grade.

Students come from a variety of ethnic backgrounds including Hispanic, African American, Native American, White, and Asian. Forty-five percent of the students in the school district are English learners with some schools having a much higher percentage. The languages represented include Spanish, Arabic, Vietnamese, Korean, Mandarin, Romanian, Portuguese, Russian, French, Filipino, Navajo, and Other Non-Indian and Indian languages. Eighty-three percent of students within this district participate in free and reduced lunch programs.

Dearborn Public Schools, Dearborn, Michigan

Dearborn Public Schools, the seventh largest school district in Michigan, includes the city of Dearborn and a small portion of Dearborn Heights. The K–14 district partners with the Henry Ford Community College and educates 17,500 students in 33 schools. Dearborn Public Schools was one of the first districts in the United States to implement the SIOP® Model districtwide. Students come from a variety of ethnic backgrounds including Hispanic, African American, Native American, White, and Asian, with the majority of Arabic descent. More than a third of the students in Dearborn are English learners. Forty-eight percent of the students enrolled in Dearborn Public Schools are in the free and reduced lunch program.

Fresno Unified School District, Fresno, California

The Fresno Unified School District, located in Fresno, California, serves approximately 79,046 students from kindergarten to twelfth grade within 104 schools. California's fourth largest school district, Fresno Unified is an urban district located in central California. The school district is composed of students from a variety of ethnic backgrounds including, but not limited to, Hispanic/Latino, White, African American, Native American/Alaskan Native, Indian, Filipino, and Asian/Pacific Islander. Seventy-six different languages have been represented over the last five years within this district including, but not limited to, Spanish, Armenian, Hmong, Khmer, Lao, and Vietnamese. Fresno Unified School District is composed of 28.5 percent English learners. In addition, 79.2 percent of the students are enrolled in the free and reduced lunch program.

Houston Independent School District, Houston, Texas

The Houston Independent School District in Houston, Texas, serves more than 209,879 students from preschool to twelfth grade within 296 schools. Residing in the Southwest region of the United States, the Houston Independent School District is an urban district that serves students from many ethnic backgrounds including Hispanic, African American,

White, Asian/Pacific Islander, and Native American. The school district is composed of twenty-eight percent English learners. In addition, eighty percent of students within this district participate in the free and reduced lunch program.

Isaac School District, Lela Alston Elementary School, Phoenix, Arizona

The Isaac School District, located in the Southwest region of the United States in Phoenix, Arizona, serves students in grades K–8 with approximately 9,000 students. The school district comprises a diverse ethnic population including students who are Native American, White, Hispanic, African American, and Asian. The languages represented within this district include Spanish, English, Arabic, French, Mandarin, Vietnamese, Cantonese, Filipino, and Other Non-Indian languages. Ninety-four percent of the students within this district participate in the free and reduced lunch program.

Lela Alston Elementary School is located within the Isaac School District. The native languages of the 450 students at this particular K–3 school include sixty-five percent English learners. The languages served at this particular school include Spanish, Arabic, Mandarin, and Other Non-Indian groups. As a high poverty school, ninety-one percent of the school's students participate in the free and reduced lunch program compared to the state average of forty-nine percent. Approximately ten percent of the school's population is identified for special education services, and all such students are included in their regular grade-level classes (no pull-out classes).

Kansas City Public School District, Kansas City, Missouri

The Kansas City Public School District, located in the central portion of Kansas City, Missouri, serves more than 38,285 students from preschool to twelfth grade within eighty-six schools. Kansas City, Missouri, is located in the Midwest region of the United States. This rural school district includes students from ethnically diverse backgrounds including Alaskan, Native American, African American, Asian/Pacific Islander, White, and Hispanic. The school district is composed of fourteen percent English learners. Sixty percent of the students within this district are enrolled in the free and reduced lunch program.

Lawrence Public Schools District, Hillcrest Elementary School, Lawrence, Kansas

The Lawrence Public Schools District, located in Lawrence, Kansas, serves approximately 10,022 students from kindergarten to twelfth grade within twenty-two schools. The school district is located in the Midwest region of the United States. This rural school district is composed of students from ethnic backgrounds including

Hispanic/Latino, White, African American, Native American/Alaska Native, and Asian/Pacific Islander. English learners comprise 4.69 percent of the students within this school district. In addition, 29 percent of the students are part of the free and reduced lunch program.

Hillcrest Elementary School is located in the Lawrence Public Schools District. It is a public elementary school composed of 377 students from kindergarten to sixth grade. Hillcrest Elementary consists of students from a variety of ethnic backgrounds including White, Asian/Pacific Islander, Hispanic, African American, and Native American/Alaskan Native. Forty-five percent of the students within this school are enrolled in the free and reduced lunch program.

Lawrence Public Schools, Lawrence, Massachusetts

Lawrence Public Schools enrolls approximately 12,275 students in grades pre-K to 12. Eighty-four percent of the student population are classified as low income, with 100 percent of students qualifying for Title I services. Nearly eighty-three percent of the students have a first language other than English, and the ethnic makeup of the district is Asian (3 percent), African American (2.4 percent), Latino (85.5 percent), and White (9.1 percent). Among the language groups are Spanish, Vietnamese, Cambodian, and French/Creole.

Lewisville Independent School District, Dallas-Fort Worth, Texas

Lewisville Independent School District, Flower Mound, Texas, is in the northwestern area of the Dallas-Fort Worth metropolitan region of Texas. LISD serves more than 47,000 students from thirteen nearby cities and communities in fifty-one schools. In terms of ethnicity, sixty-eight percent of the student body is White, sixteen percent is Hispanic, eight percent is African American, seven percent is Asian/Pacific Islander, and 0.5 percent is Native American. Twelve percent of the students are economically disadvantaged. Eight percent are enrolled in the ESL/bilingual program. It is an academically acceptable district under Texas's school accountability scale.

The Oxford Schools, Phoenix Arizona (A pseudonym is used for the charter school company.)

The Oxford Schools is a privately held company that operates free public charter schools in a number of states. The Oxford School, located within the Southwest city of Phoenix,

Arizona, is the largest charter school organization in the state. Within both the Phoenix and Tucson metro areas, seventeen Oxford charter schools serve approximately 7,000 students from seventh to twelfth grade. Approximately 1,550 students or about twenty-five percent are ELLs and seventy percent are Title I.

Pacific Resources for Education and Learning

Pacific Resources for Education and Learning (PREL) works in partnership with the Pacific educational community to provide quality programs and products developed to promote educational excellence, including direct instruction, professional development, and educational materials. Their Regional Educational Laboratory (REL) Pacific is located in Honolulu, Hawaii. With a commitment to ensuring that all students have an equal opportunity to develop a strong academic foundation regardless of circumstances or geographic location, PREL serves the United States-affiliated Pacific Islands, including American Samoa, the Commonwealth of the Northern Mariana Islands, the Federated States of Micronesia (Chuuk, Kosrae, Pohnpei, and Yap), Guam, Hawaii, the Republic of Palau, and the Republic of the Marshall Islands. The purpose of the REL Pacific is to carry out applied research, development, dissemination, and technical assistance activities to serve the needs of the Pacific region. The REL Pacific serves state education agencies (SEAs) in ten Pacific jurisdictions, including one state, three territories, and three nations in free association with the United States.

South Texas Unified School District, San Antonio, Texas
(A pseudonym is used for the school district.)

The South Texas Unified School District (STUSD) encompasses 115 square miles in southern San Antonio. This K–12 district has a current student enrollment of more than 10,000 students within its thirteen schools. STUSD consists of students from a variety of ethnic backgrounds including White, Asian/Pacific Islander, Hispanic, African American, and Native American. With approximately, 1,500 English learners and growing, thirteen percent of the students enrolled are English learners, inching toward the state's average of sixteen percent. Though the state average for free and reduced lunch is forty-eight percent, more than eighty-one percent of the students within STUSD are enrolled in the free and reduced lunch program.

Waller Independent School District, Texas

Waller Independent School District in Texas is a small district northwest of Houston in a semirural, agricultural area. It serves approximately 5,000 students across seven schools: four elementary (grades K–4), one middle (grades 5–6), one junior high (grades 7–8), and one high school (grades 9–12). Approximately forty-six percent of the students are considered economically disadvantaged. Close to sixteen percent of the students are limited English proficient. In terms of student race/ethnicity, fifty percent are White, thirty-two percent are Hispanic, sixteen percent are Black, and one percent are Asian or Native American. The district offers transitional bilingual, dual language, and ESL programs.

Washoe County School District, Reno/Sparks, Nevada

The Washoe County School District is located in the urban city of Reno/Sparks, Nevada. The district serves approximately 64,199 students from preschool to twelfth grade in 100 schools. Washoe County School District, located in the Southwest region of the United States, is Nevada's second largest district. Students from ethnic backgrounds such as Native American/Alaskan Native, Asian/Pacific Islander, African American, White, and Hispanic attend this school district. Fourteen percent of these students are considered English language learners. Thirty-six percent of students within this school district participate in the free and reduced lunch program.

SIOP® National Faculty

This SIOP® implementation book has been further informed by a number of the National Faculty of the SIOP Institute® for Pearson Achievement Solutions (see Appendix A for a history of the development of the SIOP® and Institutes). These individuals were all experienced teachers, administrators, staff developers, and/or SIOP® implementers before they joined the National Faculty. Their background with the SIOP® Model is extensive, and their reflections on professional development, building capacity, formative data collection, dealing with resistant teachers, sustaining change, and much more have been invaluable additions to this book. The National Faculty who participated in these interviews include Melissa Castillo, Amy Ditton, Alvaro Hernandez, Wanda Holbrook, Kendra Moreno, John Seidlitz, Nicole Teyechea, Martha Trejo, and Liz Warner.

Chapter Summary

The stories of these districts and schools provide rich detail to the process of SIOP® implementation. In the chapters that follow, readers will find that the information and advice shared by school district staff and SIOP Institute® National Faculty are readily applicable to many settings. The resources provided, such as lesson plan templates, workshop agendas, staff development timelines, and list of coaching services will help school and districts at all stages of SIOP® implementation, from beginning to advanced.

Questions for Reflection and Discussion

1. As you review the descriptions for each of the districts that participated in this book, which, if any, resemble your own context?

2. If you are beginning the process of implementing the SIOP® Model, what questions do you currently have? List them, and as you read the following chapters, keep track of which questions are answered. With your colleagues, discuss possible answers for questions you still have. Keep in mind that learning to implement the SIOP® Model is an ongoing process—as you and your colleagues engage with this process, additional questions will undoubtedly emerge.

chapter 2

What the Research Says about Professional Development

Effective teaching leads to positive student performance, and effective professional development is the key to improving both.

Martinez-Beck & Zaslow, 2005

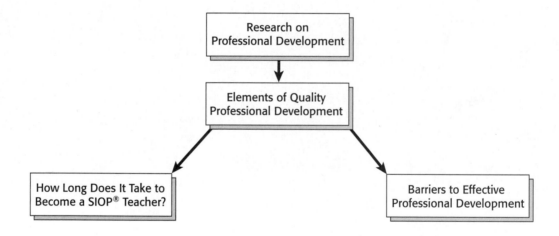

Professional development is a hot topic. It has been receiving attention on all levels—federal, state, district, and building. There is growing awareness that teacher preparation is a process; one doesn't "become a teacher" after completing a certain number of teacher education (or preservice) courses. In order to remain current on educational topics and issues, to hone skills learned in teacher education courses, to stay informed, and to learn new skills and practices, ongoing professional development (or inservice education) is part of comprehensive teacher preparation.

Although the SIOP® Model is used in many college and university teacher education programs, the focus of this book is on the way the SIOP® Model has been used effectively for professional development or inservice SIOP® programs and activities. We will describe a variety of models of professional development that have been used successfully in different types of settings. However, it is important to bear in mind that context is everything. One SIOP® implementation approach may not resemble the same approach in another context, even if the same training format is followed and the same professional development materials are used. Therefore, there isn't only one right way to develop or implement a SIOP® professional development program. Consider your context—the staff, administration, students, and community; then examine the experiences presented in this book and plan your own strategy for implementation.

What Are the Elements of Quality Professional Development?

While little research delineates the specific elements of effective professional development, there is general agreement on the main features of quality programs. As seen in Figure 2.1, the National Staff Development Council has classified standards into three areas: the context, process, and content of effective professional development (National Staff Development Council, 2001). The discussion that follows reflects research on professional development that has been organized around these categories (PREL, 2005). The principles these standards are based on are present in many of the effective SIOP® professional development programs described in this book.

Context. The context of effective professional development has several features. First, the purpose of the program is well articulated to all participants, and the participants know what they are expected to do with the information being presented. For example, will teachers' SIOP® lessons be observed after the initial training? How will SIOP® professional development align with current practice and other professional development sessions teachers have participated in? (See Epilogue for a discussion of alignment.) Will participants be expected to train others in the SIOP® Model after attending? These are some of the important questions that should be addressed prior to beginning a professional development program.

Second, everyone in the school or school district needs to be encouraged to get on board (see Chapter 3). Many educators have reported that schoolwide implementation of the SIOP® has, among other positive outcomes, facilitated communication between administrators and staff, and between mainstream teachers and specialists since everyone "speaks the same SIOP® language" of teaching and learning. Also, when the staff is committed, the SIOP® Model will be sustained over time and maintained after an administrator or key teacher leaves.

Third, effective professional development programs generally take place in the setting or context where the teachers work so that they can deal with the actual issues and challenges faced when implementing the SIOP®. Observation of live or videotaped SIOP® lessons provides teachers with the opportunity to use the SIOP® protocol and discuss specific aspects of the features and their implementation.

FIGURE 2.1 *National Staff Development Council Standards for Staff Development (Revised, 2001)*

Context Standards

Staff development that improves the learning of all students:
- Organizes adults into learning communities whose goals are aligned with those of the school and district. *SIOP® Model promotes acquisition of state standards and improved EL student achievement.*
- Requires skillful school and district leaders who guide continuous instructional improvement. *May be district EL coordinator, school administrator, coach, or lead SIOP® teacher who keeps teachers focused on deepening SIOP® knowledge and strengthening implementation.*
- Requires resources to support adult learning and collaboration. *May include release time, staff position as SIOP® Coach, SIOP® book for each teacher to deepen knowledge, instructional materials, designated staff development time, etc.*

Process Standards

Staff development that improves the learning of all students:
- Uses disaggregated student data to determine adult learning priorities, monitor progress, and help sustain continuous improvement. *Student data drives the focus of SIOP® lesson plan teaching and learning cycle.*
- Uses multiple sources of information to guide improvement and demonstrate its impact. *Videotaping, observation, coaching, discussion, and team lesson planning all contribute to improved implementation of SIOP® lessons.*
- Prepares educators to apply research to decision making. *SIOP® Model is research based and scientifically tested.*
- Uses learning strategies appropriate to the intended goal. *SIOP® training includes presentation of the model, interactive discussion, rating and discussion of videotapes, and demonstration of techniques and application activities.*
- Applies knowledge about human learning and change. *SIOP® professional development introduces the model, teachers practice with guidance, apply it independently, and evaluate and adjust practice.*
- Provides educators with the knowledge and skills to collaborate. *Collaboration is key to effective SIOP® implementation.*

Content Standards

Staff development that improves the learning of all students:
- Prepares educators to understand and appreciate all students, create safe, orderly and supportive learning environments, and hold high expectations for their academic achievement. *Features of the SIOP® promote these, including using students' background experiences, using students' native language to clarify, meeting standards through differentiation, and scaffolding to meet L2 needs.*
- Deepens educators' content knowledge, provides them with research-based instructional strategies to assist students in meeting rigorous academic standards, and prepares them to use various types of classroom assessments appropriately. *SIOP® features are based on best practice research. Most content area educators don't have a knowledge base of second language acquisition or ESL methods for working with ELs. SIOP® builds that base.*
- Provides educators with knowledge and skills to involve families and other stakeholders appropriately. *SIOP® teachers respect diverse families and encourage their involvement.*

Finally, effective professional development programs are consistent in message. Presenters draw from the research on the SIOP® Model as well as the research underpinnings of the components. Effective presenters of the SIOP® Model use the *Making Content Comprehensible for English Learners: The SIOP® Model* text as the basis for their presentations. This ensures a consistent message.

Process. In addition to context, the process used for professional development is important in meeting its goal, which is improved teacher practice and student achievement. Teachers are far more likely to implement new instructional approaches when they have to do the following (modified from Joyce & Showers, 1996):

1. <u>Theoretical Knowledge</u>. The training provides an opportunity for participants to learn the SIOP® Model and its theoretical underpinnings, and understand why the features are important for English learners. An important part of SIOP® professional development is presentation of information on second language acquisition. The SIOP® Model is more than "just good teaching"—it addresses the unique second language needs of English learners. Understanding of the second language acquisition process provides a foundation for SIOP® Model implementation.

2. <u>Modeling</u>. Teachers have the opportunity to observe classrooms in which SIOP® teachers or coaches show how to organize their classes for SIOP® teaching and model the features during SIOP® lessons. Video examples of how the SIOP® looks in a classroom setting may also be used as a school begins the process of developing SIOP® teachers and coaches.

3. <u>Practice</u>. Participants practice implementing SIOP® features with guidance and support. Typically, after teachers understand the SIOP® Model, they plan SIOP® lessons collaboratively with peers and a more experienced teacher, coach, or administrator. Also, teachers may practice by modeling SIOP® lessons for one another and receive constructive feedback on the lesson.

4. <u>Feedback and In-Class Coaching</u>. Teachers' SIOP® lessons are observed by coaches or their peers, and teachers are provided with constructive feedback on the lesson. The SIOP® protocol is especially useful for this part of the process. The initial professional development sessions (#1 above) follow the model component by component, and the observation protocol is exactly aligned with what has been learned in those sessions. The protocol becomes a feedback form for assisting and supporting high-quality implementation of the SIOP® features.

5. <u>Independent Application and Analysis</u>. After the initial process of learning and practicing is followed, teachers begin to apply the SIOP® Model independently, usually though independent lesson planning and teaching. Teachers evaluate their lessons and analyze the features, adjusting and refining as needed. They may go back and relearn a feature if necessary.

The final stage demonstrates a teacher's ability to plan and execute SIOP® lessons independently; however, the analysis will be richer when done with a group of colleagues. Forming a learning community provides educators with an opportunity to extend learning and improve practice within the shared context of their school setting. Activities may include analysis of lessons through reflection or videotaping the lesson, discussion of SIOP® features that need a more focused implementation, and refining lesson plans or implementation of specific features. The Creighton School District, which serves students in grades K–8, used their coaching cycles process as a form of learning community. The district administrator, Marilyn Sanchez, who oversaw successful districtwide implementation of the SIOP® Model, credits the work of the coaching cycle groups because "otherwise it would never have grown." Marilyn continued,

I've watched things . . . mandated and . . . as soon as the grant went away their . . . program was gone. The SIOP® grew through the coaching cycle because people liked it. The teachers liked having time and getting the support. And then they get all this positive feedback about what they did and they learn so much from each other.

In Lawrence, Massachusetts, Resident Classrooms were established so that teachers have an opportunity to observe SIOP® instructional strategies and practices in a real classroom setting, then share and collaborate with colleagues. A debriefing session follows the classroom visitation.

Using student data helps to inform lesson planning, monitor student progress, and sustain continuous improvement (National Staff Development Council, 2001). An example of using student data was in Houston, where approximately twenty teachers at Waltrip High School formed a group of "critical friends" to learn the SIOP® Model. Led by instructional coordinator Suzanne Meador, they met every other week for a year and a half during their lunch break. Suzanne introduced them to the book *Making Content Comprehensible for English Learners: The SIOP® Model.* She explains that at the meetings, "[We] had a chapter study of the book, and I gave them extra strategies and we would use them and then come back and talk about them." Once teachers learned a component of the model, they used student work to inform their practice and refine lessons.

Another example of a learning community activity is seen in Figure 2.2. Teachers at Hill Middle School in Long Beach, California, focused on improving the way they provided writing instruction and feedback to students, many of whom were English learners. This type of activity strengthens a SIOP® teacher's practice in the area of Review/Assessment, which is improving the quality of feedback given to students on their work.

The process outlined above may be cyclical in nature. As you will see in the chapters that follow, some teachers went through the process with one component at a time. For example, at Hillcrest Elementary in Lawrence, Kansas, one component was introduced and covered in depth. Lesson planning, observations and coaching focused on that one component. The cycle began again with the next component, and so forth. A number of districts followed the same process.

Another important aspect of the process of professional development is that effective programs are evaluated continuously to ensure they have led to changes in teacher practice and gains in student achievement. We encourage educators to evaluate the impact the SIOP® Model is having in their schools, at the classroom and school level. In collecting data for this book, we found that most programs were so engaged in having teachers learn and implement the features that they did not document teacher change or student achievement gains. These kinds of data help teachers, coaches, and others to understand where changes in the professional development program are needed.

Content. Finally, the content of professional development or inservice sessions matters. The two factors that had the greatest effect on teachers' knowledge and skills and led to changes in instructional practice were 1) a focus on content knowledge and 2) program coherence (consistency in message, as mentioned above) (Garet, Porter, Desimone, Binnan, & Yoon, 2001). SIOP® professional development activities are likely to improve both teaching practice and student achievement when they focus on knowing and understanding SIOP® content (the eight SIOP® components coupled with information on second language acquisition), and when they consistently reflect the SIOP® Model.

FIGURE 2.2 *Teachers' Writing Instruction Self-Assessment*

	4	3	2	1
Point of View	• Articulates how the use of writing in all content areas improves students' skill in writing as supported by research • Can articulate how the use of writing improves student mastery of their own content area	• Articulates how the use of writing in all content areas improves students' skill in writing • Explains that writing is good for students, but may not believe it will result in increased content knowledge as reflected on a multiple choice test	• Agrees that all teachers should teach the district writing prompts • Believes that writing must be taught in isolation from content that is measured on multiple choice tests	• Believes that writing instruction should be left up to the language arts teachers • Does not see a link between improved writing and increased multiple choice test scores
Process	• Purposefully pulls out common misunderstandings or mistakes from student writing to design minilessons • Can break writing instruction into manageable chunks for students in a developmental sequence using the rubrics as guides • Models frequently, clearly, and includes think-alouds • Provides constant and timely feedback • Explicitly teaches and uses rubrics as part of writing instruction • Provides students opportunities to analyze their own and others' work • Teaches students to reflect on their own writing and set goals • Uses content to provide opportunities to develop writing proficiency and understanding of the content • Assigns writing on a weekly/biweekly basis	• Shares examples of writing as part of a minilesson with students • Uses student writing performance date to design minilessons • Provides feedback • Has taught the rubric • Provides some opportunities for students to analyze their own work • Allows some class time for students to look at their own writing • Develops some activities which require students to write about content • Uses district-generated writing prompts and/or writes own prompts if none are available, and includes scoring criteria	• Provides students with examples of work to be completed • Assigns writing to students that occasionally (2–3 times per semester) requires a full essay (ex. Own or uses district prompts) • Thoroughly explains all of the parts of writing task • Creates writing assignments (ex. Write an essay about your career for the future and why you picked that career) but may or may not include scoring criteria	• Students are asked to write without examples of completed work • Rarely (1–2 times per semester) assigns writing to students that goes beyond a paragraph
Results	• Accurately scores student writing using the expository rubric and identifies next steps for instruction • Provides specific feedback to individual students based on rubric (Good lead because . . .) • Develops a system for tracking individual and class progress based on data • Uses writing results to share instructional goals with students and plan future lessons	• Accurately scores students' writing using the expository rubric • Gives feedback from rubric (good lead) • Develops a system for tracking class progress based on data • Uses writing results to plan future lessons • Meets with grade level and/or team members to collaboratively score student work	• Scores writing with the expository rubric with some errors in application • Gives general feedback (e.g., good work) • Collects results for grading purposes and submission to department chair • Plans sequential lessons based on basic writing skills	• Does not know the elements of expository rubric • Gives letter grades or % grades with no feedback, or records grades in gradebook • Plans random writing lessons • Does not use the expository (or the appropriate district-approved) rubric to score student work

Hill Middle School, 2001–02 *(Kahl, Kerns, Pendray 2002)*

It is critical that presenters and others responsible for educating English learners remain faithful to the SIOP® Model in its entirety and not dismantle the model by exposing teachers only to certain components or features. The research demonstrating the model's effectiveness, reliability, and validity was based on the eight components and thirty features in combination, not just certain components or features. In fact, one motivating factor for developing the SIOP® Model was that in the past, practitioners were picking and choosing techniques and approaches for teaching English learners without consistency and coherence, which led, for the most part, to poor academic outcomes for ELs.

The SIOP® Model is a cohesive framework for lesson planning and delivery, and educators should be wary when someone promotes an "adapted SIOP®" or individual pieces at the expense of the whole. This is *not* the SIOP® Model. In the Epilogue, we discuss alignment of the SIOP® Model with other research-based programs; this alignment is possible and practical when the model as a whole is considered.

A word about "research-based" practices is in order as we discuss the content of inservice trainings. As the National Staff Development Council Web site cautions:

> A problem in the use of the term "research-based" is that it is applied equally to practices that vary considerably in the scientific rigor used in their investigation. For instance, a person who reads an article in a professional journal in which the author advocates the use of a particular practice without providing any supporting evidence for that assertion may later carelessly describe that practice to others as "research-based." Other studies may cite only teachers' reports of changes in their own teaching practice and improved student learning as sufficient evidence for the value of the innovation. Still other studies may have methodologies that include pretests and post-tests of students and teachers, classroom observation of teachers' instructional practice, and random assignment of students to control and experimental groups.
>
> Consequently, it is critical that teams of teachers and administrators take the time to study methodically the research that supports the claims made by advocates of a particular approach to instructional improvement or whole-school reform.
> www.nsdc.org/standards/researchbased.cfm, retrieved January 18, 2007

It seems everything is called "research-based" these days. But as the report of the National Literacy Panel on Language-Minority Children and Youth (August & Shanahan 2006) indicates, there is a paucity of studies with English learners that used the type of methodology described in the quote above, such as pretests and posttests of students and random assignment of students to control and experimental groups. As Chapter 8 shows, while we report teacher testimonials as well, the SIOP® Model has been scientifically tested with positive results, and more studies are under way to strengthen the research base of the model.

How Long Does It Take to Become a SIOP® Teacher?

Effective professional development programs are implemented and sustained over time. As outlined above, they follow a process of initial training coupled with extensive follow-up with teachers in their classrooms. Research suggests that the professional development process is a difficult one since teachers may have to go through a number of changes to fully implement new instructional strategies and methods (Hawley & Valli, 1999). "Perhaps the most important aspect of teaching is that one never reaches perfection, and that constant striving to learn and improve is part of the job" (Duffy, 2004, p. 15).

Teachers and administrators often ask how long it will take to become an effective SIOP® teacher. The answer depends on a number of factors including:

- Effectiveness of the initial SIOP® training. Presenters must have sufficient knowledge in and understanding of second language acquisition to articulate the importance of the SIOP® Model for English learners. Perhaps more importantly, presenters must have a deep understanding of the SIOP® Model and its application in classrooms. Teachers learn the model and are able to begin implementing it more quickly and effectively when their staff developer is knowledgeable about the SIOP® Model, has taught English learners using the SIOP®, and can adequately address participants' questions about its theoretical underpinnings, the research that supports the model, and how it can be used with the lesson planning, teaching, and learning cycles.

- Quality and duration of the follow-up support. Research tells us that it can take as many as thirty instances of practicing a new instructional strategy or technique before teachers incorporate it effectively into their own practice (Joyce & Showers, 1996). Teachers need time to practice the features of the SIOP® Model, with feedback from a coach, peer, or other support person. SIOP® implementation and student performance were most effective in those professional programs that had ongoing, high-quality follow-up support activities.

- Level of collaboration with teachers and leaders. Isolation can be fatal to professional development because it is difficult to sustain practice in isolation. When educators collaborate, they provide valuable ideas, feedback, and encouragement to one another. Also, collaboration assists in planning service delivery, developing lesson plans, addressing problems, and improving instruction. Collaboration is critical to SIOP® Model implementation.

- How closely aligned the SIOP® Model is with existing instructional practices. Professional development is often unsuccessful when teachers are asked to learn and use instructional strategies that are very different from their familiar practices (RAND Reading Study Group, 2002). Since the SIOP® Model is based on best practices of teaching, many of the features are familiar to teachers, such as having objectives, reviewing previous learning, checking for understanding, and assessing student progress. Teachers who have a background in ESL or bilingual education have an advantage, with fewer new ideas to add to their teaching repertoire.

- Administrative support. Administrative support is an essential factor in determining how quickly and effectively the SIOP® Model is implemented in classrooms. Effective administrators are trained in the model along with their staff so they know what to observe in classes and how to structure postobservation conferences. As Marilyn Sanchez, director of ELL services in Creighton School District, said, "I'm teaching them [administrators] because these are our core instructional strategies. They need to know how to write a language objective [because] they need to observe [it]." The leadership group in Creighton who received SIOP® training consisted of all the principals and educational directors such as director of special education. Sometimes they included assistant principals as well.

- Level of resources allocated to SIOP® implementation. Release time, materials for professional development, instruction, and coaching all facilitate learning and practice with the model. For example, teachers who worked in settings where each had his or her own SIOP® book (Echevarria, Vogt, & Short, 2008) to study, notate, and through it, deepen their understanding of the model, tended to become effective SIOP® teachers more quickly than those who did not have that resource.

- Level of classroom management. Any professional development program is enhanced when the teacher is able to focus on implementing the approach without having to spend time with management issues. Successful SIOP® teachers are well prepared and they know how to manage time, materials, and student behavior to maximize student learning. They establish classroom routines and monitor their effectiveness. In this way, they are able to concentrate on SIOP® features, such as teaching students to use learning strategies or encouraging interaction.

Our experience indicates that it takes about one to two years of learning and practicing the SIOP® Model for the average teacher to become proficient as a SIOP® teacher. The factors previously discussed are the variables that will impact the ease with which teachers implement the model consistently with the anticipated gains in student achievement.

Barriers to Effective Professional Development

While a number of successful professional development research projects have included some form of ongoing support to ensure that the practices were implemented (Klinger, Ahwee, Pilonieta, & Menendez, 2003), even under these conditions, not all teachers implemented the practices. From these and other studies, we have learned about some of the barriers to implementation.

Resource and Time Intensive. Effective professional development programs require a long-term commitment and effective use of money (PREL, 2005). This requires vision and a strategic plan for professional development. In the Oxford Schools, the director of bilingual programs, Melissa Castillo, led a team that took five months to develop a plan for SIOP® professional development in their fourteen high schools. The result was systematic implementation over time with all teachers being trained in a similar way.

Lack of Accountability after Training. Most school districts lack a clear-cut mechanism for monitoring teachers' implementation of the practices they learn through professional development programs. Perhaps teachers would respond more positively to professional development and implement the practices more often if there were accountability at the district or school level. At Alston Elementary School in Phoenix, Arizona, and at Hillcrest Elementary in Lawrence, Kansas, the principals took part in the inservice sessions at their school site and participated in follow-up support that resulted in high levels of implementation with resultant gains in student achievement.

Teacher Turnover. Staff turnover is a characteristic of many urban schools and can be disruptive to professional development programs. In a study of professional development, researchers found that in schools that lacked a cohesive focus, the notion of learning communities never took (Stein, Smith, and Silver, 1999). In their words, there is a "need for teachers to participate in a common set of activities as the glue that holds the community together" (p. 267). Our work reinforces the conclusions of this study. At Alston Elementary in Phoenix, as new teachers replaced SIOP® trained teachers, they were partnered with an experienced SIOP® teacher, which made the transition easier for the new teacher and maintained the school's status as 100 percent SIOP® teachers. At Hillcrest Elementary in Lawrence, Kansas, as new teachers were hired, they were sent to SIOP Institutes® so that they received the same training as the SIOP® teachers at the school.

Impossible Situations. Some situations present so many obstacles that it is almost impossible to be an effective teacher to all students. A case in point is when teachers told us that a SIOP® tenth-grade biology teacher had three underprepared newcomers "dumped" into his Advanced Placement Biology class. That is an in-house policy and scheduling issue that is best addressed through communication with school or district administration; it is not an issue that any particular instructional approach will resolve.

Distance. Some districts or service regions cover large geographic areas with a few schools in remote locales. Quality professional development for all teachers is a challenge that may be resolved with technology (NSDC, 2001, 2007). Technology can provide for the individualization of teacher and administrator learning through the use of CD-ROMs, e-mail, the Internet, and other distance learning processes. Educators in rural or remote areas have received initial SIOP® inservice through videoconferencing. As follow-up, they may download SIOP® lesson plans, conduct action research, or compare their students' work with that of students in other schools (or even other countries) who are participating in SIOP® professional development. Technology also makes it possible for teachers to form virtual learning communities with educators in schools throughout the country and around the world. For example, teachers may become members of online subject-area SIOP® networks, take online SIOP® courses (see www.pearsonachievement.com for information about SIOP®online courses), and contribute to action research projects being done in various locations. Professional developers in the Pacific island region used technology coupled with other options for support, seen in Figure 2.3, with a positive response from participants.

Chapter Summary

In this chapter we discussed the critical importance of professional development for improving instruction and student achievement, summarized in Figure 2.4 on page 22. Research provides some guidance in how inservice training for teachers is effectively

FIGURE 2.3 *PREL SIOP® Training Options*

Pacific Resources for Education and Learning (PREL) recognizes that support in the way of a follow-up is needed after an initial SIOP® training session in order to fully implement the model. Listed below are different options to consider as a form of follow-up to assist with local educators providing training for the teachers at their site.

Option 1: Distance Delivery Support for SIOP® Trainers

- After an initial regional weeklong training, a team of trained SIOP® participants will receive follow-up sessions from a PREL trainer via a distance delivery system such as the program called Elluminate or a VTC or an audio conference. The purpose of the follow-up sessions is to work together to plan an agenda and a facilitator's guide for implementing a local training session. The number of times the group will convene will vary from site to site depending on the needs of the local team.

Option 2: Distance Delivery Plus On-Site Coaching for Trainers

- A PREL trainer provides leadership to the previously trained SIOP® educators through a form of long-distance communication such as Elluminate, VTC, or audio conference. The participants in the follow-up group are the local SIOP® Implementation Team who were already trained in SIOP®.
  - With the help of the PREL trainer, the local SIOP® Implementation Team preplan the date, the participants, the location, the agenda, and the facilitator's guide for providing a local one-week-long SIOP® training session.
  - The number of distance delivery meetings will vary between two and four, depending on the needs of the site.
  - After the initial planning is complete, the PREL SIOP® trainer travels to the site and provides coaching to the local SIOP® Implementation Team while they are presenting the SIOP® training.

Option 3: SIOP® Overview and Classroom Implementation for Training of Trainers and Other Educators

- Two-week SIOP® training sessions are offered to entities that include the following:
  - Two PREL trainers provide the two-week training.
  - Teams of three educators from buildings and/or villages attend including:
    - An administrator
    - An elementary teacher
    - A secondary teacher
  - The above participants become the local Implementation Team.
- Week one, the participants are provided the initial SIOP® training.
- Week two, in cooperation with one of the local schools, the participants plan and implement SIOP® lessons as well as prepare to be part of a SIOP® Implementation Team.
  - Monday: Work in partners or triads to plan SIOP® lessons.
  - Tuesday: Participants go into classrooms and teach their lessons.
    - Person one is the teacher of the lesson.
    - Person two is the coach and completes the observation using the SIOP® protocol.
    - The partners debrief the lesson.
  - Wednesday: The partners switch roles and person two teaches while being observed by person one followed with debriefing.
  - Thursday/Friday: The participants plan an agenda and a facilitator's guide for providing a SIOP® training to a specific group of teachers in their school, village, or municipality.
- Follow-up: PREL trainers provide follow-up support through regular scheduled Elluminate, VTC, or audio conferences.

In order to help facilitate the implementation of SIOP® at the entity level, it is highly recommended that one person be designated the SIOP® coordinator or chair.

Draft developed by Susan Hanson, PREL, 2006

FIGURE 2.4 *Do's and Don'ts of Effective Professional Development*

Do's	Don'ts
• Make a **long-term commitment** to SIOP® Model implementation to sustain effective instruction for students over time.	• Offer a series of **one-shot workshops** with little or no continuity between sessions and no commitment to an ongoing, supportive program of professional development.
• Provide initial training that is effective and interactive delivered by a **presenter with deep knowledge** of all the SIOP® Model components and of second language acquisition.	• Provide initial training where the presenter has **only a surface knowledge** of the SIOP® Model or of second language acquisition.
• Provide participants with a **variety of follow-up activities** including small group and individual work, observation and coaching, readings and discussion, reflection and analysis that extend the teachers' understanding of the model and lesson delivery, and offer continuity between workshops.	• Decide to train teachers on only **some of the components**—the research findings support the SIOP® Model as a complete system.
• Provide **resources** for ensuring success with SIOP® implementation such as release time, materials, and SIOP® coaches.	• Neglect the importance of quality **follow-up activities**.
• Establish **learning communities** of SIOP® teachers. May be with grade-level or subject area peers; should include specialists (ESL, special education, bilingual).	• **Separate mainstream teachers** from bilingual and special education teachers.
• Include a **site administrator** on a SIOP® team to learn the model, support the implementation process, and learn how to observe in SIOP® classrooms.	• **Give up** on teachers slow to implement well; most need about one year of training and support, some need closer to two.
• Conduct **formative evaluations** of the intervention: collect baseline data on teacher and students beforehand and ongoing data on teacher change and student achievement during the implementation process.	• Don't treat the SIOP® Model as a **remedial teacher program**.
• Make **plans** for incorporating new teachers into the SIOP® implementation process.	
• Collaborate, **collaborate**, collaborate (e.g., coaches and teachers, teachers and teachers, administrators and teachers).	

conducted (NSDC, 2001). First, the context of the offerings should be considered. Participants need to know the expectations of a professional development program, and steps should be taken to promote complete staff buy-in. The message of the program should be consistent with what we know about effective instruction for English learners. Second, the process should include initial training focused on theoretical understanding, followed by demonstration and modeling, practice, coaching, and independent implementation and lesson analysis. The most effective and productive way to carry out the process is through some type of learning community that provides support and feedback to teachers implementing the SIOP® Model. Third, the content of a professional development program matters. SIOP® training must be based on the core text, *Making Content Comprehensible for English Learners: The SIOP® Model* (2008), to ensure fidelity to the model.

We also discussed some variables that impact how long it takes teachers to become high-quality SIOP® teachers. In our experience, it usually takes about a year, but that time will vary depending on the considerations presented. Finally, research shows that barriers exist that make implementation of the SIOP® Model—or any professional development program—challenging.

We hope that a discussion of the various aspects of professional development will assist you in strategizing and planning your own professional development efforts.

Questions for Reflection and Discussion

1. Read through the elements of quality professional development (context, process, content). Which of these elements have you and your colleagues considered thoroughly for SIOP® professional development? Which one(s) will you need to spend some time considering?

2. Based on what you have read in this chapter, how do you get buy-in from staff, especially resistant teachers?

3. Think about the idea of learning communities. Does your school have this type of support group? If so, how well does it work? How can it be improved? If not, whom would you approach to begin such a group? What steps will you take to organize a learning community?

4. A number of barriers to professional development were presented in the chapter. How might you address some of the barriers that have been experienced at your school or district?

chapter 3

Getting Started and Building Capacity with SIOP® Professional Development

The SIOP® observation protocol is the key to the whole thing. Too many times I have seen in staff development that we go to a workshop and when we come back, we tend to fall back into our old habits. The protocol really makes us accountable for what we should be teaching. To me, the protocol is extremely important.

Wanda Holbrook, Lela Alston Elementary School and SIOP® National Faculty

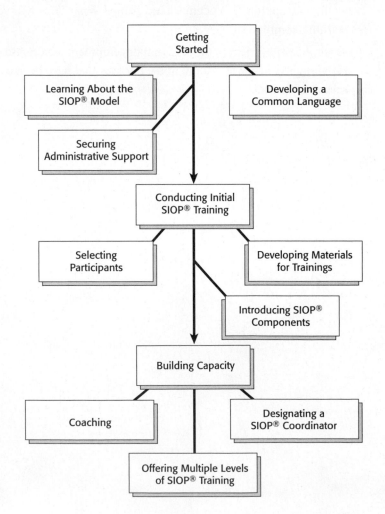

Getting Started

When teachers and coordinators of ESL and bilingual programs learn about the SIOP® Model, whether from a conference presentation, a research article, the reading of *Making Content Comprehensible for English Learners,* or even attendance at a SIOP Institute®, they often ask how to take it back to their school or district and get started. There is no single approach for beginning SIOP® implementation; the plan depends on resources, needs, interest, and administrative support. The districts and schools spotlighted in this book chose paths that were in some ways similar and in some ways different. We tell their stories in this chapter and the chapters that follow.

Learning about the SIOP® Model and Bringing It to the District or School

In conducting our research for this book, we asked our interviewees why they chose the SIOP® Model and how they learned about it. Many of them reported poor performance by English learners on standardized exams as one reason for embracing the SIOP® Model. Others cited a need to improve the training of content area teachers who had more and more second language learners in their classes. A few had learned about the SIOP® Model in one district and brought it with them when they moved to another or attended a session at a professional conference where it was featured. Quite a number explained that they wanted a research-based program that showed results with English learners, and the SIOP® Model was the only one in the research literature that worked with English as a second language programs. All of them mentioned that the systematic design of the SIOP® Model to lesson planning and teaching was appealing. The questions in Figure 3.1 are a compilation of the Top 10 asked by the districts as they began the SIOP® implementation process.

Once the staff member learned of the SIOP® Model, the strategy for establishing it in the district varied. Isaac School District's English language development coordinator, Marcy Granillo, was concerned about the low performance on the Arizona statewide tests that several of the elementary schools experienced. She examined research on improving the achievement of English learners and read about the SIOP® Model. She wrote a federal Title III grant application for funding SIOP® professional development and then contacted a relatively new site, Lela Alston Elementary School, with an enrollment of 400 and approximately 89 percent English learners to serve as a pilot school. She explained the model to the school's principal, Debbie Hutson, and staff to see if they would be willing to serve as the pilot school. Marcy also requested that staff be assigned to coordinate and oversee the training and implementation. The reading coordinator, Wanda Holbrook, and a third grade teacher, Kendra Moreno, volunteered to get more information.

At this point, those two teachers plus three others attended a SIOP I Institute® in Long Beach, California, along with the district English language coordinator and Alston's principal. After the training, the Alston team was expected to provide professional development

---

FIGURE 3.1 *Top 10 Questions for SIOP® Implementation*

---

1. Who will be the school or district SIOP® point person?
2. Who will be initially trained on the SIOP® Model, perhaps at a SIOP I Institute®?
3. How will administrators be approached and convinced of the SIOP® Model's value?
4. What funding sources are available for SIOP® implementation (e.g., for materials and resources, staff development, coaches)?
5. Who is responsible for setting the staff development program? Who will give input or review it?
6. How, where, and when will teachers be trained in the SIOP® Model? Over what period of time?
7. Which teachers will be selected for the first SIOP® cohort?
8. Will implementation be built slowly over several years or rapidly expanded across the site? Do the resources and staff development plan support this approach?
9. How do you get staff buy-in after the initial interest?
10. How can SIOP® implementation be sustained?

---

for the rest of the school staff. It was also expected that districtwide workshops would be held to educate others in the SIOP® Model. Teacher attendance at these district workshops would be voluntary.

Debbie Hutson explained the process:

> We started with the staff and did a presentation about what we learned [at the SIOP I Institute®] in Long Beach and gave a really general overview [of the SIOP® Model]. With us having just built this new school and having a new staff as a team, we all looked for something to help us with language development . . . so we just went at it as an entire group. [We] gave an overview and gave them some grade-level tasks to talk about [regarding SIOP® implementation] in the grade-level meetings . . . and we met with individual teachers and answered a lot of questions. [We] had a vote if they were willing to commit to the SIOP®Model.

In contrast, another elementary school, Hillcrest School in Lawrence, Kansas, began slowly with only a few teachers. In the first year the principal, Tammy Becker, took a team of primary teachers to a SIOP I Institute®. They started with first and second grade teachers, then subsequently sent a group of teachers from grades 2 through 6 until at least two people at every grade level had been trained in the SIOP®Model. Over time, not only did all teachers in the building receive staff development in the SIOP® Model, but teachers across the entire district did as well. The trainers and principal emphasized that using a group-by-group approach was most effective for them. Selecting teachers to receive training created a desire in the others to be included. As Tammy said,

> Doing it in steps has been powerful to us. You know for a building to be able to say that everyone is going to do this would be very tough. We found there was this jealousy thing with the other staff after the first group went: "Why didn't we [get to] do this?" It was a hard thing for them but a good thing for our building. The positive thing was that the second and third time [teachers went to a SIOP I Institute®], I had teachers asking me to go. So we sent the primary staff, and not even a month after they were back, I had other teachers saying, "Well, why didn't we get to go?"

Another approach was taken by a K–8 district in the Phoenix, Arizona area, Creighton. That district started at the grassroots level, driven by the philosophy of the director of English language learners, Marilyn Sanchez:

> If you start with someone who really wants to do it and they have a good experience, then that's what spreads it. It never spreads from the top down; it spreads because teachers are empowered.

However, the district's desire was to implement the SIOP® Model quickly throughout the district. Training began with several dual immersion schools and expanded to training all teachers in the district—more than 400 teachers had been trained in the SIOP® Model at the time of the interview. The district accomplished widespread implementation through a system of support at each school site involving TOAs (Teachers on Assignment) and part-time SIOP® Coaches who were also teachers. Their goal was to build a critical mass of SIOP® teachers districtwide as soon as was feasible.

With a rapidly increasing EL population and lack of success on numerous standardized measures by EL students, the ESL-Second Languages Department of Charlotte-Mecklenburg Schools (CMS) in North Carolina made a commitment to SIOP® Model implementation in the 2004–2005 school year. Initially, one staff member of the department (Joan Rolston) learned about the model at a conference and brought it to the director, Dr. Katherine Meads, and the second languages specialist, Jennifer Lupold Pearsall. They learned about it, attended a SIOP I Institute® and presented it to the associate superintendent of educational services, Dr. Frances Haithcock, who approved the plan and resources necessary for implementing the SIOP® Model in pilot sites in CMS. Over time all ESL-Second Languages Department members became trained in the model and formed a team to support implementation at school sites. A yearlong staff development program was provided to fifteen pilot sites (five elementary, five middle, and five high school) in 2004–2005 and to twenty sites (fifteen original plus five new) in 2005–2006 by the Center for Applied Linguistics where coauthor Deborah Short worked. The following year CMS hired a full-time district SIOP® Coach, Ivanna Mann Thrower, to coordinate SIOP® training, curriculum development, and implementation across the sites. Additional schools joined the pilot program, reaching thirty-four sites by the 2006–2007 school year. Moreover, besides the site-based training, all the ESL teachers in the district participated in staff development on the SIOP® Model.

Ivanna explained the process for bringing sites on board:

The pilot sites were chosen by the regional superintendents. The principals chose the teachers who would participate, initially. I give input into the selection of new teachers now. Originally, the ESL teacher was the lead teacher for each pilot site, but in some schools the buy-in wasn't as strong. Self-selected site coaches worked out best. . . . This year I'm requiring an administrator to be part of the [school] team, and most administrators are interested.

The start-up process in Waller Independent School District in Texas involved learning from another district. In 2002, the bilingual/ESL director invited a secondary literacy specialist from a different district in the region that had seen improvement in its English learners' performance to introduce the SIOP® Model to some of the Waller ISD teachers in the summer of 2002. The goal was to improve instruction for ELs at the middle school, junior high, and high school. The initial training was well received, and the trainer was asked to conduct three follow-up workshops plus some online coaching and technical assistance. The SIOP® trainer, Martha Trejo, explained,

When teachers began to see that they were going to actually be able to teach their content to English language learners, they went crazy. Buy-in began at the junior high and middle schools.

SIOP® Model training was implemented more formally in the 2004–2005 school year, when Martha was hired as the new bilingual/ESL director (upon the retirement of the former one). Since that time, approximately 85 percent of the teachers in the school district have received initial training in the SIOP® Model.

Several states have taken a statewide approach to educating English learners. In Idaho, for example, the SIOP® Model was part of a larger reading initiative as Leslie Beebe clarified:

It began as a reading improvement initiative. Initially, twelve school districts were selected and one representative from each district became a reading fellow responsible for facilitating implementation of reading strategies throughout the district. Over the course of eighteen months, these reading fellows received training from a number of reading experts and they attended a SIOP I Institute®. After receiving training, they brought those strategies back to the school district and worked with teachers in grades K–8.

Securing Administrative Support

For many of the districts described here, gaining administrative support was a critical early step. Although a group of teachers might conduct a book study on their own or the ESL department might sponsor a summer workshop session, in order to have ongoing staff development, those interested in the SIOP® Model needed to secure administrative approval and an allocation of resources, both time and funding.

Train Administrators on the SIOP® Model. When Martha Trejo became the bilingual/ESL director in Waller ISD in 2004, she sought "a more formalized approach to systematic SIOP® implementation." She met with the curriculum directors for the different content areas and the special education director and they agreed the SIOP® Model would benefit all the teachers. As a group, they attended a SIOP Institute® and upon return, sought the approval of the school principals. Martha arranged a full-day SIOP® retreat for them and the central administration the following summer:

> We invited all the directors, principals, and assistant principals. From 8 am to 2 pm, I gave an overview of the SIOP® Model and our goals. [During this time] each central administration department person [such as the curriculum directors] had to stand up and say why the SIOP® Model would be good. This convinced the principals. From 2 pm to 4 pm we had a gallery walk of ideas for district implementation. School teams met and established a plan for their site and we put [this information] on posters around the room.

The schools in the Waller district decided on different approaches to implementation. One elementary school, for instance, asked Martha to train staff during the faculty meetings every Wednesday morning. The junior high school planned to train all new teachers over the summer and set aside two days for training current staff during the school year. In addition, two teachers attended a SIOP Institute® so they could act as site facilitators.

As mentioned above, in Charlotte-Mecklenburg Schools (CMS), the associate superintendent for educational services was engaged in developing a SIOP® plan early on. With her approval, the district gave significant support to SIOP® professional development in terms of resources for staff and consultants, time for training teachers, and ultimately the creation of a position for a full-time SIOP® coach who would work districtwide. While much of the funding for the SIOP® implementation is drawn from a Title III grant, the administration has had to authorize the specific allocation to this purpose.

The involvement of the central administration in CMS did not stop at the initial stages. The ESL-Second Languages Department wanted to develop an understanding of the SIOP® Model among central office and site-based administrators. To that end, they have offered an administrative workshop on the model each year. During these workshops, the administrators have learned about the SIOP® components, have explored ways to look for SIOP® instruction when conducting walk-throughs, and have discussed the role of SIOP® school teams in developing professional learning communities. As the district began to collect data on the implementation effort, the ESL-Second Languages Department staff shared results with the administrators as well.

Link Administrators to SIOP® Instruction. Mark Crossman, who is the former ESL bilingual program specialist in Beaverton, Oregon, one of the first districts to adopt the SIOP® Model as its professional development initiative, explained that after the initial year, the SIOP® trainers decided to make more connections with the administrators:

> I think a lot of it [the successful implementation] has to do with the level of administration involvement, and that was when we started to rethink our strategies and were probably not doing enough work with the administrators. We wanted administrators to do more than just sign their teachers up or prompt or encourage or require their teachers to come but to be more directly involved in what it was all about. Some were doing it like, okay, I can check off that box now, we're done.

When asked if there were differences in schools that had more administrative support, he replied,

> Absolutely. . . . You could say that some places were successful with grassroots efforts, but usually it took at least a district person to get something going. Not always the principal, but it really helped.

The importance of having an administrator trained in the SIOP® Model cannot be overstated. In one Arizona school, principal David McNeil used staff meetings as professional development opportunities. Nicole Teyechea, one of the SIOP® National Faculty who has observed the principal, said,

> I know one principal who does the training [for] an hour of every other week, focusing on one component. He does the content and language objectives for it himself. So when he goes into teachers' classrooms [there is] a completely different reaction than someone who doesn't do that.

> [At meetings he says] "Can someone share something you did with Preparation today?" He's using it as an instructional tool rather than an evaluative tool to really support teachers in engaging kids. He was tired of seeing teachers at the copy machine and he was tired of seeing kids coloring.

Focus on Results. Sometimes administrators want to see results before they are willing to commit resources to professional development. In the Creighton School District in Arizona, Marilyn Sanchez, a district administrator, reported that one principal's success was a catalyst for the others to get on board. The success came when a principal had a struggling teacher who started participating in the SIOP® coaching cycles (see the description of Creighton's coaching cycles in Chapter 4). When the principal went back later and observed her teaching, it had markedly improved. She asked, "Where did you learn all this?"

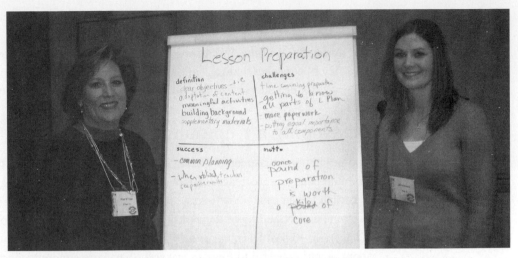

During SIOP® training two teachers focus on successes and challenges for Lesson Preparation.

and the teacher replied that it was the SIOP® training through coaching cycles. The principal talked about this experience with other principals, who were impressed. That one experience was cited as the way that enthusiasm for the SIOP® Model spread in the district. As a result, the director of ELL was given several days to provide SIOP® professional development to administrators in the district, and districtwide implementation followed.

Similarly, in Kansas City, Missouri, the focused SIOP® professional development efforts at one school yielded positive student achievement gains as well as teacher enthusiasm for the model. Other principals became interested, and the director of language services, Alicia Miguel, and the instructional coaches, Charlotte Daniels and Manuel Solaro, began offering professional development to other schools as well as to principals. Charlotte reported,

> What we were doing was we had a principals' meeting . . . and at the meeting we showed them the [SIOP®] video and we modeled the protocol . . . and we tried to get them interested in SIOP®. . . . We showed them data on the Missouri assessment test . . . and it showed schools that are implementing the SIOP® Model next to schools that aren't implementing the SIOP® and how [well] the students do in the SIOP® schools.

Highlight Benefits to Schools. A different approach was used by EL staff in Fresno, California's large urban district to gain secondary principals' interest in having their teachers learn the SIOP® Model. In this case, the EL coordinators approached several principals and explained that the training would not affect class time and that teachers would receive a wide variety of instructional and professional development materials. Most were eager to have their teachers participate. The ELL resource specialist, Elizabeth Fralicks, commented,

> The principals have been totally supportive. Who wouldn't be when someone is [providing a set of] materials? That's how we got a lot of [SIOP® training] going. We've made it so the school gets something out of it too. And what happens a lot of time is that the district has a lot of money and they have to [spend money by a certain date],

and so they buy materials. You have to make it easy for the school site. We do evening trainings that have made it easier to operate so we're not pulling teachers out during the daytime. [We meet] from 4 pm to 8 pm and we provide food. And then they [the teachers] always get, if we're talking about cooperative learning, they'll get a packet of materials so that they have the materials that we're referring to.

Developing a Common Language

Another important aspect of getting started with the SIOP® Model was developing a common language. As teachers and administrators began to learn about the model, they were able to converse about instruction and student learning using the same terms with the same understanding of their meanings. Scaffolding, language objectives, engagement, connections to past learning, and comprehensible input were no longer vague notions about practices useful to English learners, they were concrete concepts that teachers could see occurring in classrooms.

Liz Warner, Elementary ESL Coordinator of Washoe County School District, Reno/ Sparks, Nevada, and SIOP® National Faculty expressed the value of having a common language:

> . . . [I]f you're an instructional leader, then your staff needs to have a common language about what's going on in the classroom. And here's a way to have a language about improving instruction which I think is the basis of AYP [adequate yearly progress], and it's the basis of a successful classroom. It's all about teachers and the quality of instruction. And I think also that if you all have a common language that it makes it easier for the administrator to do follow-up and to support teachers because they're all speaking the same language—the SIOP® language.

Conducting Initial SIOP® Training

For those new to SIOP® implementation, the initial effort is apt to be on training teachers. This initial training is important, but so is the follow-up. Without ongoing staff development, the glow of a three-day SIOP Institute®, for example, will wear off. Planning for the staff development works best with several months' head start. Several aspects need to be considered, such as securing time for staff development (getting on the district staff development calendar is important and usually needs to occur in the spring of the year before the training takes place); allocating funds for materials and teacher stipends; and acquiring or creating materials for the teachers and staff developers.

A number of the districts told us that they took time to strategize and plan the professional development program. Alvaro Hernandez of Lewisville ISD, who is also SIOP® National Faculty, worked for two to three months with Amy Washam to organize the syllabus, materials, and presentation resources for the districtwide SIOP® course. Al said that the questions that guided their course development were "Are we on the right track and will this work? What will our teachers think of this [point of information or activity]?" The first course they offered ran for two hours per week for eight weeks. It was open to all staff in the district and introduced them to the SIOP® Model components. In time they referred to it as their level one SIOP® course.

Selecting Participants

The consensus from the districts interviewed for this book was that it is best to start with willing participants. "Begin with volunteers and treat them like professionals" was a sentiment that many expressed. Treating the teachers like professionals often involved giving them stipends for the extra training time and effort in the classroom. As a result, the number of initial participants may have been limited by available funds. Another way to treat the teachers professionally is to offer credit, either graduate course credit or required inservice hours, such as those needed to renew teacher licenses.

John Seidlitz, one of the SIOP® National Faculty, cautioned against viewing the SIOP® professional development as a remedial course for less-than-competent teachers. Instead, he recommended that those who select teachers should choose "high fliers"—those who have the respect of their peers in the schools. The district administrator in the Creighton school district, Marilyn Sanchez, suggested a similar approach:

> Start small and with people who really want to do it, and they will be excited. One teacher told us, "I can't believe it—the kids are actually listening!" So that success made other teachers interested in the model too.

Mark Crossman explained what happened when he was in Beaverton:

> We started in most of our middle schools. They are organized around teams or halls. Essentially you have one team with teachers in sixth, seventh, and eighth grade. We would identify a team in the building, not try to do the whole building. We usually looked for the team that already had people who were predisposed to being group leaders and wanted to reach out to the population that we were serving. We wanted to start off with the people who would give it the best chance for success in the building, and then as other teachers saw the success and really needed things to happen in their classrooms, that would be the time to start working with the reluctant teachers or the ones who need a little bit more prodding or nurturing. . . . [W]e would ask the principal to help us identify a team that would be a good starting team.

Introducing SIOP® Components

Overall, the majority of professional development efforts have introduced the SIOP® components in the same format as the text *Making Content Comprehensible for English Learners: The SIOP® Model* and the companion training manual (see www.siopinstitute .net). However, how time for trainings was allocated and the way training was delivered varied considerably across districts.

Begin with Second Language Acquisition Theory. Nearly all interviewees stated that it was critical to begin with an introduction to second language acquisition so that participants understood that the SIOP® Model is more than just good teaching—it is an approach that addresses the specific language needs of English learners. Laurie Beebe from American Falls, Idaho, commented,

> One of the things that really surprised me was that we had to develop on our own, information about second language acquisition. I was not aware of the implications of developing a

second language. . . . Knowing that some of my kids speak wonderfully, that doesn't mean they are necessarily getting what I'm [teaching]. One of my little ESL gals whose family speaks only Spanish said, "You know, sometimes I don't understand what you're saying," and I'm going, "Oh great, I'm a SIOP® teacher and I'm supposed to be comprehensible and I'm not doing a very good job of that." And to hear her say that to me made me really aware of how conscientious you have to be in instructing.

Tammy Becker, the principal from Lawrence, Kansas, concurred,

One of the things that would be critical if you're talking about starting a professional development program is to begin by going over second language acquisition and some of the theories and issues behind it. I saw that there is a distinct line of appreciation for the SIOP® Model when teachers do have that understanding [of second language acquisition].

Choose Order of Components Strategically. Once the foundation of second language acquisition was established, components were typically introduced one at a time. The first component introduced depended on the trainers' expertise in some cases and the participants' needs in others. As John Seidlitz, a SIOP® National Faculty member, suggested, "Begin with a component that aligns with the familiar or what the teachers perceive a big need to be."

Tammy, the elementary principal, stated,

We began with what we were comfortable with . . . there were four of us, and two of us were good with working with vocabulary but we struggled with language objectives; the other two were great with the objectives but weaker with the vocabulary, and so we really tailored what we were doing based on what our strengths were. And then added from there . . .

Laurie Beebe from American Falls explained further,

The components we introduced depended on the opinions of the group we were talking to. . . . What we found is that the schools that had been really involved—like grades 4–8 really had been involved with teaching reading strategies—they were very open to the next step. But for the people at the high school, this was brand new to them, and the implementation has been very slow there.

At Alston Elementary School, where the entire staff was trained together in the SIOP® Model, the trainers, Wanda and Kendra, chose the order of components based on the needs of the staff (see Figure 3.2 for their implementation plan). After a quick preview of all the components and a brief introduction to Lesson Preparation, they started with their first targeted component, Lesson Delivery. Wanda explained,

After looking at the components, the SIOP® team decided to not present the components in [protocol] order. We felt that the teachers did not know enough about the model to plan effectively. After a brief overview and introduction to Preparation, our team concentrated on Lesson Delivery. Having and posting objectives was a

FIGURE 3.2 *Elementary Implementation of SIOP® Model*
Wanda Holbrook, Lela Alston Elementary School in Phoenix, AZ

Alston's SIOP® Implementation Timeline

1st Quarter '02–'03	2nd Quarter '02–'03	3rd Quarter '02–'03	4th Quarter '02–'03
General Overview Lesson Delivery	Building Background	Interaction	Comprehensible Input

1st Quarter '03–'04	2nd Quarter '03–'04	3rd Quarter '03–'04	4th Quarter '03–'04
Strategies	Practice/Application Review/Assessment	Lesson Preparation Protocol	Observe

Workshops
- One component a quarter
- Staff development day
- Half day with substitutes
- After school (make and take)
- Staff meeting mini-trainings
- Usually 2 – 3 hours training per component

Coaching
Attitude
- Coach is a learner also
- Encourage — validate
- Expectations — professional
- Help you

Ways to get in the classroom
- Everyone included
- Introduce some new ideas
- Harder concepts — requests
- Cooperative teachers
- SAT9 — interaction with student data
- Check lists

Once in
- Training
- Modeling
- Team Teaching/Planning
- Team Planning
- Feedback

Feedback
- Point out the strengths
- Pick out one area to strengthen
- Give many ideas

Uses of the Protocol
- Recognize strengths and weaknesses
  - Assess the modeling
  - Choice of types of observations with feedback
  - Video taping of lessons with feedback
- Planning lessons
  - Record of lessons taught

Special to Lela Alston
- Have 'Content Objectives: and 'Language Objectives: ' signs for the white boards
- Have 'Today my job is…' signs for the boards
- Use Arizona's ELL Proficiency Objectives to make a list of language objectives

powerful and defining start. Our district had been emphasizing student engagement, so this was nothing new. We just were more accountable for it. Refining pacing was easy also. Our biggest challenge was writing the objectives. We just began with the attitude that we could refine later. . . . We began with Lesson Delivery because we knew that lessons had to revolve around objectives that were posted and the students were to be engaged. This way content and language objectives are considered and addressed at the beginning of our training. We knew that we would not be proficient at writing language objectives at first, but we had to start somewhere. Our district was already emphasizing student engagement.

Building Background was the next component introduced because it was "very observable and it usually took place at the beginning of the lesson," with links to previous learning. As in most cases, developing vocabulary was an identified need of students, so the SIOP® team decided to focus on Building Background toward the beginning of training.

The Interaction component was presented at the time of year that the students needed to review for standardized testing. It was an opportune time for practicing different grouping structures. As each structure was introduced, the coach modeled it in each teacher's classroom. Each grade level sought application of the structures, especially in the areas of testing review. During three years of implementing the Interaction component, more than fifteen grouping structures were introduced.

Comprehensible Input completed the first year of SIOP® training for this school. The team believed that, in retrospect, they could have introduced this component earlier, because the teachers were actually using Comprehensible Input techniques to get the objectives across effectively to the students.

The second year of SIOP® implementation began with the Strategies component. This decision was made because Wanda and Kendra thought the teachers would be fresh at the beginning of the year and able to learn a component that required a deeper level of thinking for the teachers. The next component introduced was Practice and Application. In this training, the trainers concentrated on designing more meaningful lessons. Review and Assessment was combined with Lesson Preparation so that the last quarter of the school year could be used for videotaping and official observations.

The teachers were encouraged to assess all lessons. A partial SIOP® protocol with the components listed in the revised order was provided each quarter to the teachers; new components were added cumulatively each time. Teachers were asked to place the protocol on their desks as reminders.

In summary, Lela Alston Elementary School in the Isaac School District approached the components by introducing the ones that were most familiar and therefore easier to implement, then moving on to the ones the SIOP® team thought would be more challenging for their staff.

A more unconventional approach was taken in one Phoenix district where English learners had been part of their schools for decades. In Creighton, many teachers had a fairly solid foundation in second language acquisition and sheltered instruction techniques. Features of the SIOP® Model were presented all at once. Teachers used the protocol while watching model lessons taught by SIOP® Coaches. So rather than studying each component of the SIOP® Model in a particular order, these teachers were asked to match what they were seeing in the coaches' lessons to specific features on the protocol. This unique "learning by doing" approach worked because of the strong peer support that was provided.

Developing Materials for Trainings

Wanda Holbrook reported that Alston trainers developed some unique items to use in staff development and to help teachers in their classrooms:

> We made signs with magnets on the back with Content Objective on one and Language Objective on another [for teachers to use when posting objectives]. The first and second grade teachers wanted signs that said, "Today your job is . . ." . This

[phrasing] started when I would go into those classes and write this on the board because I felt that "content and language objective" would mean nothing to them [the young learners].

We also took our state's ELL Proficiency Objectives and placed chosen ones in a matrix that our lead SIOP® teacher had created. Each grade level chose objectives from the state list that they wanted to make sure they were covering. This list was very usable as language objectives were chosen for each lesson.

Other districts created PowerPoint presentations and videotaped teachers to show the SIOP® Model in action in their classrooms. These resources could be shared with other training cohorts. Alvaro Hernandez reported that the videotaping was particularly effective in Lewisville Independent School District.

Building Capacity

Districts and schools varied in their approaches to developing a critical mass of SIOP® teachers and administrators. Some intentionally started slowly with a few individuals while others set out to train large numbers of people as quickly as possible.

Coaching

One district, Creighton, that wanted to build capacity quickly, implemented a site-based peer support system. Teachers on Assignment (TOAs) worked at every school in the district to train coaches. Securing release time for SIOP® Coaches was an obstacle to training large numbers of teachers, so the district ELL director came up with a solution:

> We hired three substitutes at the district so we've been able to schedule them between school sites. So that's one of the things that has built capacity because it hasn't been just the district saying, "Do this." Before this, I had three SIOP® trained teachers who worked at the district level and each one of them had two different schools. That was fine, but it just wasn't building enough critical mass. Now we have one TOA at every site, and they provide training. So it's coming more from the sites [rather than from the district office].

Creighton staff have credited coaching cycles with building capacity and sustaining SIOP® implementation throughout the district. Inservice sessions were considered positive experiences largely because teachers were teaching their peers to use the SIOP® Model. The model was more easily accepted by teachers new to it because its implementation was being encouraged by their colleagues:

> We think that we get the most bang for our buck by having the classroom teachers get excited, and they sell it to their peers. Because when you have somebody who's a coach and not in the classroom, teachers say, "Well, yeah, you're not in the classroom." But when you have somebody like [one of their coaches] that I just saw teach an amazing SIOP® lesson, I mean she's in the classroom and it still looks like this. And you ask her how she does [such an effective lesson] and she looks at you and says, "How else would I do it now that I know?" So teachers are just so powerful with other teachers.

Offering Multiple Levels of SIOP® Training

In Lewisville ISD, the district continues to offer its level one SIOP® course to any teacher each semester. With the support and encouragement of the ESL/bilingual director, Pam Creed, Alvaro and Amy have increased the time to nineteen hours distributed across an entire semester with two weeks between each session so that participants would have time to implement what they have learned. They also require teachers to submit a videotape of themselves teaching a SIOP® lesson, and participants collaboratively observe and assess their videos. To further build capacity, the Bilingual/ESL Department continues to support teachers' implementation of the SIOP® Model by offering a second level course, SIOP® II, which is school based and provides models of SIOP® lessons through videos of district SIOP®-trained teachers using the techniques outlined in the book *Teaching Ideas for Implementing the SIOP® Model* (Vogt & Echevarria, 2005).

Designating a SIOP® Coordinator

One important step in building capacity is designating one individual as the SIOP® coordinator. While names might vary—SIOP® Coach, SIOP® Specialist—the role is similar: to oversee and support SIOP® implementation. Earlier we described Charlotte-Mecklenburg's decision to fund the position for a districtwide SIOP® Coach. In this case, some of the

FIGURE 3.3 *PREL SIOP® Coordinator's Role*

The SIOP® Coordinator will function as a leader in developing a training-of-trainers approach to implement the SIOP® Model. The coordinator will develop and adapt SIOP® materials to train other professional development providers to implement the SIOP® Model at their site.

The role includes such things as

- Assist with identifying key educators to be trained as trainers for the SIOP® Model.
- Plan and implement a one- to two-week SIOP Institute® for training trainers who will then plan training for the schools they work with.
- Once the trainers are trained, assist them with implementing a SIOP® training for their schools.
  - Work with them to develop their training materials, including PowerPoints and handouts.
  - Make sure each trainer has a training manual that includes their PowerPoints and other presentation material.
- Plan and facilitate biweekly Study Groups to further discuss SIOP® issues with the trainers and provide ongoing support. Encourage the trainers to start similar Study Groups at the school level.
- Based on the needs of the trainers, plan and implement approximately two mini-institutes per year for the trainers to review and reinforce SIOP® components.
- Demonstrate SIOP® lesson plans in classrooms for the trainers and teachers to observe.
- Offer support to the trainers based on their needs as they begin implementing the model.
- Facilitate the ordering of the textbooks and binders to implement the SIOP® training at each site.
- Observe in classrooms using the SIOP® protocol to provide feedback to the teachers regarding the implementation of the model.
- Observe the trainers providing feedback to teachers they observed. Provide the trainer with separate feedback concerning his/her coaching.
- Teach the trainers to use the SIOP® protocol for observing in classrooms and providing individual teachers with feedback.
- Plan and implement a second week of the training for the trainers with the goal of having the trainers write lessons using the SIOP® lesson plan format and teach the lessons in the classrooms.
- Plan and implement an overall evaluation of the SIOP® Model implementation at each site.

Draft developed by Susan Hanson (PREL, 2006)

staff at the ESL-Second Languages Department collaborated to write a job announcement and interview candidates.

In other instances, such as at PREL, the Pacific Resources in Education and Learning Center that services the territories and freely associated states of the Pacific region, staff have provided professional development and support. One island, Pohnpei, decided to formalize the role of SIOP® coordinator, and Susan Hanson from PREL assisted by drafting a formal job description to make a SIOP® Coordinator position more permanent. (See Figure 3.3.)

Chapter Summary

This chapter has presented a variety of strategies that schools, districts, and even states employed to begin training teachers in the SIOP® Model and helping them implement it in their classrooms. There is no best way to get started; rather it depends on resources, interest, need, and the background knowledge of the teachers who will learn the model. While getting started often involves a flurry of staff development workshops, we encourage you to think beyond the first steps and plan a long-term program of SIOP® implementation. How some districts did just that is featured in the next chapter.

Questions for Reflection and Discussion

1. You are interested in bringing the SIOP® Model to your school. Prepare a series of talking points to convince your principal that this is the best professional development program for the teachers you work with. Consider the demographics and current level of academic achievement among your English learners, the training your teaching colleagues have had to date, and the overall benefits the SIOP® Model might offer.

2. You have been selected to lead SIOP® Model professional development at your district. Who will be the first teachers you decide to work with? Why have you selected them? How can you build a community of learners with the group you have chosen?

3. Write a memo introducing teachers to the SIOP® Model and inviting them to join the professional development effort. List the benefits they will gain by learning about the model and how you envision the staff development to take place. Counter in advance potential opposition to the SIOP® implementation endeavor.

chapter 4

Models of SIOP® Implementation and Professional Development

I've slowly come to the realization that there is no one magic way to implement the SIOP® model. If districts are willing to take the necessary time to train, build momentum, and effectively provide follow-up and support, they can be successful. I've seen too many examples of successful districts with different approaches to believe that there is a precise formula that everyone must follow.

John Seidlitz, SIOP® National Faculty

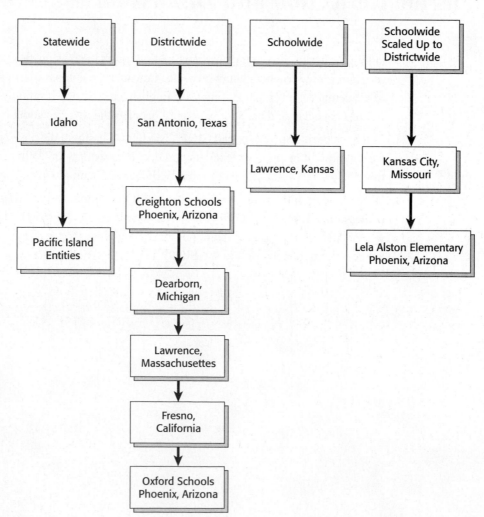

GUIDING YOUR PRACTICE

This chapter showcases various professional development (PD) programs that have resulted in effective SIOP® implementation. Consider your context as you read. You may find features of a PD program that would enhance your own professional development as a teacher or features that you want to add to PD that you organize or deliver. We invite you to focus on the successful aspects of these PD programs as well as the pitfalls to avoid.

In this chapter we showcase a number of SIOP® professional development programs. As mentioned in the Introduction to this book, these examples are by no means the only schools and districts where effective SIOP® implementation and professional development is happening. We meet countless dedicated educators in the United States and abroad who are working diligently to provide quality SIOP® instruction to second language learners, many with impressive results. Our goal here is to provide a variety of examples to reach the widest audience possible: rural schools and urban schools; elementary settings and secondary settings; small districts and large districts; funded programs and unfunded programs; programs at a single school or statewide programs; all from various geographic locations.

We will begin with an overview of implementation options and then present specific implementation and professional development situations.

Statewide SIOP® Implementation

In some states, the SIOP® Model is part of an overall educational reform effort. For example, in Idaho, SIOP® training began as part of a reading improvement initiative. Initially, twelve school districts from across the state were selected and one representative from each district became a reading fellow responsible for facilitating implementation of reading strategies throughout the district. Over the course of eighteen months, these reading fellows received training from a number of reading experts, as well as learning the SIOP® Model through attendance at a SIOP I Institute®. After receiving reading and SIOP® Model training, the reading fellows brought their new expertise back to their school district and worked with teachers in grades K–8.

In the one district that was the focus of the interview, a reading fellow, Laurie Beebe, spent half a day meeting with teachers during their collaboration time. She helped teachers develop reading strategies and showed teachers where the strategies fit into a SIOP® lesson. The district superintendent was supportive of the SIOP® Model and reading strategies "marriage" and promoted the idea that all teachers are teachers of reading and the SIOP® Model. His support provided the impetus for that thinking throughout the district.

The role of the SIOP® Model was described by Laurie Beebe in the following way:

> Most content teachers are not aware of how to teach reading. So, what (SIOP®) provided was an avenue to take content and demonstrate to teachers that language can be taught within content subjects: how to use vocabulary, comprehension, and decoding strategies with the older grades, and what can be done as an intervention with kids who are simply not understanding. Along with that . . . we had to have something in the area of, How do we help our second language kids? . . . In fact, that's really our main focus: How do we get academic information to the kids who have really limited backgrounds and limited language? They are expected to take (standardized) tests when they don't even have strong academic language.

> With SIOP®, the whole learning process gels together. SIOP® has demonstrated to teachers how to plan a lesson, how to use reading strategies during that lesson, and how to review at the end of the lesson. Reading strategies were being stressed to teachers before SIOP®, so that foundation was already present when SIOP® was presented to the district.

Since the time of the statewide initiative, many universities in Idaho have formed a collaborative, and faculty provide SIOP® professional development at the teacher education level as well as for inservice teachers.

Districtwide SIOP® Implementation

Many districts have made SIOP® professional development and implementation a district priority or district initiative. For example, two urban districts, one in Phoenix and one in Kansas City, Missouri, had similar experiences in quite different settings. Creighton School District in Phoenix has nine schools, serving students in grades K–8. It is located in the Southwest, and English learners have been part of the fabric of the schools for decades. Kansas City Missouri School District (KCMSD), on the other hand, has seventy-two schools and serves students in grades K–12. In both these cases, districtwide SIOP® implementation began with one dedicated individual at the district office. In Kansas City, Alicia Miguel was the director of language services for KCMSD, and Marilyn Sanchez was director of English language services for Creighton. In both cases, they worked in selected schools to introduce the SIOP® Model and, through extensive coaching and support, deepen teachers' understanding of the model. From there other schools became involved. In Creighton, the first cohort was thirty teachers, and in 2005–2006 the number had grown to 400. Professional development with the SIOP® Model really accelerated when the district administration took notice. As Marilyn describes,

> Last year our leadership decided to look at core instructional strategies because our evaluation instrument is really old, so they looked at SIOP®, they looked at [other regular education programs], and then we tried to merge those. Then one of our principals said, "I don't know why we're doing this. Ninety percent of our district is ELL and the other children are in poverty, and they need this just as much." So then the leadership council chose SIOP® as a basis of our core instructional strategies . . . This is our first year. We also use SIOP® to do our own SEI training—Structured English Immersion training—required by the state . . . We use it [SIOP®] as a basis for that. So with those two things our critical mass is growing.

In Kansas City, Alicia worked extensively at one school site for a year, then involved other schools. She plans during the 2007–2008 school year to bring in SIOP® National Faculty to train 60 percent of the nearly 4,000 teachers in the district, with the remainder to be trained the following year.

Schoolwide SIOP® Implementation

In several places, SIOP® Model implementation began at one school. While widespread implementation is impressive, recommendations made in the Epilogue sometimes suggest that starting small is useful so there is a model school for the others to follow. For example, Lela Alston Elementary School in Phoenix was the only SIOP® school in the district for almost four years. Their focus was on developing high-quality SIOP® implementation in every classroom, and they had a strong SIOP® support component (see description in the next section of this chapter). Their student achievement gains on the state standards test brought attention to the school, and interest in the SIOP® eventually spread to other schools in the district.

However, being the only school may create vulnerability. A change in district personnel threatened continuation of the SIOP® Model at Alston School. Although other schools were scheduled to begin SIOP® implementation as well, when a new assistant superintendent for instruction (who is no longer in the district) joined the district, he wanted to have his own "stamp" on the district and did not support SIOP® training. For some time it appeared as though SIOP® training would not be continued, but grassroots support overcame district resistance. Currently, a number of schools in the district have received SIOP® professional development.

Another district reported that a difficulty of being the designated SIOP® school is that while the school staff is focused on sustaining SIOP® professional development activities, the district may have a number of other initiatives that compete for time, effort, and funds. Sometimes there may not be a good understanding at the district level of the focused effort required to implement any program to a high degree and have it impact student achievement.

In conclusion, there is not necessarily one best way to implement the SIOP® Model. The decision depends on many of the factors discussed in Chapter 2.

Sample SIOP® Professional Development Programs

In this section, we will present a number of examples of implementation from around the United States. Essentially three types of models emerged from the interviews:

1. A district representative or team attended a SIOP Institute®, then returned to the district and carried out a professional development program (see Appendix A for a description of SIOP Institutes®);

2. A district representative or team attended a SIOP Institute®, returned to the district, and developed a plan for sending the rest of the staff to SIOP Institutes® or contracted with SIOP® National Faculty to provide staff training.

3. An individual or group began a book study of *Making Content Comprehensible for English Learners: The SIOP® Model,* and began learning and practicing the components of the SIOP® Model.

These professional development plans have not been empirically tested, so we are not endorsing them as effective models of professional development. However, they reflect practices that are taking place around the country and have some elements of what we know to be effective professional development, as discussed in Chapter 2.

Teachers Trained with No Start-up Cost

Kansas City, Missouri. As part of the district's strategic plan, every teacher in this midwestern urban district of 27,000 students and 4,000 teachers will be trained in the SIOP® Model. In 2002, the director of language services, Alicia Miguel, attended a SIOP Institute® and took the training back to her district. The district practiced job-embedded professional development wherein grade-level or content area teachers are released together during the school day to receive professional development. In elementary schools, specialists (art, music, PE teachers) work with the children during teachers' release time, and secondary teachers meet during their planning periods.

Alicia targeted one school, Gladstone Elementary, for initial SIOP® training. During the first year, she went to the school twice a week, each time meeting with grade-level teams, the support teachers such as ESL, art, music and PE teachers, and the instructional coach. There were four teachers at each grade level, and there were three ESL teachers; Alicia met with seven groups each week. For example, on Tuesday mornings, she met with kindergarten teachers and the primary ESL teacher from 9:00 to 10:00, then first grade teachers from 10:05 to 11:00, and so on. Each grade-level team met once per week and learned one SIOP® component per month starting with Preparation and ending with Review/Assessment. During the meetings, the group discussed the chapter that corresponded to the component they were focusing on and they watched video clips and discussed them so that they fully understood each component. As Alicia worked with the teachers, she was deepening her own knowledge and understanding of the SIOP® Model as well. All eight components were introduced and studied in the first year.

The second year focused on implementation. The instructional coach, Charlotte Daniel, met with teachers once per week to plan lessons, observe the lessons, and debrief. She also modeled SIOP® lessons as needed. Then Alicia met with the school's instructional coach and the teachers once per month to ensure that the components were adequately represented in the lesson plans and that the observations and debriefing sessions were productive. Some of the lessons were videotaped and used in the meetings. The computer teacher at the school assisted the teachers in videotaping the lesson at the same time that teachers were observing and taking notes. The following week, during the regular SIOP® meeting, they watched the video clip together and discussed the notes, questions, or suggestions that teachers had written during the observation. Videotaping was very useful because they could rewind and replay if something was in question or if teachers did not remember how something was done. Lessons were also observed in person by peers. For example, during the third grade teachers' release time, they would visit a second grade classroom and observe a SIOP® lesson. In this way, the teachers had an opportunity to see a SIOP® lesson implemented and could debrief a specific lesson.

In the third year, Charlotte, the instructional coach, worked with the teachers through weekly grade-level meetings. At this point, all staff knew the SIOP® and had developed "the language of SIOP®," which facilitated implementation. Observations were done with their own grade levels, e.g., third grade teachers observed a third grade lesson. Teachers felt it was more meaningful to observe a lesson that they would teach themselves.

Aside from the cost of the SIOP® book for each teacher, there were no additional costs to the district for comprehensive training at the pilot school. As professional development expanded districtwide, SIOP® National Faculty (professional developers) were brought in to assist with the district's widespread effort. The goal for the first year of expansion was to have 60 percent of the district's 4,000 teachers receive SIOP® professional development and the remaining 40 percent the following year.

New School . . . New Vision

Lela Alston Elementary School, Phoenix, Arizona. This endeavor was funded by a federal Title III grant for professional development. A new K–3 school, Lela Alston Elementary School, had been opened in the district and was selected to receive SIOP® training as a pilot site with other schools in the district to follow if the project was successful. At the end of Alston's first year, a team of seven people attended a SIOP Institute® in Long Beach, California. The team included two district office personnel, Marcy Granillo and Irma Pastor; two district language specialists, Rueben Huerta and Lisa Kempton; and three people from Lela Alston Elementary School, principal Debbie Hutson, coach Wanda Holbrook, and trainer and lead SIOP® teacher Kendra Moreno. The Alston team consisted of the principal, the coach, and a third grade teacher. After the training, the Alston team was expected to train the rest of the school. The second and third years were when implementation and training took place (2002–2003 and 2003–2004). It was also expected that districtwide workshops would be held to educate others in the SIOP® Model. These districtwide workshops were on a volunteer basis.

The Title III grant provided stipends for training, money for supplies, a full-time coach (Wanda), and a stipend for a lead SIOP® teacher (Kendra). The funding was also used for staff training both years, a weekend staff retreat twice a year for the entire staff, and for substitute teachers. Substitutes were brought in to allow one grade level at a time a day or half a day to work out of their classroom together with Kendra and Wanda. Each teacher at the school received the SIOP® book and some supply materials.

The training team—the lead teacher, principal, and coach—completed a time line for the two years. As they went through the two years, they implemented one component per quarter with a cumulative effect.

The staff was provided training and support in a number of ways.

- The SIOP® coach (Wanda) and lead teacher/coach (Kendra) conducted whole staff trainings (twenty-three teachers, including special education teachers, plus paraprofessionals). The district's staff development program provided for one early release day per quarter, so those four days were used for SIOP® trainings. The staff met for four or five hours after the children were released. At the training, the staff was introduced to each feature of the selected component, watched the SIOP® videos, and had discussions around the practices they had seen. It took the entire two years to get through all the components in a comprehensive way.

- Substitutes were used to allow Wanda and Kendra to work with individual grade level teachers wherein they did lesson planning, preparation, and sometimes a more in-depth look at the component.

- Each quarter Wanda modeled and/or teamed with each teacher, including the special area teachers, to present a lesson. Wanda and the teacher planned a lesson during a preconference and discussed the lesson later. Most of the lessons were reading based. During the first two years the lessons were given a number rating, and a detailed discussion followed. As the value of the discussion became more obvious, the number rating was discontinued and the observations more focused on the features observed in the lesson.

- Teachers' lessons were observed and rated. During the first year, teachers used the entire protocol to conduct peer observations with another teacher they felt comfortable with. During the second year, teachers were comfortable enough with the process that their lessons could be rated on the specific components they had studied. Wanda observed a lesson from every teacher using the SIOP® protocol. She met with the teacher during prep time or after school and discussed the observation.

- Videotaping of teachers' lessons began in the spring of 2004 and continued in the 2004–2005 school year. A video camera was purchased with some of the SIOP® grant funds, and the coach videotaped every teacher doing a SIOP® lesson. Afterward, she and the teacher watched the video together and completed the SIOP® protocol. Then the tape was given to the teacher to guarantee privacy; it was meant for their professional growth only. In the fall of 2005, they began the second round of videotaping, with the teachers taping one another and rating the lesson or asking the coach to be involved. Peer videotaping proved to be more stressful and more of a risk than working with the coach, with whom trust had been built.

Struggling to Get It Going

San Antonio, Texas. This district, located on the south side of San Antonio, had a student enrollment of more than 10,000 students. The schools were experiencing rapid growth resulting from the construction of a new Toyota plant and other satellite industries. At the time of the interview, nineteen new housing developments were accommodating the migration of families to the district, which is expected to double in size over the next few years. The school system was being transformed from a small rural district to a growing suburban one.

In 2005, the district hired a new superintendent and later hired several key administrators, including the assistant superintendent for instruction and support services and the director of bilingual/ESL programs. All had previously worked in larger districts where the SIOP® Model was implemented effectively. When they arrived, their intent was to provide professional development and facilitate use of the SIOP® Model in the schools using an implementation model similar to one they had used before. With approximately 1,500 English learners and growing, and declining test scores at the secondary level, the need was clear. However, there were some struggles they had not anticipated that prevented them from making rapid progress in the implementation of SIOP® Model.

Understanding district culture and systems has been the topic of many "Leadership 101" classes but is sometimes overlooked when creating new initiatives. This case was no exception and required some rethinking of the initial SIOP® implementation plan. While many of the administrators understood ELs were not successful in core subject areas, only a few had an instructional background in effective approaches for English learners. Some were unfamiliar with sheltered instruction strategies and did not know what to look for when they went into classrooms already impacted with English learners.

The second issue that had to be dealt with was the lack of understanding of the importance of academic language. The relationship between academic language and school success had to be understood before SIOP® could be made a priority. Laying the foundations of the interplay between academic language and academic achievement continues to be an area of constant staff development. Administrators and mainstream staff understand the importance of vocabulary instruction; however, explicit teaching of specific language structures that are found in cause and effect relationships, comparisons, etc., needs development. These structures make up a large part of the formation of language objectives, a major feature of the SIOP® Model.

Third, there were programmatic service delivery issues. For example, some students in secondary schools were placed in ESL classes by grade level, not English proficiency level, so that all seventh grade ELs were in the same class regardless of English proficiency, while one school had a sheltered team and the others did not.

Also, funds were used differently from the way to which the new administrators were accustomed. In their previous experience, English learners generated 50 percent more of the regular ADA, so there were ample funds to develop a district program replete with SIOP® coaches, resources, a staff development plan to train all teachers and administrators at the secondary level in SIOP®, and a resource library for sheltered core teachers. Title II and Title III funds were used for intensive staff development of the SIOP® Model and ongoing monitoring and evaluation measures. In this state, funding formulas were different—the use of funds, especially local funds, was more conservative. Keeping ample reserves of funds was prudent, so that the program was not funded to its maximum.

Finally, some teachers had been trained in SIOP® at a regional service center or as part of a university grant, but there was no systemic district program of implementation or monitoring.

In facing these and other obstacles, the director of bilingual/ESL programs saw the need to 1) provide a systematic implementation plan; 2) educate principals and administrators in the effectiveness of the model; 3) use student data and various state monitoring reports as the rationale and impetus for the planned SIOP® training; and 4) develop some key people at campuses to learn and incorporate the SIOP® Model well in their classrooms so that they could eventually become SIOP® coaches and provide support and model lessons for others.

The first year was spent "understanding the system" and forming relationships with key principals. After the state test scores came back in the spring, a group of secondary principals and assistant principals were sent to the Administrative SIOP® training using Title III funds. That fall a new junior high principal, a former bilingual teacher with instructional expertise, attended the three-day teacher training of SIOP®. With her understanding of the model she was then able to go into classrooms of a few teachers who had been previously trained and had instructional conversations about the SIOP® components. In addition, this principal understood the immediate need to have all of her staff trained in SIOP® and a specific sheltered team established in her building.

The following fall, a group of ESL teachers and an assistant principal developed a database that is evolving into a rubric of language proficiency and achievement scores, using the LAS assessment, the state annual language proficiency scores, benchmark scores, and Reading Proficiency Test in English (RPTE) and TAKS scores. Writing scores using writing traits, as well as other reading assessments, will be added to the database/rubric to determine proficiency levels. ESL classes were then structured around proficiency levels. The bilingual/ESL director advised the group as to the content of ESL classes so that they not only developed English language, but were the foundational classes of academic language for success in sheltered classes. They established ESL blocks so that beginning students could have concentrated time to improve their English proficiency around the specific areas of vocabulary and content discourses they would encounter in either their SIOP® or content classes.

At the time of the interview, a state report requesting a plan to improve state testing results of ELs was just completed. All of the secondary principals and their teams were able to review the current programs at their sites and agree to a number of plans: a consistent model of ESL courses for the district; the formation of SIOP®-trained content teams; a plan for more teacher and administrative training in SIOP®; and a building coaching model. (Some content teachers from the secondary schools have attended SIOP® training and have begun learning and practicing the model. Implementation has been quite uneven in classrooms without follow-up support and currently, the bilingual/ESL director is watching for some strong SIOP® teachers to emerge so that they could become SIOP® coaches.) These coaches would facilitate high-quality implementation of the SIOP® Model.

Once all teachers knew the model, the goal was to have the ESL, sheltered, and mainstream teachers on teams so that the ESL teachers understood the expectations of the sheltered and mainstream classes and vice versa. Collaboration among the teachers would enhance service delivery to students by improving instruction through an analysis of student data and using targeted proven interventions to those English learners at risk.

While all schools have agreed to the new model, the degree of " buy-in" is relative to the instructional leadership at the campus level and the marshalling of support from the central office and other entities. The ultimate goal is to have one school serve as a model to others—and generate interest in replicating it—once those teachers have improved instruction to students; student achievement will improve as a result.

Statewide Literacy Initiative That Includes the SIOP® Model

Idaho. As part of a statewide introduction to the SIOP® Model, district staff attended a SIOP Institute® in 2003, learned the model, and then began training teachers in their district. Ten people in the district received training, and those individuals worked together to teach the eight components to the entire district staff, K–12.

Training was tailored to the different grade levels. In K–5, the eight components were presented once a month. Wednesday afternoons were scheduled as collaboration time, and one day a month during teachers' regular collaboration time, one of the components would be presented to them.

At the middle school, they had weekly collaboration time. Collaboration teams were grade level teachers who met weekly to discuss student issues and schedules, and received professional development instruction. One of the district SIOP® trainers had as part of her job description to go to the middle school once a week and teach reading strategies. Within those reading strategy discussions they would talk about a component of SIOP®. For example, in discussion of a reading strategy she would point out that in order to use the strategy, students' background needs to be built first. Then she would present the SIOP® component for building background effectively. SIOP® lesson planning and instructor modeling were used to present the instructional segment of the collaboration meeting.

Training was more actual modeling for those teachers in grades K–8—mostly the core teachers—because when the core teachers have their block time for collaboration, that's when the students go to PE and art and music. In 2005 the specialists (art, music, PE) formed a collaboration team also.

At the high school, teachers were offered inservice days, and some of the teachers took a SIOP® class that was offered during the summer. It was a three-day intensive SIOP® training. The teachers that did not take the SIOP® class in the summer were required to spend three inservice days throughout the school year learning about the model. Those SIOP® inservice trainings were given by the district SIOP® trainers at the school site.

After all teachers in the district were trained in the SIOP® Model, the following year an "observational protocol" class was offered to teachers interested in deepening their implementation of the model. Two or three teachers from the same school attended, for a total of twenty-five teachers. Five class sessions and five peer observations were held, focusing on coaching/observing using the protocol, learning strategies to encourage student engagement, and studying the eight components in greater depth. The class was a two-credit continuing education class that lasted all year. Peer partnerships used the protocol as a tool in observing and conferencing. Those twenty-five teachers have continued implementing the model in their classes.

A SIOP® National Faculty member, Melissa Castillo, conducts a workshop.

From the Ground Up: A Successful Grassroots Effort

Creighton, Arizona. This district of nine schools began by using the SIOP® Model in five dual language schools and later expanded training to all teachers in the district. (After English-Only became state policy in 2000 there were seven SEI or Structured English Immersion schools and two dual language schools.) The SIOP® was the basis for their state-mandated sixty hours of Sheltered English Immersion training, which was structured in four modules of fifteen hours. The district employed a system of Teachers on Assignment (TOAs) who had an assigned school site and facilitated collegial coaching clusters at their site. The TOAs had been trained at SIOP Institutes®, typically SIOP I® and SIOP II®. At the school site, coaches were selected based on their knowledge of second language acquisition and the SIOP® Model. If a coach was not familiar with the SIOP® Model, they were required to receive training in the model through a university course or a SIOP Institute®. Widespread, grassroots SIOP® training was accomplished through the collegial coaching process.

Collegial Coaching Cycles. The district's coaching process was a cycle involving planning, teaching, and debriefing. First, a TOA worked with a site-based coach, assisting him or her in planning lessons and understanding the SIOP® Model to a higher degree. Then the coach planned a lesson that was modeled for a group of three to five peers, with the group debriefing the lesson and discussing the components of the SIOP® Model. Each participant had a copy of the SIOP® protocol with the rating numbers removed. Since the planning was done collaboratively, the Preparation component wasn't pertinent to the debriefing and was removed from the protocol. Participants wrote what they saw the coach do and described it on the protocol under the corresponding indicator. The TOA also attended the session to provide support and guidance. For example, when a teacher mentioned something observed, the TOA may say, "Oh, right, when she did that it was part of building background." In this way, the teachers were learning the model through practice rather than direct teaching of the SIOP® Model.

Next, one of the teachers in the group volunteered to model a lesson during the following quarter (nine- or ten- week period). The coach assisted teacher volunteers in planning the lesson that was modeled for the group. Feedback from the group was not evaluative (see Figure 4.1 for debriefing form) and was limited to positive comments and a discussion of how the lesson matched SIOP® features. The teachers were instructed to "Please use statements that remind the teacher we're not judging what we see. We're here to observe and reflect, never to evaluate a teacher!" Because of this type of setting, there wasn't a problem getting teachers to volunteer to model a lesson for their peers. This cycle resulted in having a different teacher each quarter go through the cycle and model a lesson for the group.

Coaches were teachers practicing the SIOP® Model in their classroom, and as coaches they were responsible for first setting up their room so it was "SIOP® compatible." The district offered two types of coaching models. One involved providing a coach for grade level clusters, i.e., K–2, 3–5, and 6–8. Those coaches received a stipend of $3,000 and were responsible for conducting four coaching cycles. In this process, with three coaches per site there are twelve coaching cycles, which impacts a large number of teachers.

The other model of coaching is similar but requires less participation. Some school sites wanted a coach for each grade level. In that case, the coach focused on one grade level and received a stipend of $1,000. Responsibilities included keeping their room arranged in a way that supports SIOP® teaching, sponsoring one coaching cycle, and participating in "book talks" with other SIOP® coaches at their grade level.

Coaches were funded through a matching program wherein the district paid for two coaches for every one that the school site funded. For example, at a K–8 school there were nine coaches: six that the district funded and three that the school funded.

SEI I (fifteen hours). This first level of training begins with an overview of the model. The components that we introduce are Building Background, Comprehensible Input, Strategies, Interaction, Practice/Application and Review/Assessment. Although Lesson Preparation and Lesson Delivery are not presented until the second level of training, these components are modeled for the teachers. The rationale for omitting these two components is to focus on objective writing at the next level.

Instead of using videotape examples of the components, actual lessons are modeled by the presenters. There are two model lessons and a simulated coaching cycle. As a follow-up to the SEI I training, teachers participate in a coaching cycle at their school.

SEI II (fifteen hours). The focus of this level of training is on Lesson Preparation, with specific attention given to understanding and writing language and content objectives, although the other components are reviewed. Teachers are introduced to writing content and language objectives, and they are provided opportunities to practice writing objectives. In addition, the district has videotaped model lessons showing a variety of language levels. Teachers are asked to identify the language level reflected in the videotape and then write a language objective appropriate for the child.

FIGURE 4.1 *Creighton's Collegial Coaching Debriefing Form*

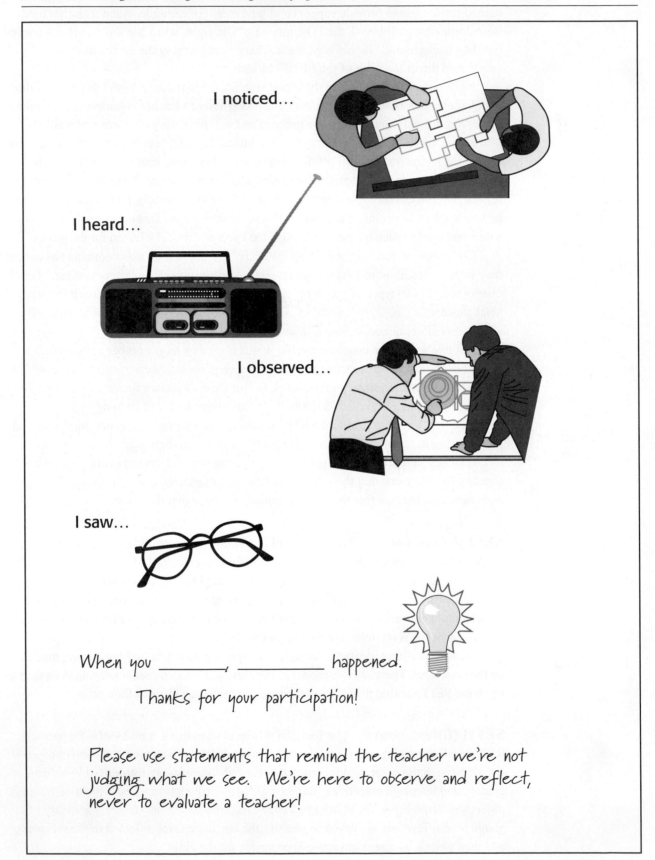

I noticed...

I heard...

I observed...

I saw...

When you _____, _____ happened.

Thanks for your participation!

Please use statements that remind the teacher we're not judging what we see. We're here to observe and reflect, never to evaluate a teacher!

The other six components are reviewed and reinforced using video analysis. Through video analysis, teachers gain a deeper understanding of the features. As a follow-up to SEI II training, teachers participate in a coaching cycle at their school.

SEI III (fifteen hours). This advanced training involves twelve hours of instruction and three hours of planning. This module is dedicated solely to lesson planning and lesson delivery. Since the teachers have had extensive experience with each of the components, they are responsible for pulling it together and writing a SIOP® lesson plan. The lesson writing is done during the twelve hours of instruction. Each teacher will model his or her lesson for one of the TOAs.

As a follow-up to the training, the teachers will teach a practice lesson for peers.

SEI IV (fifteen hours). This training is dedicated to using SIOP® in guided reading groups and other literacy settings. (All eight components are adapted to literacy, with a heavy emphasis on contextualizing critical literacy strategies such as prediction, revision, determining importance, etc.).

A University Partnership Yields Results

Lawrence, Kansas. Tammy Becker, the principal at this midwestern elementary school, made a commitment to have teachers learn the model through SIOP Institutes®. Working with Dr. Socorro Herrera from Kansas State University, as part of a teacher preparation grant, Tammy initially attended a SIOP Institute® for Administrators and then attended three SIOP I Institutes®, each time with a different team of her teachers. First she attended with a team of primary teachers from first and second grade as well as the ESL Newcomer teacher. Later, she attended another SIOP Institute® with a group of teachers from grades 2–5. At a third SIOP Institute®, she brought teachers from a variety of grade levels so that at the school there would be at least two teachers from each grade level trained by SIOP® experts.

After the first group was trained, they formed a study group so that they could support one another and deepen their understanding of the SIOP® Model. Once two groups of teachers had been trained, these nine teachers began implementing the components of the SIOP® Model focusing on certain features at a time.

A trainer from Kansas State, Shabina Kavimandan, (funded through the grant) conducted mini-sessions at the school introducing the SIOP® components to the other teachers who had not attended an institute. The idea behind this training approach was to select one person from each grade level to be trained by SIOP® experts at the Institutes. These teachers became grade level resources to the other teachers who had been trained by Shabina, the university trainer. Later, more teachers from each grade level were trained so that there were two SIOP Institute®-trained teachers per grade level.

Teachers, along with the support of Shabina and Tammy, the principal, spent two full years learning the components in training sessions and then implementing them in their classrooms. At each mini-session, Shabina introduced one component at a time and reinforced what had already been introduced. Those teachers who had been trained at the SIOP® Institutes helped with the trainings at times, and they often used video clips from their classrooms to show the remaining staff. Shabina also went into the classrooms once per week and supported teachers by discussing the focused areas they were working on, such as language objectives or vocabulary.

In the fall of 2006, the teachers who had not previously done so attended a SIOP Institute®, so by 2007, all teachers and specialists in the school had received the same training and were consistently implementing the SIOP® Model in all classrooms.

Start in the Middle Grades and Expand throughout the District

Dearborn, Michigan. In this large urban district of 18,000 K–12 students (7,500 ELLs), the district Bilingual and Compensatory Education staff targeted middle school for the first wave of SIOP® training. A six-member district team, consisting of district and building administrative staff and Bilingual/Title 1 Resource Teachers, attended a SIOP Institute® in Long Beach, California, in June of 2001. The core of the team who have continued providing SIOP® professional development over the years included Dr. Santina Buffone, coordinator, bilingual and compensatory education; Megdieh Jawad, coordinator, bilingual and compensatory education; Maura Sedgeman, resource teacher leader, bilingual and compensatory education; and Saada Charara, classroom teacher. The team returned to the district motivated and energized to recruit more teachers into the training.

Thus, another team of fifteen individuals from the middle schools (administrators, assistant principals, and bilingual teacher and general education teacher teams from each of the middle schools) participated in the August 2001 SIOP Institute®. With a strong school-based SIOP® team and vital support from administration, this group of Institute-trained educators planned for districtwide SIOP® training for teachers, administrators, and paraprofessionals.

The districtwide kick-off was a two-part SIOP® training on six Saturdays, with district SIOP® trainers leading each component. Approximately eighty teachers and paraprofessionals participated from various district elementary, middle, and high schools. Attendees were paid at workshop rate. Each Saturday focused on four components of the SIOP® Model. (The district has continued this practice every year to the present—especially important for new teachers to the district).

After the initial districtwide Saturday training, SIOP® expanded to the building level. For example, at one of the middle schools, district trainers attended grade level meetings and presented each component. Over time, all teachers in the building were trained in SIOP®. The building staff focused on embedding SIOP® techniques and strategies into daily teaching, whether the content area was science, math, social studies, or language arts.

Because the principal and assistant principal were also SIOP® trained, teacher evaluations included SIOP® components. Evaluations reflected use of language objectives and content objectives written and explained to the students. Evaluations also affirmed that teachers brought lessons to closure with strong review and assessment.

Another way the district has promoted SIOP® implementation is through "book talks" in some of the schools. A small group of teachers met either before or after school to review the book chapter by chapter to deepen their understanding and keep the ideas fresh in their minds. One of the first people trained at the SIOP Institute® became an assistant principal at one middle school and has used the "book talk format" as a means for effective SIOP® implementation.

To ensure a successful teaching staff for the districtwide Accelerated Summer Academic Program involving more than six hundred Bilingual and Title I students, SIOP® training is included as a part of the summer staff development. One component is presented per day in an interactive session. In the past seven years this training has impacted some eighty teachers and paraprofessionals *each year*, widening the district pool of SIOP®-trained staff.

SIOP® training has become a mainstay of each year's professional development plan for the districtwide professional development days. As well, all SIOP® training in the district is tied to State Board Continuing Education Units or college credit. District SIOP® trainers teach SIOP® as one of the endorsement courses as part of a district-sponsored Bilingual/ESL endorsement cohort program. After the initial SIOP® inservice in each component, teachers write lesson plans using the SIOP® format. Teachers are also observed in their classroom implementing SIOP® strategies. The SIOP® book *Making Content Comprehensible for English Learners: The SIOP® Model* is used for the Dearborn cohort class, as well as by Wayne State University in teacher preparation courses.

The district-developed SIOP® bookmarks (see Chapter 6) synthesizing each component and the overview have aided teachers in remembering strategies and techniques as they work with students and plan lessons appropriately. Many teachers have laminated the color-coded, tagboard bookmarks and put them on a ring for convenience.

Whether through the comprehensive district professional development plan, adding specific techniques to each SIOP® component, or just ensuring that some component of SIOP® is a part of every content area inservice, Dearborn has increased teachers' capacity to reach English learners and other students. Through these various ways, the district has trained approximately 650 teachers, 30 administrators, and 150 paraprofessionals since 2001. As new teachers join the district, many SIOP® opportunities await them—as one of the district music teachers, Jim Walters, who was trained in the SIOP®Model, put it in an original "SIOP Song":

> Just use the S-I-O-P®!
>
> You need the S-I-O-P®!
>
> Because with sheltered instruction,
>
> Both language and content grow in unity.
>
> Yes, with sheltered instruction,
>
> The children will all SI OPportunity!

Using SIOP® National Faculty for Expert Training

Lawrence, Massachusetts. In this urban district of more than 12,000 students, English was not the first language of more than 80 percent of the students, and special education services were provided to 18 percent of the students (2005–2006). Under an English-only state mandate, the superintendent, Dr. Wilfredo Laboy; assistant superintendent for curriculum and instruction, Gail Rosengard; and Dr. Dalis Dominguez, began to tackle the district's low achievement. They contracted with Pearson Achievement Solutions to bring SIOP® National Faculty to their district and provide a capacity-building model of professional development. In spring 2006, a two-day SIOP I Institute® was conducted in Lawrence for a "Master Cohort" of fifty teachers and fifteen Central Office staff. The group was referred to as a Master Cohort because they were already recognized as being knowledgeable and skilled in the content and pedagogy of instructing English learners and would receive extensive training to become site SIOP® professional developers.

At the Institute, participants were introduced to each of the eight SIOP® Model components, along with the research base for each. In fall 2006 (August–November), the following professional activities took place:

- One-day overview for all PK–12 teachers in the district. During this overview, four of the eight SIOP® components were emphasized: 1) Lesson Preparation; 2) Building Background; 3) Strategies; and 4) Lesson Delivery.

- Formation of districtwide SIOP® Implementation Team consisting of the superintendent of schools, the assistant superintendent for curriculum & instruction, the coordinator of curriculum and instructional measurement, the supervisor of ELL Programs and ELL districtwide facilitator, and several content area curriculum specialists.

- Coaching and preparation of SIOP® Resident Classrooms, which emphasize a strengths-based model and the concept of making teaching public for collegial professional learning. They provide an avenue for highlighting SIOP® instructional strategies and practices, which support the common goals, philosophy, and objectives established in the district's Comprehensive Education Plan and Essential Learning Outcomes, aligned with state standards. They maximize opportunities for collegial sharing and collaboration and offer teachers a unique opportunity to observe instructional strategies applied within real classroom settings. A debriefing session follows the classroom visitation.

- The role of the Lawrence Public Schools Instructional Content Coaches is aligned with the Strengths-based Model of Professional Development. Forty-eight specialized content area coaches and facilitators provide ongoing, school-based professional development and training in the areas of Literacy, Mathematics, and Science.

- Selected staff attended a two-day SIOP Institute® in Florida to become trainers approved to train using SIOP® online course materials. The selected staff consisted of four members of the Master Cohort.

- SIOP® Walkthroughs began. SIOP® Walkthroughs are conducted by the SIOP® Implementation Team as well as school administrators, e.g., principals and assistant principals. The purpose of these walkthroughs is to monitor the implementation of the SEI program as well as the SIOP® Model, not to evaluate teachers. The district developed a SIOP® Walkthrough Tool, which is organized around the four SIOP® components being implemented the first year, and around principles of an effective learning environment. Users of this tool have been trained in its use. The data gathered during these visits forms the basis for professional conversations with faculty or individual teachers for the purpose of informing instructional decisions, strengthening teachers' ability to deliver effective SIOP® lessons, and improving the academic success of English Language Learners. During these visits SIOP® features, as well as best practices observed, are recorded in detail. After Walkthroughs are completed, the administrator from the school schedules a debriefing session with the teacher(s) within a day of the Walkthrough to provide feedback and discuss next steps.

- A schedule of Resident Classroom openings was developed and distributed.
- Job-alike half-day professional development. During fall 2006, ESL teachers from the Master Cohort attended a workshop titled " From Preparation to Lesson Delivery: Using SIOP® for Coaching." This workshop focused on how to help mainstream teachers successfully implement the SIOP® Model and how to answer the most frequently asked questions (i.e., How do I develop and choose a strong language objective? What is the difference between the content objective and language objective? How do I present the language objective for students who represent different language development levels?, etc.). New teachers in grades 1–8 attended a workshop titled "From Preparation to Lesson Delivery: Using SIOP® for Instruction: ESL Strategies." This workshop provided an overview of the four SIOP® components being implemented by the district as well as additional instructional strategies that can be used within the SIOP® Model.
- SIOP II Institute®. During winter 2006 and spring 2007 (December–June), the Master Cohort (original cohort of fifty teachers and fifteen Central Office Staff) participated in a SIOP II Institute®, which is an advanced training designed for those who have attended a SIOP I Institute® and have been implementing the SIOP® Model. The teachers and staff received six days of follow-up training with the SIOP® National Faculty.
- School-based trainings. Once the Master Cohort had received this extensive training, they conducted school-based trainings that varied in implementation. Some have given a course outside the school day; others have been part of the half-day early release professional development agendas; others have led team discussions. Job-embedded professional development is tailored to the needs of the school. It is a strength of this implementation plan that the Master Cohort members are recognized by colleagues as a resource within their building.

At the time of the interview, the district planned to continue the SIOP® professional development in 2007–2008 in order to sustain the components learned in 2006–2007 and to focus on the remaining four components. The goals of the two-year SIOP® professional development effort included:

- Teachers will increase their knowledge of ELL students' educational needs.
- Teachers will be able to formulate and deliver clear, educationally sound student-centered SIOP® lessons.
- Teachers will develop an understanding of the connections between the delivery of content in the classroom and the disparate language needs of their students, resulting in increased educational outcomes.
- Teachers will develop SIOP® lessons that will be guided by language and content objectives appropriate for LEP students at different levels of proficiency.
- Teachers will analyze the language needs of their students and develop SIOP® lessons and educational strategies to assist them in gaining the requisite knowledge.
- Teachers will use the SIOP® protocol to plan, implement, and analyze classroom lessons.
- Teachers will use the features of the SIOP® protocol to assess content learning of students who are at different levels of English proficiency.

SIOP® Lesson Study: A Unique Approach

Fresno, California. In this large, urban K–12 school district (78,000 ELs or 1/3 of the student population), the idea for SIOP® implementation began after some district EL staff attended a SIOP Institute®. One of the philosophies in the EL department was that instruction only changes if you put the quality of the contact between teachers and students in the forefront of professional development. In order for the quality of instruction to change, this interaction has to be the focus; if teachers' instructional needs aren't met, neither are the students'. Their goal was to support teachers, sustaining that support over time.

Before beginning a professional development effort, the staff spent considerable time doing research on which students were struggling and determined that they would begin with secondary students. They also researched what secondary English learners needed. They discovered that social studies was a subject area in which ELs were struggling, so they began by collaborating with the district social studies coordinator. They worked with a committee of about twenty teachers from sixth grade to twelfth grade, spending a year strategizing ways to train most effectively. They wanted to involve the people they would be working with and approached the training of teachers as having "all their ducks in a row."

During the planning year, the group developed a number of materials and strategies to prepare for training teachers. The group:

- Aligned the standards to materials. Publishers were asked to show how their materials would supplement the adopted textbooks and assist in meeting the standards.

- Adapted standards to various language acquisition levels (see Chapter 7, Figure 7.20).

- Identified key vocabulary from the social studies standards, and adopted text (see Chapter 7, Figures 7.17 and 7.18).

- Identified the academic language of the social studies standards needed to complete tasks and how to differentiate for students (see Chapter 7, Figure 7.19).

- Adapted chapters from the text, demonstrated highlighted text and rewritten text.

- Prioritized standards and identified "focus" standards.

- Demonstrated how to go back to key lessons and extract the key concepts.

- Coordinated with the district content person so teachers didn't get a different set of demands from him or her.

- Identified necessary professional development and used the SIOP® as a framework for introducing it (see Epilogue, Figure 9.2). For example, technological applications, Japanese lesson study.

- Invited presentations by several EL-friendly publishing companies at selected training sessions where "gift certificates" were offered to teachers to provide a sampling of materials that supported SIOP® implementation.

Once these things were in place, in the second year, teachers were selected to participate in SIOP® training. The social studies coordinator recruited teachers, and fliers were distributed to advertise the training. Enrollment was limited to forty teachers because the goal was to have a focused training with teachers from a variety of schools.

This group spent two years together going through the SIOP® components. The training sessions were held in the evenings from 4:00 p.m. to 8:00 p.m. and food was provided. The trainings were hands-on to make them meaningful, and teachers were given the SIOP® book *Making Content Comprehensible for English Learners: The SIOP® Model*, along with supplementary social studies materials and staff development.

Once the teachers learned the components, they began doing Japanese lesson study with SIOP® lessons. Japanese lesson study (JLS) is a collaborative process through which teachers improve instruction and is based upon the way teachers in Japan learn to teach and develop lessons and curriculum (see Chapter 4, Appendix page 62 for further discussion).

Teachers also engaged in self-observations. They used the SIOP® protocol to self-evaluate their lesson and used the information to prompt discussions about how the feature furthered the teacher's instructional goal. They used this process as a way of establishing a "comfort zone" so that later the teachers would be able to participate in JLS and allow other teachers and observers in their classrooms.

All Across the Pacific

There are districts across the United States that service large geographic regions, which can be a challenge for providing ongoing professional development. Some ideas may be garnered through the experience of professional developers in the Pacific. The largest geographic SIOP® professional development effort to date was conducted by staff from Pacific Resources for Education and Learning (PREL), which serves the Pacific region. They work with teachers on the islands of Hawaii, Guam, American Samoa, the Northern Mariana Islands, Chuuk, Pohnpei, Palau, Yap, and the Marshall Islands.

The SIOP Institutes® held in Hawaii in 2005 were attended by PREL staff and teachers from the region. After the PREL trainers learned the SIOP® Model, they began working with individual teachers in their service area. Susan Hanson and Canisus Filibert co-presented a SIOP® training on Chuuk in the spring of 2006, and Susan presented an overview of the SIOP® Model at the Pacific Education Conference in Palau in July 2006. Canisius provided a SIOP® training in Pohnpei in August 2006 and in January 2007, he presented a SIOP® training in Majuro, Marshall Islands. At the SIOP Institute® held in Guam in 2006, educators from around the region attended and received intensive training in the SIOP® Model.

After the institutes, the PREL staff stayed in touch with and provided support to the teachers. In West Hawaii, a Listserv was created through which they communicated, and staff distributed to the teachers additional classroom activities to supplement those they received during the trainings. The PREL staff also used local resources such as the ESL coordinator, Precille Boisvert, in West Hawaii, who helped with training presentations and provided some follow-up. West Hawaii sent two school teams to the SIOP Institute® in Long Beach, California, in June 2006, and Precille Boisvert and two colleagues attended the SIOP II Institute® in Long Beach as well. At the time of the interview, she was preparing a SIOP® professional development course for the staff at one of the high schools for 2007.

With the more isolated islands, it wasn't possible to offer after-school or one-day professional development sessions. For example, from Hawaii to Chuuk involves four island stops, so one day isn't possible. Thus, a five-day training was held. On the afternoon of the fifth day, participants wrote SIOP® lesson plans. The trainers collected their lesson plans, typed them up, and sent each participant a booklet of everyone's lesson plans as a resource. These teachers were invited to the SIOP Institute® in Guam, and one was able to attend along with four other teachers who had not attended the initial five-day SIOP® training. These five teachers planned to work as a team to conduct SIOP® training in Chuuk. They were enthusiastic about implementing the SIOP® and made plans for future professional development, including requesting that one of the PREL staff assist them with a summer training.

On the island of Pohnpei, Canisus worked with a group of teachers, teaching them the SIOP® Model. The group started a Pohnpei SIOP® Club that met monthly. At the meetings they talked about how they implemented the SIOP® components and ways that they could train others. Three of the club's participants attended the Guam SIOP Institute® along with two other teachers. One of the new participants was given the task of coordinating implementation efforts in Pohnpei. Some of her responsibilities included giving orientations on the SIOP® Model to the DOE administrators and building principals, coordinating the Pohnpei SIOP® Club and participation on the education Management Council. The education director of Pohnpei was very supportive of the teachers' efforts and communicated that he wanted to see the SIOP® Model implemented throughout the island.

The professional development program initiated and supported by the staff at PREL offered a number of service options, found in Chapter 2, Figure 2.3. Their experiences illustrated ways that teachers in expansive geographic regions can receive high-quality professional development and ongoing support.

High Schools Start with the Boss

Phoenix, Arizona. In this charter high school district, the ELL director was responsible for seventeen schools. In order to comply with the state's SEI requirements, she decided to implement the SIOP® Model in the schools. She began by taking a team to a SIOP Institute® to be trained together. The team consisted of her assistant director, two curriculum coaches, one of whom was also the assistant principal, and one classroom teacher.

When they returned from the training, they spent five months developing the training they would use in the schools. Their intent was to understand the model deeply themselves and to "live" the model a little before they began to work with teachers. A significant piece of the planning was to ensure that the team would be able to train the teachers using the SIOP®. Planning began by aligning every session to the State Professional Teachers Standards. The thinking behind this approach was that if teachers are expected to align instruction to what students are supposed to do academically (state standards), the team must do the same for teachers. Ultimately they made certain that the training delivered mimicked exactly what effective instruction looked like. It was crucial that every component be clearly modeled and practiced by every participant. During the five months, the team practiced presenting the components to each other and studied together the SIOP® book, *Making Content Comprehensible for English Learners: The SIOP® Model*.

Perhaps most importantly during this time, they educated the superintendent, and he decided that all administrators would be trained on the SIOP® Model. Once the team of core trainers felt comfortable with the training they had developed and with their understanding of the SIOP® Model, they conducted professional development sessions for all administrators and the curriculum coaches (there was a curriculum coach at every site). Starting with administrators provided the buy-in they would need for districtwide implementation.

Naturally, not all administrators wanted to move forward with schoolwide training, but the majority did. They had so few resistant administrators because of the superintendent's support, and as they developed a better understanding of the SIOP® Model, they recognized it as appropriate and necessary for their students.

Initially, the core trainers provided a three-day professional development session for thirty individuals with the idea that these site trainers would take the SIOP® Model back to their own schools (Training of Trainers). Those thirty trainers were the curriculum coaches and one ELL facilitator from each school. During the three days, the core trainers presented the entire SIOP® Model and worked on lesson planning. In addition to the SIOP® training, the core trainers provided site trainers' support in developing and delivering their own three-day training.

Site trainings that were conducted during three allocated professional development days involved every teacher on staff. At each of the site trainings, one of the core trainers presented with the site trainer, who actually did the majority of the training since he or she had a much deeper understanding of the model. For instance, the site trainer would present one component of the model to establish credibility with her teachers, and the core trainer would do the rest. They both worked with the teachers on SIOP® lesson planning.

After the teachers attended SIOP® training, the site trainers mentored them in a number of ways. They assisted them with lesson planning, conducted observations, and worked with them at grade level meetings. Some schools did this once a week, others once a month, and the rest once a quarter, all depending on schedules and administrative support. At schools that met once a week, teachers at each grade level had common prep time. Schools who met once a month did so in lieu of a weekly staff meeting, and those who met quarterly did so on early release days.

Frequency of observations depended on the school. Some schools only had part-time ELL facilitators (depending on the number of ELs), and some curriculum coaches had responsibilities for content-specific initiatives in addition to SIOP® so that frequency varied from one observation per quarter to one per year.

In addition to the observations, teachers were coached and mentored. The curriculum coaches were trained in cognitive coaching, which is the approach they used as they worked with teachers.

Ongoing support from the district level was also provided for curriculum coaches and ELL facilitators. Mini-trainings reinforcing individual components from the SIOP® were done by the ELL director at designated facilitator and curriculum coach meetings. There were also designated districtwide professional staff development days where all teachers, administrators, and support staff received training. Lesson Planning, Language Objectives, Vocabulary Development, and Lesson Delivery were a few of the sessions provided during these days.

Chapter Summary

In this chapter we presented many different ways that the SIOP® Model is implemented around the United States. Since the effectiveness of these programs has not been researched, we are not endorsing them as effective models of professional development. However, in the descriptions you will see reflected some elements of what we know to be effective professional development.

Questions for Reflection and Discussion

1. Which one of the various professional development programs in this chapter most closely reflects your current situation?

2. As you consider the professional development needs of your school or district, which features of the programs described will you begin to implement? Why did you select those features? What are some potential difficulties you may encounter? (See Barriers to Effective Professional Development in Chapter 2.)

3. Create an ideal professional development program using the ideas described in the chapter. Where would you begin if you were to actually implement the program you've created?

Appendix: Japanese Lesson Study

The Japanese lesson study (JLS) process used in Fresno, California, is based on the work by James Stigler and James Hiebert (1999). These researchers used the results of the Third International Mathematics and Science Study to show that although American teachers are often competent at implementing American teaching methods, these teaching methods themselves are severely limited. They propose a new plan for improving classroom teaching in America. Their proposal is based on six principles: (1) expect improvement to be continual, gradual, and incremental; (2) maintain a constant focus on student learning goals; (3) focus on teaching, not teachers; (4) make improvements in context; (5) make improvement in the work of teachers; (6) build a system that can learn from its own experience.

The Fresno staff used a resource by Professor Catherine C. Lewis titled, *Lesson Study: A Handbook of Teacher Led Instructional Change* (2002) for thinking about and helping teachers use analysis of their lessons as a means of improving instruction for English learners. One aspect of the process is to think of a research question or general theme around which lessons are designed. (See Figure 4.2 for a sample of possible Lesson Study questions.)

The social studies teachers worked together to plan SIOP® lessons where they set up a research goal. For instance, one group's goal was to preteach vocabulary in an explicit way and then implicitly teach during the lesson to see if it furthered both language acquisition and content acquisition. So the research question that they planned their lesson around became: Does vocabulary instruction improve language and content acquisition? The teachers sometimes held five or six meetings to plan just one lesson. They met together and planned the lesson out using the SIOP® protocol and Japanese lesson-setting protocol.

Each group taught the one SIOP® lesson they had designed twice—first a selected teacher from the group taught, then the group revised it based on feedback, and another teacher retaught the lesson. When they taught the lessons, they invited outside experts to observe, such as EL specialists, social studies teachers, the social studies coordinator, or site and district administrators, and each observer was assigned a cooperative group of students to watch. The focus was on watching the students, not the teachers. Then the

FIGURE 4.2 *Samples of Lesson Study Research Questions and Themes*

Please choose a specific research question or a general theme around which to design your lesson. Examine the specific features of the SIOP® Model, features of a specific approach (Thinking Maps), or curriculum (TCI, WRITE, adopted text, etc.). Your group may also decide to spotlight a particular level or levels of ELs in the classroom. The focus is on English Learners and what instructional approaches facilitate their learning, their integration into society, and their general growth and well-being. The questions below are just samples. Please feel free to modify or create your own.

- What is the effect of integrating **explicit vocabulary instruction** into a social science lesson?
- Does developing **language objectives** for a history lesson promote content acquisition? Language acquisition?
- Will a **primary language preview** and follow-up review increase comprehension of a lesson in English?
- Does **adapted text** (highlighted, margin notes, simplified text, etc.) increase the use of content area text for comprehending content?
- What types of **speech modifications** by a teacher provide the most comprehensible input for ELs?
- Do **simulations** (act-it-outs, drama, readers' theatre, etc.) promote deeper EL engagement in and comprehension of content lessons?
- (How many, what kind of) lessons for **academic background building** in the area of cause/effect words are required to promote actual student use in writing?
- Which **SDAIE techniques** (modeling, visuals, hands-on activities, demonstrations, gestures, questioning, etc.) are most useful to us in making content comprehensible?
- What kinds of language objectives are useful for content area teachers?
- What teacher activities promote the **independent use of graphic organizers** by EL students (such as Thinking Maps)?
- Does establishing **personal and cultural connections** to the content being taught expedite content acquisition?
- What amount of **primary language support** promotes mastery of content standards for pre- and early-production ELs?
- What **grouping configurations** and protocols best support language learners?
- What type of **outlines and study guides** facilitate textbook use for English Learners?
- Does the use of **wait time and question preparation** increase the participation of English Learners in classroom discussions?

Created by Elizabeth Fralicks, Title III, Fresno Unified School District

teachers were provided feedback and had the time to revamp the lesson and review. Feedback is presented by all observers directly after the lesson is taught—it is recorded on video and in written form. The feedback focused directly on what was observed: what the students were doing and saying. Observers record precisely what they observe and collect student work as evidence. The revision process is based on the research question and whether or not the students learned what the teachers intended; the revision attempts to address any issues in the lesson that did not further the goals of the lesson. It was through this process that teachers developed a deeper understanding of the SIOP® Model and used it to meet the specific needs of their students.

chapter 5

Coaching with the SIOP® Model

[A] coach is most effective when he or she is a good listener and responds in ways that are nonjudgmental and nonthreatening. Answering questions honestly, responding to concerns quickly, sharing classroom stories, celebrating progress and successes, and making time for the teachers you are coaching, all help to build trust and reinforce a positive coaching relationship.

Vogt & Shearer, 2007, p. 199

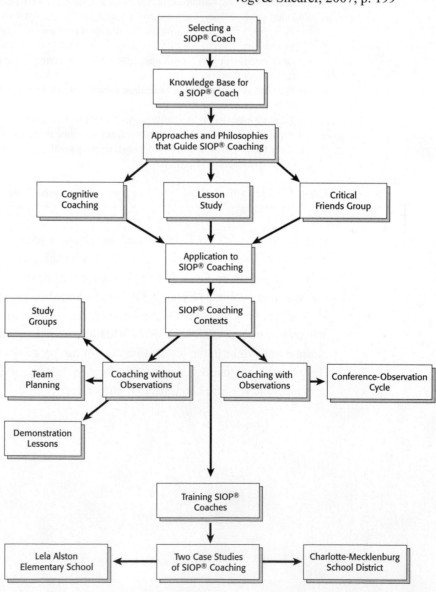

Becoming a SIOP® Coach takes knowledge, experience, leadership skill, and practice. You will find guidelines for coaching across several contexts as well as case studies of two exemplary SIOP® Coaches in this chapter. If you are participating in a coaching process or setting one up, you will see how you might become a better coach or work more successfully with one. Administrators gain insights into selecting SIOP® Coaches and supporting their implementation efforts.

Learning to be an effective SIOP® teacher takes time—time to learn and time to transform one's instructional practice. Our experience with districts implementing the SIOP® Model has shown that teachers with support from SIOP® Coaches learn the model more deeply and implement it better in their classrooms than those without such coaches. Our anecdotal evidence matches research on coaching and mentoring: by working with a more capable other, teachers gain knowledge and are guided to higher levels of implementation (NCTAF, 1996; Tharp, Estrada, Dalton, & Yamauchi, 2000). Similarly, learning to be an effective SIOP® Coach who develops and executes a coaching program also takes time as

well as sensitivity, knowledge, and practice. In this chapter, we offer guidance on SIOP® coaching grounded in the experiences of districts successfully implementing the model.

Selecting a SIOP® Coach

A SIOP® Coach is a facilitator, mentor, and advisor who can learn to work effectively with teachers implementing the SIOP® Model by building trust and sharing a commitment to professional growth. Being a SIOP® Coach requires a certain level of knowledge about the SIOP® Model, about second language acquisition, about the established curricula of the courses where the SIOP® Model is being implemented, and about coaching in general. That is why a literacy coach, reading specialist, ESL teacher, or any other educator cannot become a SIOP® Coach simply by adding another label to his or her job description. In addition, a SIOP® Coach is not an evaluator, and it is best if the individual does not have direct supervisory responsibility for the teacher, because the teacher might be unwilling to take risks when trying new techniques or applying new ideas to the lessons.

Numerous educational specialists can become SIOP® Coaches with the appropriate professional development and experience. A SIOP® Coach may be one of the following:

- District level coach
- Site facilitator
- Teacher mentor
- Peer teacher
- External staff developer

The relationship between the coach and teacher may be one of expert-novice or of equal partners. In the former case, the coach is often an experienced SIOP® implementer, with the teacher just beginning to learn about the SIOP® Model. In the latter, teacher colleagues may be coaching one another as they implement the model in their classes. In some cases, an ESL teacher and a content or grade level classroom teacher may collaborate as peer coaches.

The Knowledge Base for a SIOP® Coach

It is important for a SIOP® Coach to have a wide range of professional knowledge and experiences. The following list represents several important areas of expertise (Hasbrouck & Denton, 2005; Short, Vogt, & Echevarria, 2008).

- <u>Deep Knowledge of the SIOP® Model.</u> The coach needs to be well versed in the theory and research that support the model and must understand what high-quality SIOP® instruction looks like in a variety of classrooms and subject areas. The coach must be able to translate his or her understanding of SIOP® lessons into concrete suggestions for teachers in terms of their lesson planning and delivery. It is especially valuable if the SIOP® Coach has taught classes using the SIOP® Model because that background will provide a shared experience with the teachers. Ideally, a SIOP® Coach has also taught English learners, using the model to design and deliver content lessons.

- <u>Basic Understanding of Second Language Acquisition and Literacy Development for Children and Adolescents.</u> Because the SIOP® Model presents two goals to teachers and students, namely learning the content topics and learning the related academic language, the SIOP® Coach needs to help teachers manage both goals strategically. To assist them, coaches need to convey how language learning occurs, how literacy can be fostered through content area instruction, what the relationship between first and second language literacy is, which individual and sociocultural factors affect second language development, and so on.

- <u>Knowledge of ESL Methods.</u> Many of the content area and grade level classroom teachers that a SIOP® Coach will work with are unlikely to be trained in ESL or sheltered instruction methodologies. As a result, they will look to the coach for training and guidance as to which techniques and strategies to use in their SIOP® lessons. Coaches may also work with ESL teachers who need assistance in applying their traditional ESL techniques to content-based ESL lessons.

- <u>Experienced in Teaching.</u> Credibility is essential for a coach so that feedback given to classroom teachers is considered by them as valuable. Generally, a minimum of three years of teaching experience is necessary for a coach to be effective in his or her role. As SIOP® Coaches, it is preferable that they are experienced SIOP® teachers.

Deborah Short (far right) works with teachers on SIOP® lesson design.

- <u>Basic Understanding of the Content Area Curricula.</u> In order to help teachers design lesson activities and plan objectives, general knowledge of the content area curricula is indispensable. SIOP® Coaches need to know enough about a subject to help teachers identify key concepts and the academic language students need to learn. Having an outside perspective on the syllabus of a course may also allow a coach to cut through extra details and help teachers focus on the core material.

- <u>Leadership Skills.</u> A SIOP® Coach must be a leader because he or she is guiding teachers along a path of new knowledge. This path may have some rough spots, and strong leadership skills will help teachers stay the course, maintain focus, and reach their goals.

- <u>Coaching/Mentoring Experience.</u> Individuals who already have experience as coaches or mentors are strong candidates for a SIOP® Coach if they add knowledge of the SIOP® Model to their coaching background, and have the other characteristics discussed here as well. Coaching experience will help them determine how fast or how slowly to move along a teacher new to the SIOP® Model and how to develop the trust and respect needed between a teacher and coach.

At this point, we would like to call attention to the relationship with literacy coaches, a growing and popular resource for schools. For these literacy specialists, the issue of first language literacy development is generally well covered in their preservice or inservice training; less so is second language literacy. Therefore, in setting standards, the International Reading Association (2006) has called for secondary level coaches to receive training in specific subject areas and on ESL issues in order to provide appropriate guidance to content teachers. The *Standards for Middle and High School Literacy Coaches* (IRA, 2006) complement the goals we have set for SIOP® Coaches, both elementary and secondary. The standards recommend, for example, that coaches:

- Share a positive vision for students' learning with teachers, including understanding and educating teachers about the second language acquisition process.

- Encourage ESL teachers to serve as resources for content-area teachers to help them understand how ELLs learn language.

- Serve as the experts for their schools on research and practice for adolescent ELL language development, and share new findings with colleagues.

- Help teachers design instruction that helps improve ELLs' ability to read and understand content-area information, and identify teaching strategies that take into account ELLs' different proficiency levels while moving them toward grade level literacy.

Approaches and Philosophies That Guide SIOP® Coaching

It is important for a SIOP® Coach to develop a coaching philosophy and make it transparent to teachers. The coach may embrace an approach that has been described in the professional literature, such as cognitive coaching, lesson study, or critical friends, or the coach may develop a hybrid approach. Whatever philosophy is espoused, we recommend that it be based on trust, respect, and a mutual desire for professional growth.

Cognitive Coaching

Costa and Garmston (2002, 1994) have written extensively on the cognitive coaching process. They view the process as a means for understanding a teacher's thought processes (while planning and delivering lessons) and for encouraging teacher reflection. In their approach, the coach observes the teacher who is learning a new technique or strategy. Cognitive coaching involves a planning conference (preobservation), the observation, and a reflective conference (postobservation). The cognitive SIOP® Coach should be nonevaluative but must guide teachers and move them forward professionally. As Vogt and Shearer (2007) point out, "Knowing how to interact with another teacher—when to question, model, coax, prod, and gently nudge—requires sensitivity and caring" (p. 199). Pajak (2003) also reminds us that teachers may have different teaching styles, and coaches should be prepared for a style that does not match his or her own. Therefore, the coach needs to keep an open mind while observing. In effective cognitive coaching situations, mutual learning takes place.

Lesson Study

Lesson study is a teacher-led approach to professional development and dialogue about effective lessons. Long utilized among Japanese teachers, it gained notice in the United States as a result of the 1995 Third International Mathematics and Science Study (TIMSS) and the 1999 TIMSS Video Study, which revealed that many Japanese students performed better on mathematics and science exams than American students. In studying what teachers did in high-performing schools, the practice of lesson study came to light (Hiebert & Stigler, 2000).

In a lesson study approach, a group of teachers co-develop a lesson in response to a research question they have generated (e.g., how to get students to consider multiple solutions to an algebraic problem) that is tied to a long-term goal of improving student learning (Lewis, 2002). One teacher in the group teaches the lesson while the others watch. They regroup and discuss. They may revise the lesson. If so, another teacher teaches it and the rest observe. After two cycles (usually), the lesson is finalized and made available to other teachers in the school, or as used in the United States, the district. Sometimes an administrator joins a lesson study team, sometimes an outside advisor. It is a very collaborative process. (See pages 62–63 for more details.)

Critical Friends Group

Developed by the Annenberg Institute for School Reform at Brown University and utilized widely in Coalition for Essential School sites, critical friends group (CFG) is generally a cadre of teachers (numbers vary, from four to twelve) who meet about once a month to examine student work using a specific protocol (Bambino, 2002; Cushman, 1998). The CFG may stay in operation for two years. The goal is to seriously consider one's own classroom practice and improve it, sometimes directed toward a specific reform model. The group is often led by a trained facilitator who guides the process and manages the time for each stage. The group usually sets a goal for improving student learning and identifies some strategies for teachers to implement.

During a CFG session, one teacher presents student work while the others listen. Then the other teachers **ask questions** or **provide feedback** (sometimes characterized as "warm" such as praise, and "cool" such as critique) while the teacher listens. Then the teacher reflects on the comments aloud while the colleagues listen, and finally the whole group debriefs with an open discussion. In some cases, a member of CFG will observe the lesson of another and make the presentation of his or her observation points to start the CFG meeting.

Application to SIOP® Coaching

All three approaches described here empower the teachers in some way. That is a valuable philosophy for SIOP® coaching as well. John Seidlitz, SIOP® National Faculty member and experienced SIOP® Coach, explained that all of these approaches need some modification in order to assist teachers with the SIOP® Model. Cognitive coaching, for example, "is too open for the SIOP® Model, which is more specific. It can only be so open to goal setting by teachers because the teachers need to set SIOP® goals." Nonetheless, he likes cognitive coaching as a framework:

> It develops less dependence on the coach and develops expertise in the practitioner. It's not just about reflection but about getting someone to do independent thinking. The teacher begins to see that he or she can do this.

In his work with the SIOP® Model, John has also found ways to integrate CFG and lesson study. "I think it's okay for teachers to ask for advice and it's okay for coaches to give advice." Although the coach-teacher dynamic is a bit different from the critical friends' dynamic (unless peer SIOP® coaching is occurring), he has found that coaches can respond to such requests for advice within the context of the SIOP® components and features. It is also useful for teachers to develop a SIOP® lesson as a team, in his view. He has seen a modification of lesson study occur when all teachers try out the same co-developed lesson and then report back. The ensuing discussion leads to revision of the lesson.

SIOP® Coaching Contexts in Schools and Districts

SIOP® coaching has been accomplished in numerous contexts. One major distinction between the contexts is whether or not the SIOP® Coach carries out classroom observations with feedback. In some schools and districts, SIOP® implementation and coaching began without the observation component but was modified over time to include classroom visits once teachers became more comfortable with the model and with the coaching process.

Coaching without Observations

Study Groups. One common setting for coaching without observations is the study group. A coach convenes a group of teachers interested in the SIOP® Model, usually for after-school meetings, to read and discuss *Making Content Comprehensible for English Learners: The SIOP® Model* (Echevarria, Vogt, & Short, 2008). They may decide to read one chapter at a time and practice the associated techniques. In October, for example, they might read and discuss the chapter on Preparation and begin writing content and language objectives for their lessons. In November when they meet again, they report back on the Preparation features they tried to implement and share ideas for effective practice. At this meeting, they also discuss the next chapter, in this case Building Background, and plan to apply those features over the course of the following month. The group may continue on a monthly schedule for the rest of the year. The study group approach can also function with a peer group of SIOP® teachers, with individuals taking turns leading the book discussion each month. In fact, a group of high school teachers in Lee County Schools (Sanford, North Carolina) began their exploration with the SIOP® Model in just this way in 2000 and now the model is well established in the secondary schools there. The critical friends group approach can also be applied to a SIOP® study group, especially after teachers have learned the model and want to review and assess their SIOP® teaching through an examination of student work.

Team Planning. SIOP® coaching may also occur in team planning periods. This type of coaching was common in the Lela Alston Elementary School as the teachers were being introduced to the SIOP® Model over a two-year period. The coach joined the SIOP® teachers during a dedicated planning period to demonstrate new techniques, develop language and content objectives for upcoming curriculum units, work on lesson planning, and the like. In one of the elementary schools in Waller ISD in Texas, the bilingual/ESL director introduced the SIOP® components at monthly faculty meetings but followed up with grade level teams during their planning periods. The goals of these team meetings may shift as teachers become proficient in one area and are ready to focus on another. This type of coaching may also occur after school at regular intervals.

Demonstration Lessons. Another type of coaching is the demonstration of model lessons. Ivanna Mann Thrower, the Charlotte-Mecklenburg district coach, and Martha Trejo, the Waller bilingual/ESL director, have utilized this approach, among others. The coach prepares and delivers SIOP® lessons in a teacher's classroom, and that teacher observes. Sometimes the coach might invite another teacher or two into the room as well, depending on factors such as the size of the class, space in the room, and the comfort level of the collaborating teacher and students. Some coaches also videotape their model lessons for use in future staff development. Before a coach engages in model lessons, however, current SIOP® coaches offer the following advice:

1. Don't teach "cold." Visit in the classroom several times before guest teaching. Get to know the students and let them become familiar with you.

2. Be sure you comprehend the lesson topic well, especially if the sheltered lesson is for a subject you have infrequently or never taught.

3. Set a focus for the teacher observing you. Although you want to demonstrate a full lesson, with most of the SIOP® features, you can adjust what the teacher looks for

according to the teacher's level of SIOP® implementation. For example, a teacher new to the SIOP® Model may watch how the coach introduces vocabulary and incorporates activities that encourage students to use the new terms throughout the lesson. A more experienced SIOP® teacher may concentrate on the coach's discourse to track the use of higher-order questions and techniques for eliciting elaborated speech from the students.

4. **Debrief.** Find time to talk about the lesson with the teacher. Discuss what he or she noticed, the focal features, and what the teacher might try next.

This example of coaching is a bridge between coaching without observations and coaching with them. Demonstration lessons take the pressure off the SIOP® teacher to perform and allow the coach to show a teacher how sheltered techniques can be effective with his or her students. However, the follow-up conversations can incorporate some of the features of cognitive coaching as the coach elicits the teacher's reaction to the model lesson and encourages the teacher to reflect on instructional adjustments he or she might make for future lessons. Likewise, the coach develops a realistic perspective on the teacher's classroom culture and student abilities. This knowledge helps the coach provide more targeted support in the future.

Coaching with Classroom Observations

SIOP® observations can occur in several ways, ranging from less to more formal. A less formal observation may be a three-minute walkthrough to "catch SIOP®," as Ivanna Mann Thrower describes, or a class visit with unstructured note taking. Slightly more formal might be using the list of SIOP® features as a checklist to mark the presence or absence of the features in the lesson; recording information about a component (as the Creighton School District does in Figure 5.1); or note taking in a T-chart format that

FIGURE 5.1 *Creighton SIOP® Observation Checklist*

The Sheltered Instruction Observation Protocol (SIOP®)
Echevarria, Vogt, & Short, 2000
(Modified by Creighton School District Collegial Coaching Program, Phoenix, AZ, 2001)

Observer: _____ Teacher: _____
Date: _____ School: _____
Grade: _____ Subject: _____
Language: _____

Directions: Cite under "What Happened" any specific examples of the behaviors observed.

Building Background	What Happened:
7. Concepts explicitly linked to students' background experiences	
8. Links explicitly made between past learning and new concepts	
9. Key vocabulary emphasized (e.g., introduced, written, repeated, and highlighted for students to see)	

captures classroom events and discourse in one column while recording related comments about SIOP® feature implementation in the other (Hillyard, 2007). A very formal observation would involve the SIOP® protocol and the rating of the lesson. This last option is rarely recommended, especially not with teachers new to the SIOP® Model unless it is part of a research project. The coach who rates with the protocol needs to be very experienced, with a high level of reliability in scoring SIOP® lessons.

Additional skills are needed in a SIOP® Coach who also conducts observations and gives feedback to teachers. Of particular importance is the ability to foster trust. When teachers allow coaches into their classrooms as they are learning a new technique, or in this case the SIOP® Model, they are opening their instruction to potential criticism. This is a risky situation, and the teachers need to feel comfortable with the coach; they need to trust the coach to be supportive and considerate. Tension may rise, yet an effective coach knows how to put teachers at ease and still elicit insights about instruction and visions for change. Therefore, the coach should be well-versed in one of the coaching philosophies discussed so far: cognitive coaching, critical friends, or lesson study.

The SIOP® Coach who conducts observations must also be very experienced in observing SIOP® classrooms and very consistent in assessing how well a teacher implements the features of the model. In other words, the coach needs to know what an engaged classroom looks like, how scaffolding should occur according to the proficiency level of the students and the complexity of the content material, when and how much feedback on student output is needed, and so forth. This knowledge comes with the experience of observing numerous classrooms (in person and on videotape) over time.

If the coaching process leads to rating observed lessons, then intra-rater reliability is needed. A coach needs to rate a similar lesson in a similar way even if several months have passed between observations, or if different teachers are teaching. Furthermore, if more than one coach is involved in helping teachers implement the SIOP® Model, inter-rater reliability is *required*. The teachers should know that no matter which coach observes, the coaching perspective on a lesson will be the same. It takes time and effort to develop a high level of inter-rater reliability but it is critical if teachers' lessons will be scored with the SIOP® protocol.

Although the SIOP® Coach is the one most apt to conduct observations, SIOP® teachers may observe one another as peer coaches or critical friends. Peer coaching is part of the program at Lela Alston now, as the coach Wanda Holbrook explained. "We do peer coaching because you learn more as you coach each other. So it deepens teachers' understanding as they coach each other." In other instances, mentors may observe SIOP® teachers and provide expert-novice guidance. Staff developers may provide workshops on the SIOP® Model and incorporate classroom observations into the professional development program. Information gleaned from the observations should be used in subsequent staff development.

Conference-Observation Cycle

Although it can be difficult to schedule, coaches and teachers will benefit the most from using the conference-observation cycle for their interactions. This cycle begins with a preobservation meeting, sometimes referred to as the planning conference, continues with the actual classroom observation, and concludes with a postobservation meeting, or reflecting conference.

- Preobservation: Planning Conference. Before observing a class, the coach should meet with the SIOP® teacher and discuss the lesson plan and the SIOP® goals for the observation. If the teacher is learning the SIOP® Model, the goals may focus on one SIOP® component at a time. Eventually, additional components and features are added. In some cases, the coach may have time to review the lesson plan a day or two in advance and make suggestions for improvement before the observation (Short & Echevarria, 1999). The coach might pose questions during this planning conference such as, "What are your goals for student learning in this lesson?" and "What SIOP® features would you like me to look for while I watch?" It is beneficial if the teacher helps establish some criteria for the observation.

- Observation Procedures. While in the classroom, ". . . the coach's role is that of data collector, observing and recording data based on the planning preconference during which specific lesson goals and objectives were developed" (Vogt & Shearer, 2007, p. 201). The coach is a nonparticipant observer. He or she does not make comments to the teacher while the lesson is ongoing. SIOP® Coaches usually record notes during the observation, using running records, T-charts, SIOP® feature checklists, and/or the SIOP® protocol to organize their data.

- Postobservation: Reflecting Conference. The data collected during the observation phase drives the postobservation conference. However, Costa and Garmston (2002, 1994), among others, caution coaches to refrain from starting in with a list of mistakes or suggestions. Instead, the observed SIOP® teacher should be asked to reflect on the lesson—in terms of the selected observation focus—and be provided with a chance to ask the coach questions first. Examples of coaches' questions might be: "Upon reflection, how do you think the lesson went?" "Do you think you accomplished your objectives?" "When do you think student learning occurred?" "As you plan your next lesson, what will you do differently and what will you try again?" As the teacher responds to questions like these, the coach can refer to the recorded notes to support the discussion.

At Lela Alston Elementary School, the observations often followed a sequence of activities similar to this cycle. As the coach explained,

> A routine was followed when coaching a teacher. The first was a preconference. The focused component was discussed. The teacher and I chose the objectives and outlined the basic lesson. We also chose who would do which part of the lesson [if we were coteaching] or decide if it was an observation. The postconference was one of my favorite parts. I love the discussion that it generated. My understanding grew the most during those meetings.

It is clear from her comments that the coach viewed herself and the teacher as learners coming to shared understandings about how to implement the model in a particular classroom.

Training a SIOP® Coach

We are often asked how long it takes to become an effective SIOP® teacher, and we respond that for many, it takes at least one year of steady, engaged practice. We would be remiss to assume otherwise for a SIOP® Coach. Becoming an expert coach takes some time too. Many of the SIOP® Coaches in the districts that we interviewed attended a SIOP II Institute® as a first step in honing their SIOP® coaching skills.

John Seidlitz has trained SIOP® Coaches and he highly recommends on-the-job training that is practical and linked to the SIOP® Model. Just as we suggest introducing one component to teachers at a time when they are learning the model, John suggests developing one coaching skill at a time that is embedded in the SIOP® components. For example, when coaches are getting ready to observe teachers who have recently worked on Lesson Preparation, John teaches them observation skills. Such a session might begin with having coaches brainstorm the kinds of things they might observe in the classroom to expand their perspectives. He might discuss scripting, movement maps, behavior registers, focusing on target students, and other ways to record observations. After the coaches try out the skill, they talk about it at a subsequent meeting so they can continue to refine their practice.

John and others we have spoken with also find it important to help coaches develop effective questioning and listening skills, particularly if they will engage in the conference-observation cycle. The questions that could be posed (such as those above) are often derived from Costa and Garmston (2002, 1994). John encourages coaches to practice with a partner in a training session before a real observation. The goal, he stresses, is to help teachers, ". . . improve their level of SIOP® implementation."

Figure 5.2 is a reference guide that John distributes when working with SIOP® Coaches. He includes the information in a handy format.

Laurie Beebe in American Falls, Idaho, also trains SIOP® Coaches with questions for postconferencing. Her handout appears in Figure 5.3.

Another important topic to cover when training SIOP® Coaches is preparation for the types of SIOP® teachers they may encounter. Toll (2005, p. 41–2) describes characteristics of three groups of teachers encountered by new coaches.

Ready-to-go group: These teachers are eager to try new things. They are confident, but can sometimes monopolize a coach's time. It is useful to leverage these teachers' enthusiasm to help try out new practices. If a site is beginning with SIOP® training, start with several of these teachers in the first group. They tend to represent 10–20 percent of a school's staff.

Wait-and-see group: These teachers are eager to improve their teaching, but cautious about change. They seek quick signs of success rather than focusing on the end goal, and they may be overwhelmed by daily concerns and feel hesitant to stand out in front of others. It is best to encourage their participation by listening to and learning from their past efforts. Encourage partner work with them when trying new practices. They represent about 60–80 percent of a school's staff.

FIGURE 5.2 *Quick Reference Guide for SIOP® Coaches*

SIOP® Coaching is
- Mediating a teacher's thinking about instruction of English learners
- A way of enhancing a teacher's ability to manage, monitor, and modify one's own practice through reflection on the protocol

Great SIOP® coaches have*: • Deep knowledge of model • Basic understanding of second language acquisition • Understanding of literacy development • Knowledge of ESL methods • Basic understanding of content area curricula • Coaching/mentoring experience	**Cognitive Coaching Results:** • Application increases from 5% to 90% • Decrease in referral of ELs to special education programs • Student achievement in reading, math, and language arts • More enthusiasm and use of cooperative learning techniques
SIOP® Contexts*: • Study group • SIOP® Team Planning Periods • Peer Observation Teams • Staff development with model lessons and observations as follow up	**The Coaching Process**:** • Planning Conference • Observation • Reflecting Conference
Planning Conference:** • What is your lesson going to be about? • What SIOP® component will you be focusing on? • What do you see yourself doing first, next, and last? • What do you want me to look for that lets you know you've been successful? • Do you have any questions for me?	**Reflecting Conference**:** • How do you think it went? • Were you able to implement the component we discussed? • Do you feel you were able to . . . *(discuss each feature)* • I observed . . . • Where could you find resources to help you . . . • What will you do differently? What will you try again? • What can I do to help?
Summarization Stems • You're saying . . . • You believe . . . • So you think that . . . • It sounds like you're struggling with . . . • So you've been able to . . .	**Establishing Inter-rater Reliablity** • Samples in *Making Content Comprehensible* • Live observations with multiple observers • Videotaped lessons with group discussions • Clarification of feature definitions and what a score of 0, 1, 2, 3 or 4 means

*Echevarria, Vogt, & Short (2004)
**Conference conversation components developed by Costa & Garmston (2005).

Put-on-the-brakes group: These teachers want nothing to do with the coach and feel satisfied with their work as it is. Most have a history of resisting initiatives. Do not avoid these teachers but don't give them undue time or mental energy. Support them in an honest and authentic manner, but don't let them derail progress. Showing them student data and analyzing student work may help persuade them to try something new. They represent about 10–20 percent of a school's staff.

FIGURE 5.3 *Laurie Beebe's Postobservation Conference Questions*

Suggested Questions for the Postconference
Remember you are there to observe implementation of the components—not to <u>judge</u> the lesson.

Observer is to facilitate reflection!
Use the scores at some point during the conference to validate observations.

As you reflect on the lesson, how do you feel it went?

What did you see students doing (or hear them saying) that made you feel that way?

What do you recall about your own behavior during the lesson?

Did the lesson go as planned or did you have to make adjustments? If adjustments needed to be made, what did you do and why?

What can you say about your students' achievement?

Which SIOP® components were the strongest? The weakest?

What component would you like to strengthen for the next observation?

Two Case Studies of SIOP® Coaching

We share two stories of SIOP® coaching in this section of the chapter. One story describes the coaching program at Lela Alston Elementary School, where the decision was made to train the entire staff in the SIOP® Model over the course of two years. Effective coaching was an important factor in full SIOP® implementation there.

The other story is one of a large, urban district with a history of administrative decentralization. As explained in Chapter 3, when Charlotte-Mecklenburg Schools in North Carolina decided to implement the SIOP® Model to improve student achievement among their rapidly growing EL population, the ESL-Second Languages Department had to work with the associate superintendent for education services and regional superintendents to establish the program and ensure support. It was at the end of the first year of implementation in fifteen pilot sites that the school system agreed to fund a position for a full-time SIOP® Coach. The stories of these two districts follow.

Lela Alston Elementary School

The staff at Lela Alston decided to make SIOP® Model implementation their sole professional development initiative for several years. In 2002, Wanda Holbrook, one of the SIOP® Coaches, and several colleagues designed a two-year staff development program to introduce all faculty to the SIOP® Model as described in Chapters 3 and 4. (Figure 3.1 shows their implementation plan and delineates information about their approach to coaching.) Over time, Wanda established a set of coaching activities as shown in Figure 5.4.

By focusing on one component per nine-week quarter, the SIOP® Coach, Wanda Holbrook, and lead teacher, Kendra Moreno, could spend time making sure the teachers understood the features of the component well. They conducted workshops in various forms, such as full staff development days, half-day sessions, after school make-and-take gatherings, and staff meetings. These training sessions were followed by coaching with each teacher.

FIGURE 5.4 *Lela Alston's Coaching Activities*

- Design a two-year staff development program
- Conduct workshops and meetings on the SIOP® components, one component per quarter
- Coach teachers
- Help teachers write SIOP® lessons
- Help create tools for lesson implementation (e.g., laminated charts for language objectives)
- Demonstrate model lessons
- Observe lessons and provide feedback to teachers

Wanda believed that an important characteristic of an effective coach is having the right attitude when working with teachers. She explained,

> I believe that the coach's attitude is pivotal to strong implementation. The coach has to be a learner also. Coming in with all the answers and believing that the teacher has nothing to offer greatly hinders progress. Just as students learn the best with positive affective situations, teachers react the same way. Some of the best learning discussions came about when a lesson didn't turn out perfectly. We could then tweak the lesson. It gave us great opportunities to become self-reflectors.

Encouragement and validation of teachers and their practices were key to Wanda's coaching philosophy. She recognized that the teachers were taking a risk when inviting in an observer. As a result, she sought to develop trust so that the teacher would be open to coaching feedback.

> My role is always to encourage and validate. Most people thrive on focusing on the positives rather than the negatives. We are doing so many things right as a profession, so these need to be validated. When I was teaching kindergarten, I taught phonemic awareness. Because it was not validated, I did not continue to be consistent with the skill. It was more hit or miss. Now we have research to validate the importance of phonemic awareness in reading instruction. The information in SIOP® is not new information, but we can look at the model with new eyes and with new consistency.

Wanda also felt strongly about treating teachers as professionals. She had high expectations of the teachers and believed that they wanted to raise the standard of their teaching to meet students' needs.

> I truly believe that students as a whole really want to learn and do the right thing. I also believe that the teachers have the same attitude of wanting to do their best. I can't think of a teacher that got up in the morning and said, "Now, what can I do to be a bad teacher today?" We teach as we were taught as children unless someone came along and showed us a better way. The SIOP® Model is such a consistently better way. How can you argue with research and success? My strongest role is to help. We want to teach our students in the best way possible, so I sought out ways to make the teachers' jobs easier. My principal was very supportive and was the "strong arm" in the school. I could then come along as the support.

One of Wanda's jobs was to help the teachers create SIOP® lessons. She worked with them in grade level teams. As they developed the lesson plans, the teachers were encouraged to keep them in a notebook. Over time, more and more lessons were added until most of the grade level material was covered. Currently, several grade levels have SIOP® lesson plans for teaching the entire school year's curriculum.

Development of other products assisted teachers in implementing SIOP® lessons, especially in the area of language objectives. The trainers made a laminated chart of possible language objectives based on Arizona state standards. By having some sample objectives and starter phrases like "Students will record observations of . . . ," teachers found writing language objectives to be easier (see Figure 7.15 in Chapter 7). Some teachers placed a large clip or clothespin directly on the chart next to the objective so the students could see which objective they were working on. In a similar way, the primary grades teachers laminated signs that read, "My job today is . . . " and posted them, writing the rest of the objective information next to the sign. This procedure offered a kid-friendly way of expressing the content and language objectives for the lesson.

Another of the coaching jobs was to observe SIOP® lessons, but this was one of the most challenging aspects of coaching—gaining access to teachers' classrooms. Some teachers are very cooperative at Alston and welcomed the support, but others were cautious. Still others preferred to be left alone and not taken out of their comfort zone. As a result, Wanda began working with the cooperative volunteers first, then moved on to the others. She utilized a number of strategies to gain access to those classrooms. One way was to find an article that described a new idea or technique and share it with the teacher, often modeling it in the classroom. In one case, the school began using the reading strategy QAR (Question/Answer Relationship), so Wanda presented it in the context of the SIOP® Model and demonstrated it for the teachers.

> Because teachers really would prefer that others are not in their classrooms to make change, I had to look for creative ways to get in. Depending on the component, I would find a technique to teach. The cooperative teachers were the easiest to allow me in their classrooms at first. After word got around that the particular technique was good, other doors were opened. No one likes to be left out. Sometimes I did have to ask the teacher if they wanted to be included. That worked well.

Another way was through a focus on difficult concepts that students weren't grasping. Some teachers would ask Wanda for assistance in teaching a challenging concept, such as the cause-effect relationship.

> As the first year continued, teachers would come to me and ask if I could help them with concepts that were harder to teach and the best way to teach them. We used the SIOP® Model to plan the lessons.

For some teachers, the offer of assistance and support was not enough. In such cases, the principal played a role in helping reluctant teachers get on board. She would use student achievement data to convince teachers that they needed to improve their teaching. Wanda appreciated these efforts:

A supporting principal is invaluable. She focused on teachers that had poor test scores or observations showing that the teacher needed help. She encouraged them to talk to me and gave me the list of names. I concentrated on those.

Wanda also found that as the time for standardized testing approached in the spring, teachers were more open to participating and interested in finding effective techniques to review concepts with the students. She used this opportunity to show teachers that increasing interaction and using a variety of grouping configurations would facilitate review and also spotlight gaps in the students' learning. The teachers then taught those weak or missing concepts and reviewed them as preparation for testing.

Despite Wanda's positive approach, some teachers tried to stay under the radar. However, at Alston all the staff were required to participate in the SIOP® training, coaching, and implementation. To ensure total staff involvement, Wanda developed a checklist by which she made sure that everyone participated at a certain level. Every visit was entered into the database so she had a record of participation and knew whom to approach about doing a classroom observation.

Eventually, no one had a choice. We were all included. I used a checklist to see whom I had worked with and how often.

Once she was able to gain access to the classroom, Wanda would ask the teacher about her understanding of the component. If the teacher's understanding was weak, Wanda provided individualized training with the teacher to deepen her knowledge. Sometimes Wanda would model a lesson first or coteach one with the teacher to make sure she was comfortable with the component. In any case, there was joint lesson planning using the SIOP® protocol as a guide. The teacher and coach would sit together and, looking at the protocol, decide on the objectives and develop a lesson plan for the teacher to teach for the observation. If they were coteaching, sections of the lesson would be assigned to Wanda and other sections to the teacher.

The lesson took several forms in the classroom. Sometimes I modeled the lesson. Other times the teacher and I taught the lesson together. Sometimes the lesson was planned together and the teacher taught it independently of me. Each quarter, the teacher was observed using the current and previous components of the protocol [as the focus]. If I was the observer, I left a note to the teacher pointing out specific strengths of the lesson.

A session to discuss feedback took place after the observation when Wanda shared her reflections with the teacher. Initially, the lessons were scored on the protocol; but as time went on, more emphasis was placed on qualitative feedback and less on the numerical rating until the point where the team at Alston ceased using the ratings and only provided commentary, written and in discussion.

The teacher was first required to reflect on the lesson in general. Sometimes the teacher pointed out the weaknesses of the lesson. The focus was always switched to two or three strengths of the lesson. We then reviewed the protocol features and focused on one feature to improve. We brainstormed several ideas and rewrote the lesson. If another observation was needed, we scheduled it then.

The SIOP® protocol without the numeric scale was useful in several ways. Teachers used it to observe Wanda's model lessons, and Wanda used it to observe theirs. In this way, everyone had the same expectations and understanding of the features being observed. Teachers had the option of peer observations, and the protocol was used to provide feedback in that context as well.

The observations were first done by me. The SIOP® team wanted the focus to shift from the coach to individuals and grade level teams. Then the teacher had a choice. The observations could be done by me, peers, or by videotaping themselves. As the coach, I checked to see if the peer observations were completed and if questions had arisen. I did not sit in on the conferences.

The protocol was also used to provide feedback on videotaped lessons. Getting teachers to agree to videotaping took some effort. First, trust had to be built between the coach and teachers during the first two years of SIOP® implementation. Second, the coach and other trainer were videotaped delivering model lessons and allowed these tapes to be rated by the staff using the SIOP® protocol. These factors contributed to the teachers agreeing to be videotaped. Wanda explained how the process worked:

> I was not immune to the videotaping. Both the lead SIOP® teacher and I each taped a lesson for the staff to use the protocol to score it. That was a risk-taking adventure. Videotaping lessons is always hard for the teachers. At the end of the second year of implementation, taping a lesson was required. Sharing the tape with others was not required, therefore the tape became the property of the teacher . . . Many teachers elected to have me observe the taping of their lesson. As usual, the postconferences were informative. After getting over the initial shock of how we looked and sounded on tape and ignoring our unique mannerisms, observing the lesson from a different perspective lent itself to more objectivity.

The added support of the coach and trainer assisted teachers in implementing the SIOP® Model to a high level in every classroom. Moreover, the students benefited. Their academic achievement scores improved over time as discussed in Chapter 8.

Charlotte-Mecklenburg Schools

When Ivanna Mann Thrower was hired as the full-time, districtwide SIOP® Coach in Charlotte-Mecklenburg Schools (CMS), North Carolina, in the summer of 2005, she had been an elementary school teacher in the district and had received training in the SIOP® Model from the ESL-Second Languages Department staff. With the new position, she researched the model and read more about it; she then attended a SIOP I and a SIOP II Institute® in the summer. "I had no time to process it all. I got off the plane on Saturday [coming back from the SIOP® II training] and starting Monday, gave two weeks of SIOP® training to CMS teachers." The first week, she explained, had been intended as a curriculum development session but instead it became a week for planning site-based implementation. The attendees were participants from the first year of SIOP® training and were identified as leaders for the pilot schools. This process helped formalize the role of the site-based facilitators, and each site was able to design a plan, reviewed by Ivanna, that suited their school, personnel, and resources. In the second week, Ivanna trained staff from two additional elementary schools in the SIOP® Model that were joining the pilot so their knowledge of the model would be more on par with that of the fifteen sites already participating.

In her first year as coach, Ivanna set her main goals as developing SIOP® awareness among schools and making it concrete for teachers, such as producing a bulletin board set of SIOP® tips for the schools (e.g., "Use Think Time" with a graphic) and setting a plan for schools to review two SIOP® components per quarter as a focus of school meetings.

In her second year, Ivanna extended her efforts and developed a menu of coaching services (see Figure 5.5). Because new schools were joining the SIOP® implementation pool each year and new teachers were entering current SIOP® schools, her "challenge was to bring new staff on board and get them up to speed." Her menu of services, therefore, was designed to meet the needs of diverse learners at different levels of implementation. The site-based coaches also participated in some of these activities. As the menu reveals, the coaching contexts offered in CMS ranged from informational meetings to coaching with classroom observations.

> As schools made requests, I tried a calendar [to organize requests by area of the district]. I'd say I'll be in this area tomorrow and take appointments, but it didn't work. Now I place whatever I am asked to do first on the schedule or do what I see needs attention and go to that school.

When asked to work with a school, Ivanna usually did some variation of this process:

> I will meet with each grade level of content area, forty-five minutes to one hour per group, to do specific SIOP® training, as requested. We negotiate the topic in advance, such as language objectives. I will do up to three days per school.

Ivanna strategically organizes these types of trainings "in a box." So if another school requests staff development with the same topic, she has the materials prepared and readily at hand.

As one coach servicing at first twenty and then thirty-four sites (as of the 2006–2007 school year, the third year of implementation), Ivanna needed to strengthen capacity at the school sites. She established monthly meetings with site facilitators (aka site coaches) and provided them with a card set of verbal tips for each component that they could use in the school meetings they held for other members of their SIOP® team. The site coaches were encouraged to meet weekly.

These monthly meetings lasted one hour per group—secondary school coaches met from 3 p.m. to 4 p.m. and then elementary coaches from 4 p.m. to 5 p.m. Essentially, Ivanna would present the same information but tailor activities to the school level.

FIGURE 5.5 *2006–2007 CMS SIOP® Coaching Services Menu*

Staff Meeting Presentations (~ 30 min)

- General SIOP® Overview
- Differentiating Instruction (General, content or grade specific)
- SIOP® Strategies (General, content or grade specific)
- Create Your Own (no extra charge, but it might take longer to prepare)

Other Meetings (30 min – 1hr 30 min)

- General SIOP® Overview (same as above, different serving sizes available)
- Content/Grade Specific
  ○ Language Objectives
  ○ Strategies
  ○ Lesson Design
- Combination Platter (select as many as needed from above)
- Administrator Conference

Class Observation and Follow-Up (time varies)

All observations served with a 30-minute follow-up coaching session

- Snap Shot (15–30 min)
- One Shot (1 class period, 45–90 min)
- Lesson Development (2+ days in same class period)
- Component Focused (Can be combined with other observation types)

Model Lesson (class visit, preparation, and 1 class period)

All model lessons served with a 30-minute follow-up coaching session

- Joint Planning/Team Teaching
- Joint Planning/Coach Teaching
- Coach Teaching

Coaching (time varies)

- Check in (session after the observation/model lesson and follow-up session)
- Ongoing (sessions scheduled at regular intervals)

Provided by the ESL-Second Languages Department, Charlotte-Mecklenburg (NC) School District

I'd begin with announcements, FYIs. Then I'd do true coaching training. For example, I had two seven-minute video clips I showed. I had them use the Center for Applied Linguistics' preconferencing form [in partners]. The coaches watched the clips and recorded their observations. Then they did postconference feedback.

Ivanna also helped site coaches develop skills on the job. For instance, she did observations of a SIOP® teacher and the coach shadowed her. The coach and Ivanna discussed what they observed separately from a postobservation meeting with the teacher. When she conducts observations, Ivanna uses the SIOP® protocol as a one-page checklist and records additional information and commentary on the back.

I have the checklist on the front, and I script on the back what's happening. I make a note next to each component or feature. I use a checkmark if the feature is seen. I circle things for discussion. Sometimes I will check and circle a feature seen but weak [in its delivery]. I share the front with all the teachers. The back and front with some upon request. I will show the front to administrators if they ask. The front is to show them what the teacher is doing.

In the third year of implementation, Ivanna conducted all of the district staff development—three days of training for elementary and secondary SIOP® teachers at the pilot sites and one day of coaches' training. She has expressed the desire to develop a Level 2 SIOP® training for current teachers to deepen their knowledge and help them explore better ways to implement features they are struggling with. She would also like to train the site coaches more and have more consistency across schools in terms of the SIOP® teams' implementation practices.

Ivanna's advice for districts seeking a coach echoes what others have said:

1. Choose a dedicated person as coach and get [that person] fully trained in the SIOP® Model first.

2. Be prepared for teacher turnover.

3. Get the administration on board.

4. Take tiny steps.

5. Celebrate every step.

6. Work top down and bottom up at the same time.

7. Build community [among the teachers and administrators] and synergy.

8. Plan ahead for student scheduling and follow students for data collection.

Ivanna is committed to SIOP® coaching and to "raising student achievement by training teachers." Although her responsibilities are many, she praised her colleagues at the ESL-Second Languages Department for their support and assistance with her tasks. The SIOP® Model remains a major initiative in CMS, and the district has started to collect data on student performance and track the impact of SIOP® professional development (see discussion in Chapter 8).

Chapter Summary

In this chapter we have offered guidance for selecting a coach and for making sure the coach has the requisite knowledge, skills, and training for the position. We have explored coaching philosophies, the various contexts of SIOP® coaching that exist, and procedures for conducting conferences and observations. Lela Alston Elementary School and Charlotte-Mecklenburg Schools provided two cases of what full implementation of SIOP® coaching entails.

To those of you who are SIOP® Coaches, we would like to close with a reminder from Ivanna Mann Thrower: "Celebrate every step!" We recognize that sustained staff development is needed to help teachers expand their knowledge and skills with the SIOP® Model. As Borko (2004, p. 6) concluded,

. . . [M]eaningful learning is a slow and uncertain process for teachers, just as it is for students. Some teachers change more than others through participation in professional development programs. . . . Further, some elements of teachers' knowledge and practice are more easily changed than others.

Teachers, like students, learn at different rates, and while we want to challenge teachers to greater and greater levels of quality implementation, we also want to be sure to acknowledge their progress along the way.

Questions for Reflection and Discussion

1. Write a want ad for a SIOP® Coach. What traits and qualities would you look for?

2. Find a videotape of a teacher teaching English learners in a classroom. It does not need to be a SIOP® videotape, but could be one representing another instructional model. Prepare a set of preobservation questions as if you could meet that teacher. Watch the tape and take notes on the presence or absence of SIOP® features. After watching the tape, prepare another set of postobservation questions and identify the SIOP® features the teacher exhibited in the lesson.

Enhancing and Sustaining SIOP® Implementation

As with any new program, the buy-in is critical at the beginning. I'm just thrilled now in our third year how far the teachers have come. As they began to see their English learners—as well as the English-only children—develop skills at a faster rate and gain the knowledge they need, they got more enthusiastic about it. I'm really proud of our staff here. They're really committed to SIOP® and they're seeing the benefits now.

Debbie Hutson, principal, Lela Alston Elementary School

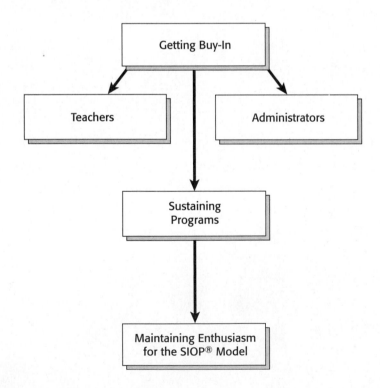

GUIDING YOUR PRACTICE

Teachers and administrators alike have told us about the difficulty of maintaining enthusiasm for new practices after initial training. In this chapter you will learn about ways that you as a teacher or administrator can get resistant teachers on board and how you can sustain practice. Included are specific ideas for teachers (e.g., SIOP® bookmarks) and for administrators and professional developers (e.g., SIOP® newsletters).

One challenge that often accompanies any professional development effort is motivating educators to participate in the reform effort or initiative beyond attendance at the initial training. Many well-intentioned professional development programs don't take root in schools or lead to change in teaching practice. In this chapter we discuss ways to get teachers and administrators to buy in to a professional development process, and we present steps districts have taken to sustain SIOP® implementation over time.

Getting Buy-In

Teachers

Teachers have many responsibilities and tend to feel overworked, so the suggestion of doing something new or different is often met with resistance. As Debbie Hutson, principal at Alston Elementary in Phoenix, reported,

> I would say the very initial problem was getting them to buy-in. Our school district puts so much on the teachers—there is so much accountability that I think even these high-achieving teachers here are saying, "Well, how much more do I have to do?" That was one of the things—it was tough to convince them that this would be really good and it would help us and our kids in the end. In the second year you didn't see that as much, [their attitude] was more, "I think this [the SIOP® Model] really is good and it really is worth the extra work that I'm doing.

Further, there may be the sense that the SIOP® Model is simply the "newest approach" and it will be replaced with another before long, so teachers don't need to put much effort into it. Alston Elementary made a two-year commitment to SIOP® implementation and after some typical, and understandable, resistance the teachers have experienced success. At the beginning, however, Kendra Moreno, one of the SIOP® trainers, was a little taken aback by some teachers' initial attitudes:

> Several teachers at the beginning of this asked, "When the two years are over, are we going to keep doing this?" And we responded to that, "Well, what do you mean, 'keep doing this?'" Hopefully it will change your teaching perspective and you'll include these things in everyday teaching." It was just kind of a weird question to ask.

It was suggested by more than one interviewee that listening to teachers and their concerns is a way to get them to buy in to a different teaching approach. Rather than "forcing" professional development on them, time was taken initially to talk about their needs as teachers and the needs of the students facilitates acceptance. Principal Tammy Becker of Lawrence, Kansas said,

> One of the things that I would advise would be to have classroom teachers meet in sort of an informal way and really hear from them. Not so much as a technical overview [of SIOP®] but more of just a time for them to share their thoughts and ideas.

A variety of approaches have been taken when addressing resistant teachers. In some cases, the teachers were brought on board because of strong administrative leadership. Alston principal Debbie Hutson required that all teachers attend the professional development sessions, participate in the videotaping of a lesson, and have a SIOP® lesson observed by the principal. Her effective leadership encouraged schoolwide SIOP® implementation. She commented,

> They have pretty much come along; one of them was somewhat resistant to begin with. But [the SIOP® Coach] has worked with her and has done a video, so she's done everything that we've said they have to do. Now I'm getting ready to do my

spring classroom observations as part of the teacher evaluation for the district and . . . I've told them that this year's observation will give feedback on the [SIOP®] protocol and even though I'm not using that as the observation form, those components will be evaluated and given feedback on.

Another way to entice resistant teachers was to help them with lesson planning and, as Marilyn Sanchez from Creighton School District said, try to "build pockets of positiveness." A number of interviewees mentioned using positive, enthusiastic teachers to win over the resisters. At Hillcrest Elementary School in Lawrence, Kansas, principal Tammy Becker asked resistant teachers to observe an effective SIOP® teacher. She said,

Part of it is the observation piece. If you can convince them to go into another teacher's classroom and just sit there and watch (you have to be careful which teacher you choose), and if those reluctant teachers will just sit there and watch and see how the kids interact, they often will come out saying, "Wow, that's something that I want to learn more about." But if they're sitting and watching a video, they are likely to say, "Well, that doesn't really apply to me."

In other cases, a number of SIOP® trainers opted to exclude those teachers in favor of building a critical mass of enthusiastic SIOP® teachers. Melissa Castillo, formerly the Title III director for Oxford Schools, said,

I always told my coaches and facilitators to put their energy in teachers who wanted them. . . . Still, their expectation was that all teachers participated in training. Resistant teachers were handled differently—it just depended. If teachers were resistant and we knew they needed the support we might model lessons for them and worked with them in getting to understand the model, and then we had others that we kind of just left alone and that was handled at the administrative end. We can't always force ourselves on everyone. What we found was as teachers were successful and kids were being successful, the resistance kind of went down and we didn't have that many resistant teachers.

As Melissa mentioned, most resistant teachers became productive SIOP® teachers with time and support. Principal Debbie Hutson reported that one of the successes of SIOP® professional development was that teachers had come to a realization that:

. . . Wow, this is really making a difference! And seeing the language growth in their kids and seeing the achievement [the teachers say], this is taking a lot of work and I'm really stretching myself as a teacher and doing a lot of things that I didn't want to do like having a peer observe me and those things. Now I can really see that it's a really good thing.

At Gladstone School in Kansas City, Missouri, every teacher was required to have a SIOP® lesson observed, which motivated even resistant teachers to get on board so that they would be able to teach a high-quality lesson when it was their turn to be observed. In addition, Alicia Miguel, director of language services for Kansas City, made SIOP® training attractive to teachers by offering college credit through the University of Missouri.

Administrators

Over and over in our interviews, we heard about the importance of administrative buy-in and support in order for SIOP® implementation to be successful. Sometimes district administrators or principals bought in to the SIOP® Model after reading about it in a professional journal or at a professional conference. More often, though, they were convinced of its importance for English learners when they were shown data on improved student achievement or were told about change in teacher practice—especially from schools in their own district.

Some administrators saw the value of the SIOP® Model to the extent that they converted their observation forms to align with the SIOP®. Melissa Castillo, currently a member of SIOP® National Faculty, has worked in a number of districts who have made strong commitments to SIOP® implementation. She reported that in one Arizona district,

> We were doing a lot of training in SEI and SIOP® . . . So this district is even changing their observation form to match what teachers are being trained on . . . when they do walk throughs, they are providing teachers with feedback that support the model.

> Likewise, Laurie Beebe from American Falls, Idaho, witnessed strong administrator buy-in. As she mentions in her comments that follow, one administrator put the SIOP® protocol into an Excel spreadsheet so that she could easily insert comments and ratings. According to Laurie,

> The administrators now have a copy of the protocol and I've gone through [it] with them and I've shown them your videos and had them score the protocol. So when they walk through classrooms looking for the use of SIOP®, they can see it. One of the administrators took the protocol and put it in the format that she was most comfortable with. Then she gave it to the other administrators so they have it as well.

In some cases, while the SIOP® protocol couldn't be used for formal evaluation, the teachers understood that being a SIOP® teacher meant that their lessons would be effective when they were formally observed. Nicole Teyachea, SIOP® National Faculty and former ELL facilitator at one of the Oxford high schools, reported,

> The way that we presented it to my staff was to say, "It's my job to support you so that when you get evaluated, you'll meet all the evaluation expectations. You know I am not an evaluator; I am here to support you . . . and the way I am going to support you is by using the SIOP® Model. And if we hit on all these eight components then you're going to be successful when other people come in and observe you."

Sustaining Programs

One constant issue with any professional development program is enhancing and sustaining practice after the initial training. After getting teachers and administrators on board, districts developed long-range plans to ensure that SIOP® implementation continued and expanded consistently and with increasing effectiveness.

One effective way for sustaining programs has been discussed in previous chapters: provide quality follow-up through some form of coaching and learning communities. A

FIGURE 6.1 *SIOP® Observation Record*

Room #	Teachers	Preparation				Building Background			
		Plan	Team Teach	Observe	Debrief	Plan	Team Teach	Observe	Debrief
1	Valencia								
2	Amos								
3	Walton								
4	Bergum								
5	DiNapoli								
6	Villalobos								
7	Kleppe								
8	Stephens								
9	Hernandez								
11	Nijdl								
19	Mangione								
14	Rushlow								
15	Painter								
16	Batterberry								
17	McCartney								
18	Scott								
21	Gavina								
23	Groark								
25	Moreno								
10	Harris								
13	Pettit								
30	Harstad								
53	Weidemann								
20	Holbrook								

Wanda Holbrook, Lela Alston School, Phoenix, Arizona.

commitment to ongoing, systematic support is critical. At Alston School, observation and coaching sessions were done systematically with all teachers and tracked using the form seen in Figure 6.1. As several interviewees mentioned, it was through consistent peer support that the SIOP® Model became part of the fabric of the schools.

Another way to sustain programs was to expand professional development beyond classroom teachers so that a SIOP® culture developed throughout the district. In Lewisville ISD (LISD) in Texas, the Bilingual/ESL Department made a commitment to devote a large part of its Title III funds for staff development on the SIOP® Model. Besides the first and second level SIOP® Model courses that were described in Chapter 3, the former elementary specialist (Alvaro Hernandez) and current secondary specialist (Amy Washam), with the support of the department director (Pam Creed), have also designed SIOP® training for district staff other than classroom teachers. At present, they offer

SIOP® training for Administrators, SIOP® Training for Gifted and Talented Teachers, SIOP® Training for Paraprofessionals, and a new course, SIOP® Training for Librarians. Each of these staff development programs lasts from one to three days and provides an overview of the SIOP® Model. The rest of each session is designed for the specific needs of the participating group. For example, the administrators' training focuses on ways they can support teachers implementing the model at school sites.

At Lewisville's Peters Colony Elementary School, in August 2005, the entire staff received SIOP® training, which was followed in August 2006 by a Peters Colony SIOP® Initiative where Assistant Principal Al Hernandez met with the staff once a month, covering one component and collaborating with each other. Additional staff members who have joined the staff this year are attending the district's SIOP® I training and attending the SIOP® Initiative on campus every month as well.

As Al said,

We met every month and covered one component a month throughout the school year. This allowed the staff and administration time to collaborate on each component.

We also began filming on campus one component a month. We ask for a teacher volunteer, take a lesson from the book, [*99 Ideas and Activities for Teaching English Language Learners with the SIOP® Model*], and then film one of teachers demonstrating the lesson. Amy and I collaborate with the teacher, either one on one or together. Prior to filming, one of us observes the lesson in a class that is not being filmed. Either Amy or I coach the teacher through the lesson. The lesson is then observed, and we normally collaborate as a group and adjust the lesson as necessary. Teachers are offered opportunities to observe each other as well.

You would be amazed how much more powerful the lessons we have filmed from the teaching ideas book become after we adjust the lessons [with coaching].

The SIOP® implementation process in Lewisville has been very dynamic and very successful. With a variety of staff development options and continual revisions to existing courses, the district has a strong vision for improving teaching to improve student learning. "It's all about the kids!" explained Alvaro Hernandez. He reported that "along the way there have been so many positives to this [endeavor]" and one of the greatest SIOP® successes has been "the ability to sustain and maintain the training and continue to grow the staff development" in LISD.

A challenge for sustaining SIOP® implementation is teacher turnover. Districts have employed a number of different ways to bring new teachers into SIOP® practice. As mentioned in Chapter 2, new teachers at Alston Elementary School in Phoenix were partnered with an experienced SIOP® teacher, who mentored the teacher and assisted with lesson planning. At Hillcrest Elementary in Lawrence, Kansas, as new teachers were hired, they were sent to SIOP Institutes® so that they received the same training as the SIOP® teachers at the school. In both of these cases, it made the transition easier for the new teachers and maintained both schools' status as having 100 percent SIOP® teachers.

Other schools have ongoing book study on *Making Content Comprehensible for English Learners: The SIOP® Model*, such as in Charlotte-Mecklenburg, where some sites conduct a SIOP® book study. This is one way to deepen the teachers' knowledge of the SIOP® Model and to involve new teachers who come to a school each year. Sometimes Ivanna Mann Thrower, the SIOP® Coach, attended these sessions, especially if a new component was being introduced. In this way she could be assured that the features of the component being studied were clearly explained before teachers try them out in the classroom, especially new teachers.

Finally, in Waller ISD, Texas, the focus was on training at least one cohort of teachers at each of the schools. After the initial training on the model, additional steps were taken to enhance and sustain the implementation and move toward the district goal of having 100 percent of the district's teachers trained. One strategy for this involves new teachers as Martha Trejo explained:

> Every new teacher is SIOP® trained in the summer before starting to teach. They receive a two-day SIOP® overview. During the interview, before they are hired, the teacher candidates are informed of the summer training dates and commit to attending.

Further, Waller requires staff development days right before school begins, and Martha has two days set aside for training the current teachers who have not been exposed to the SIOP® Model yet (or new teachers who had a conflict with the earlier summer training designed for them).

In addition to the strategies for sustaining SIOP® implementation discussed here, Chapter 4 presents descriptions of the efforts of districts to enhance and sustain SIOP® practice.

Maintaining Enthusiasm for the SIOP® Model

Once a school or district has invested in a professional development effort, even when they have taken steps to sustain it, it may be a challenge to maintain the momentum. There are many distractions in teaching that result in uneven implementation of an approach and perhaps more significantly, individuals tend to regress to their previous ways after the newness of the training (and even follow-up) has worn off. Educators have been successful in several ways in generating and maintaining enthusiasm for the SIOP® Model—keeping it "on the radar"—as they find their time and energies being pulled in a number of directions. The following are some successful ways that interest and enthusiasm have been maintained, leading to ongoing, high-quality implementation of the SIOP® Model.

e-Newsletter

In one district, the ESL program coordinator, Liz Warner, sends out a monthly e-newsletter as a way to provide teachers with SIOP® ideas and as a way to keep the focus on implementing SIOP® lessons. As you can see in the following newsletters, Liz briefly discusses each of the eight SIOP® components, beginning with Preparation (see Figure 6.2). Notice how she communicates her enthusiasm for the SIOP® Model—and for teaching—in her tone and by providing a resource for cooperative learning ideas.

In Figure 6.3, the ESL program coordinator, Liz, not only reviews some of the Building Background information in the SIOP® book *Making Content Comprehensible for English Learners: The SIOP® Model*, but she provides additional ideas for tying students'

FIGURE 6.2 *SIOP® Component #1: Preparation*

Sheltered Instruction Observation Protocol (SIOP®)
The first of the eight components of the SIOP® is Lesson Preparation. The research found that lesson planning is critical for both a student's and teacher's success. Think of those days when you went into the classroom well prepared! It felt great, right???

CONTENT OBJECTIVES: You need to know what your content objectives are! If someone asked you about what you taught today, you probably said something more than, "I taught about butterflies." Your students, if asked what they learned that day, might say, "I learned about the metamorphosis of a butterfly" or "I learned the difference in a butterfly and a moth" or even "I examined the implication of losing endangered species of butterflies in our world's rainforests."

LANGUAGE OBJECTIVES: Besides having a content objective, a successful teacher also has a language objective. What do you want students to do with the academic language you are teaching them? Do you want them to be able to define terms in writing? Would you want them to defend a position regarding the Iraq war? Would you like them to be able to read a section out loud to a partner? Think of your language arts standards here, even if you are teaching math. How will they use their Reading, Writing, Listening, and Speaking skills with YOUR content? How will they develop and use vocabulary? A good teacher has to think past just telling students the definitions of words. They must teach student to use those words in some way.

SUPPLEMENTARY MATERIALS: What materials will you need and how will you pass them out? Do you need maps for each team or will each person need a map? You might think of assigning a team "gofer" or "materials monitor" who gets materials for their teams. Will you have a central place that materials can be found? Will you post a daily list of materials students need for the lesson that day? Will you provide pictures of those things they need for students who cannot yet read?

MEANINGFUL ACTIVITIES: Will your students find the activity meaningful and helpful in learning? If YOU think they will be bored, then the activity is probably not engaging enough. How can you make it more meaningful, fun, interesting, and relevant?

The activity I will share this month is a great one for making a simple anticipatory set or review at the beginning of the lesson more exciting and fun. When doing a KWL chart (This is what I know [K]. This is what I want to know [W] and this is what I learned [L]), you will most often call on one or two students (and often NOT your English learners) who raise their hands. When you hand out a worksheet, your class lets out a collective moan. This activity will make sure all students are engaged in something meaningful—and fun!

Try Dueling Flip Charts
Teams race to fill their flip chart with ideas.
Steps
1. Teams all stand in a single file line three feet from the flip chart.
2. Teacher signals "Go." (I start some jazzy music.)
3. The person at the front of the line starts by running to the chart and filling in an answer with the team marker.
4. After recording an answer, the teammate runs back and hands off the marker to the next in line and then goes to the end of the line.
5. The next team member runs up to add to the chart.
6. Play continues until the flip chart is filled, the teacher calls stop, or one round is completed and all teammates sit down to show they are finished.

You can learn more about this structure by visiting this Web site and clicking on the Structure of the Month. There are blackline masters and content, management, and social skills ideas to go along with Dueling Flip Charts. Enjoy!! www.kaganonline.com/Newsletter/index.html

Liz Warner
ESL Program Coordinator

FIGURE 6.3 *SIOP® Component #2: Building Background*

Last month, we looked at the first component of the SIOP® Model, or Sheltered Instruction Observation Protocol. We looked at Lesson Preparation and I wrote about content and language objectives. I am hoping that everyone gave it a shot! Let me know how it is going. I think a required habit teachers should develop is that both the teacher and the student know the objectives of the lesson, and I believe we have to *teach* that instead of just having it written somewhere.

Building Background

This month, the component of the SIOP® Model is Building Background. This component is one of the easiest to incorporate into your teaching. Taking a few minutes to jump-start students' schema, finding out what they know or have experienced about a topic, and linking their knowledge directly to the lesson's objective will result in greater understanding for English learners! Keep reading to find out how you can win a prize if you are a middle school or high school teacher.

Effective teachers present information in a way that students can understand, bearing in mind their language development needs and the gaps in their educational experiences. New information is tied to the student's knowledge and skills. Building background is relating to a student's schema or his knowledge of the world. I often hear teachers say, "These students just don't have the background knowledge!" It is my thought that they *do* have background knowledge, it is just that *their* background knowledge is *different* from ours! We are the teachers. It is our responsibility to connect to *their* background knowledge to help them learn. We need to learn about their lives and things that matter to them.

Remember, we want *all* students to be able to answer the questions we ask, not just the few who raise their hands. And we should allow students to use their first language in our classrooms to share content with another student. Pair your Non-English Proficient students with bilingual students! Requiring your students to use only English in your classroom will frustrate you and your students. Just make it clear that it is always OK to use their first language to talk about content and what you are teaching them. When you have taught them academic language in English, they will know how to use those words. Just telling ELLs to use only English when they don't know any will force them to not be engaged in your class. None of us wants that.

<u>Background Building Questions</u>

How do people usually feel about . . . ?
Have you ever seen a . . . ?
What are your thoughts about . . . ? Why?
What do you already know about . . . ?
What are some things you wonder about . . . ?
What do you think this chapter is about by looking at the pictures?
Look at the title. What do you think this story is about?
Does this remind you of other things we have learned about?
What connections can you make between . . . ?
What things do you think of when you think of . . . ?
What would you predict?
What is your theory about . . . ?
What are some possible explanations?
If you were going to guess . . . ?
What do you notice about . . . ?
What does . . . mean to you?
What do you think the significance of . . . is?
If you were someone else, how might you think about this topic?
What would it feel like to be . . . ?

Timed Pair Share is a great questioning strategy. We want all of our students answering questions, not the same few who always raise their hands. I say, "If the question is not important enough to expect all to know the answer, then why ask the question?"

(Continued)

FIGURE 6.3   *SIOP® Component #2: Building Background*   (*Continued*)

Timed Pair Share (Kagan, 2004)
Set up. You need a timer of some kind. I use a *teach timer* on the overhead, but a watch works fine. You will need to have your student paired up.

1. Teacher asks a question and gives think time.

2. Teacher announces the time each student will have to share.

3. Partner A shares while Partner B listens.

4. Partner B responds ("Thanks for sharing" or "What I heard you say was . . . ")

5. Roles are switched. Partner B shares and Partner A listens.

6. Partner A responds ("To summarize your answer . . . " or "Amazing!")

Vocabulary Building
Part of building background is also key vocabulary building. We all know it is not enough to give students a list of words and share the definitions with them. "These will be on the test! Know them!" There are many exciting ways that we can teach students our important academic language.

Here are some other ideas for Key Vocabulary Building from *Making Content Comprehensible for English Learners: The SIOP® Model* (*3rd Ed.,* 2008):

Semantic Mapping
Concept Definition Maps
Vocabulary Self-Collection Strategy (VSS)
Personal dictionaries
Rich language environment
Repetition of the use of academic language

All of these can be found in the SIOP® book in Chapter 3, *Making Content Comprehensible for English Learners: The SIOP® Model* (*3rd Ed.,* 2008):

Vocabulary Self-Collection Strategy (VSS) (Ruddell, 2005)

1. Teacher models for students how to find important content vocabulary words in text.

2. Students read text.

3. Students list two or three key vocabulary words they feel are essential to understanding content concepts, either alone, in pairs, or in groups.

4. Class list is formed and the vocabulary is discussed in class.

5. Students can enter the words in their personal subject area word books, do activities with the words, be held accountable for them (through a quiz), etc.

Research has found that students picking out key vocabulary themselves instead of the teacher doing it, will make them more adept at selecting words they need to know and therefore, they learn the academic language they need to succeed. This is especially true when the teacher shows the students *how* to select key vocabulary in a passage. These words can become a personal dictionary or a picture dictionary. I found that my students *loved* highlighter tape. I had them highlight text of important words.

Word Walls are also valuable for sight words as well as content words, at any grade level. Word Walls are living, breathing, growing things—NOT those preprinted things you buy at the teacher supply store! Word Walls are used and added to each day. Students learn to use them for speaking and writing. I think it would be so cool to see a Word Wall in a high school classroom with words like meiosis and mitosis!

OK, that's it for this month. I am seeing some great things in classrooms and I would love to come visit you. Just invite me—I will do model lessons, do peer coaching, whatever you want!!! Next month, we will talk about Comprehensible Input.

Liz Warner
ESL Program Coordinator

FIGURE 6.4 *SIOP® Component #3: Comprehensible Input*

"I taught it! They didn't get it!" This may reflect a problem related to comprehensible input. Unless we can make what we are teaching understandable, we are wasting time. Comprehensible input will facilitate the lightbulbs going on! We know how much fun that is!!

The features of comprehensible input are:
- **Speech appropriate for students' proficiency level** (e.g., slower rate, careful enunciation, and simple sentence structure for beginners)
- **Clear explanation of academic tasks** (instructions are given in small, bite-size bits, steps are given in the form of visuals, and the teacher checks for understanding)
- **A variety of techniques used to make content concepts clear** (e.g., modeling, visuals, hands-on activities, demonstrations, gestures, body language)

One of my favorite ideas for comprehensible input is in the form of a door mat. The teacher writes an instruction for students on a piece of chart paper and tapes it to the floor just inside the door. Students must step over it to enter the classroom. This door mat may have instructions about the materials to have ready, the homework to have out on the desk, or may even ask the students to review what they learned the day before. Sometimes the door mat can have pictures or visuals asking students to produce a graphic organizer to be filled in later.

One friend purchased a large plain mat commonly used in front of the sink. She puts her instructions on the mat in water-based pen each day. The routine is that each student reads the mat as he or she comes in and then has a team discussion regarding the door mat instructions before beginning the task. She often uses this mat for her Daily Oral Language activities, too!

Enjoy making your door mat! Could you also make a "path" of door mats with multistep instructions?

Enjoy!
Liz Warner
ESL Program Coordinator

background to the subject and gives specific questions for drawing out students' background experiences. Finally, she offers to visit classes and model SIOP® lessons for the teachers with whom she works.

The newsletter on Comprehensible Input (see Figure 6.4) is brief but begins by grabbing teachers' attention, then it reviews the SIOP® features and provides an excellent idea for making clear explanations of tasks. This example demonstrates that regular communication of this sort need not be lengthy but serves to keep SIOP® practices on teachers' minds and offers new, fresh ideas to maintain their interest and commitment.

In the newsletter on Strategies (Figure 6.5), Liz again quotes and paraphrases some of the information in the SIOP® book but adds her own personal comments that make the communication interesting and teacher friendly.

One of the strengths of the SIOP® Model is that it is a framework that accommodates other methods, approaches, and ideas. The e-newsletters encourage teachers to incorporate cooperative learning structures into SIOP® lessons. In Figure 6.6, the newsletter on Interaction is loaded with ideas for incorporating student-student and student-teacher interaction, while referring to other district trainings in which the teachers have participated. As we've mentioned before and as the e-newsletters illustrate, the SIOP® Model organizes good instructional practices and makes them more effective for English learners.

FIGURE 6.5 *SIOP® Component #4: Strategies*

Our fifth installment of SIOP® newsletters is dealing with strategies for English learners. We hear the word "strategies" bantered around a lot. We have cooperative learning strategies, multiple intelligences, Success for All strategies. I think we sometimes confuse *teaching strategies* with *learning strategies*. Think of the word "strategic." It means to plan for success. It means to use techniques and to put them in such an order that it helps you to become successful. I always think of the football coach. He teaches his players what to do in different situations. Teaching in the classroom should be the same. We need to teach our students what to do in the event of a tough situation. So this month we are talking about student learning strategies.

There are different kinds of strategies: metacognitive strategies (students thinking about their own thinking) and cognitive strategies (students using strategies to organize their thinking).

One of my favorite quotes easily explains the word "strategy" when it comes to learning. "As teachers, we must make public 'secret things' that expert readers do" (Margaret Meek, 1993). We can't assume they "get it" or understand it just because we told them. We have to model it and practice the strategies. The strategies need a name and a process in a student's brain.

Muth and Alvemann (1999) talk about a continuum of strategies from very teacher-centered strategies to teacher-assisted ones, then from peer-assisted ones to student-centered strategies.

Teacher-centered strategies include lecture direct instruction, demonstration, and recitation.
Teacher-assisted strategies include drill and practice, discovery learning, brainstorming, and discussion.
Peer-assisted strategies include role playing, peer tutoring, reciprocal teaching, and certainly cooperative learning.
Student-centered strategies include rehearsal strategies such as repeated readings, selective underlining, and two-column notes; Elaboration strategies such as mental imagery, guided imagery, and creating analogies; and Organizational strategies such as clustering, graphic organizers, and outlining.

A graphic of the continuum of strategies can be seen in *Making Content Comprehensible for English Learners: The SIOP® Model* in Chapter 5.

Remember the term "scaffolding"? Our ultimate goal is to move students away from teacher-centered to student-centered strategies. Remember, we don't leave a scaffold on a building forever. We remove the scaffold when builders no longer need it for access into the building. ELs need similar support; we remove the scaffolds when they no longer need them.

One of my favorite more student-centered strategies is SQP2RS. Go to this site (and Chapter 5 of the SIOP® book) for an explanation. It is a perfect activity for differentiating texts.

www.siopinstitute.net/PDF/SQP2RS-Posters.ppt

Enjoy!
Liz Warner
ESL Program Coordinator

In the next e-newsletter (see Figure 6.7), the Practice and Application component is discussed in a very personal, practical way that helps teachers understand from their own background experience (learning to drive) that talking about an idea or concept is not enough; one must have opportunities to practice if learning is to take root. Again, a variety of ideas are provided to stimulate teachers' interest, along with techniques that can be used immediately in K–12 classrooms.

FIGURE 6.6 *SIOP® Component #5: Interaction*

The newsletter this month goes along with Chapter 6 in our text, *Making Content Comprehensible for English Learners: The SIOP® Model* by Jana Echevarria, MaryEllen Vogt, and Deborah Short.

Did you know that research says that we, as teachers, dominate the speech in a classroom? We speak about 80 percent of the time and students get about 20 percent of the time to speak about content. When we are calling on students one at a time, that means that in an hour time frame, each student would get about six seconds to practice and use their spoken language. If we simply have them "turn to a partner" and "take turns" sharing answers, we up that amount of time to six minutes an hour. *And*, when we realize that students learn to speak English by speaking, we start to look at how much we, as teachers, speak and we tend to talk less! I know that over the years I have had to realize that it is *not* about me, but it *is* about giving my students the chance to produce more complex language and thinking skills. They should be allowed to interact more.

Opportunities for Interaction
We need to plan for interaction time for our students in our lessons. The rule I suggest for interaction (and the one I try to follow) is that for each ten to fifteen minutes I talk, the students get two or three minutes to process the content orally with each other.

Art Costa developed an instructional technique called a 10-2 Lecture. The teacher provides direct instruction for ten minutes and then the students get two minutes to summarize or answer higher-level-thinking questions with each other. Those two minutes are the time students produce comprehensible output. I am sometimes aware that I want the participation to be equal between students (so you don't have HOGS and LOGS in a conversation), so I have adapted this strategy to be a 10-1-1. When it is time to share between partners, I put my overhead timer up and give each partner one minute to share with each other. I am excited when students are working on language and each partner gets one minute to share with the other. I am excited when students are working on language and I even hear some Spanish or Tagalog in these two minutes! I realize there is negotiation of meaning.

Grouping Configurations
There are many ways to group students! I use pairs a lot. Pair your LEP (limited english proficient) students with a FEP (fluent english proficient) bilingual student, side by side. These are called Side-by-Side Partners or Shoulder Partners. Tables of four work well also but tables of five and six start to grow into management problems for me.

There is no limit to the types of groupings you can use. You can do whole group, triads, interest groups, language groups, or your guided reading groups. The key is to be flexible and to use lots of different types of groups in your classrooms!

Wait Time
I once saw research that said we tend to call on a student in 8/10 of a second from the time we finish asking the question. I don't know about you, but I often need time to formulate an answer in my head. Like on *Jeopardy*, I know many of the answers but those smarty-pants buzz in too quickly for me to do well on that show! Think about the need for time if you are an English language learner (ELL)!

A technique I developed to help me get better at wait time is to drink my water. I keep a bottle of water on my desk. I ask a question, take a slow sip of water, and then call on someone. Once, a fourth grader asked me, "Ms. Warner, have you ever noticed that asking questions makes you thirsty?"

Clarify Key Concepts in L1 (First Language)
Best practices say that ELLs benefit from having key concepts clarified in their native language. Sheltered instruction involves teaching subject matter in English, but students should be given the opportunity to clarify in their own language with another student, an assistant, an aide, another student, or you, if you speak in his or her first language.

Liz Warner
ESL Program Coordinator

FIGURE 6.7 *SIOP® Component #6: Practice and Application*

Read more about Practice and Application in Chapter 7 of the SIOP® book *Making Content Comprehensible for English Learners: The SIOP® Model.*

This month, we look at practice and application in the classroom. Do you remember learning to drive? My first memory is sitting on my daddy's lap and steering the car. When I was old enough, he began letting us drive our Buick around the property with him in the passenger seat. He told us what to do and how to do it. He told us before we actually did it ("Now, get ready to turn on your blinker"), and then, when we did it, he praised us. Then there was Driver's Ed in high school. I hated the class where we *talked* about driving. Where I really learned to drive was actually doing it around the streets of Roanoke Rapids, Virginia. I especially remembered the bridge. There was a bridge over the Roanoke River that was too skinny to believe, and it was long. When another car was coming it was so scary, but our driving teacher, Coach West, made us drive that bridge every day, it seemed.

It was simple practice and application. Sometimes we forget that the need to practice and apply knowledge is important for our students. We feel pressure to teach material and we forget to teach our students, especially with standardized tests coming up! Practice is so important. It is especially important to your English learners. It is not enough to tell them. They need to practice! Want to show better academic results in your classroom? Schedule practice every single lesson.

Hands-On Materials and Manipulatives

Guided practice is essential, and if you can use manipulatives, then it is even more effective. All concepts in math can be taught with manipulatives at the concrete stage of learning. Think of Base 10 Blocks, unifix cubes, algebra tiles, and even a ruler!

For language arts, let students use letter tiles, sentence strips to sequence, or magnets or a personal Word Wall to sort and classify.

For science, having models to put together, doing dissections, and having a collections area are great ways to use manipulatives.

Practice

1. Practice small, meaningful pieces of your lesson. Teach for ten minutes and then practice for two.
2. Each practice should be short in duration so the student has to exert intense effort and make an intention to learn.
3. Practice any new learning with mass practice. Practice old learning with distributed practice.
4. Let students know how they did with immediate feedback from you or another student.

Application

A student does not need to know how to speak fluently before reading or writing. Each skill supports the other. Student should be using *listening*, *speaking*, *reading* and *writing* in every lesson you teach. Look for ways to incorporate all of these into all classes, even your science or PE lessons. Ask students to use the academic language you are practicing. It takes twenty-one (or more) times for an ELL to hear, say, read, and write a word for it to become a part of their vocabulary. So you can guess why practice is important.

For this, graphic organizers are a great idea, *but* instead of running off worksheets for them to fill in, teach your students to produce their own graphic organizers. Then the skill of organizing thoughts in a visual, graphic way is *theirs* . . . not just another worksheet!!!

One of my favorite activities for practice that involves listening, speaking, reading, and writing is a sort of reciprocal teaching called *Show Me Your Thinking* in which the students take turns leading the practice. I have used this strategy in kindergarten for learning to write letters, in fourth grade with kids practicing writing and saying numbers into the 10,000s, and in high school with vocabulary when I do teacher training.

(Continued)

The steps are as follows:

1. Each student needs paper and pencil (I use notepads) or a slate/whiteboard.

2. A Teaching Captain is chosen. That person reads a question or problem and says, "Everyone write your answer."

3. The team writes or draws the answer without any help from others. When done, they turn their paper over to signal to the Teaching Captain that they are ready.

4. The Teaching Captain says, "*Show Me Your Thinking!*" and everyone turns over their papers.

5. Team members read and discuss their answers. Help is given to those who need help, and then there is a Team Celebration (a handshake or team cheer). Students can use this to check notes, the text, or the text on the board.

6. A new Teaching Captain is chosen and the next question or problem is shared.

Sooo, go out there and practice! It will make your teaching easier and their learning more valuable! Want me to come model *Show Me Your Thinking* with your class? Just invite me!! I love the chance to come to classrooms and hang out with kids!

Liz Warner
ESL Program Coordinator

For Lesson Delivery (see Figure 6.8), Liz took several points from the SIOP® book and personalized them, providing teachers with ideas to use from her own experience as a teacher. In this way, the e-newsletter became something that resonated with teachers and motivated them to try the ideas in their own classrooms.

The Review and Assessment e-newsletter (see Figure 6.9) reminds teachers that review and assessing content and language learning must occur throughout each lesson. The SIOP® features are reviewed and an idea for reviewing is presented.

FIGURE 6.8 *SIOP® Component #7: Lesson Delivery*

Yesterday you wrote out your lesson plan for a class and it's almost time to deliver the lesson. Will it go well? Will it bomb? Will students understand? A well-planned lesson that looks great on paper does not guarantee success. That is why just reading lesson plans in a book or online will never make a great teacher. While a poorly planned lesson can just about guarantee disaster, a well-planned lesson must also include an idea about how to deliver the lesson. What do great teachers do that guarantees learning?

In the SIOP® Model, Echevarria, Short, and Vogt (2008) describe the importance of lesson delivery. The four features of the Lesson Delivery component include the following:

- Content objectives clearly supported by lesson delivery
- Language objectives clearly supported by lesson delivery
- Students engaged approximately 90 to 100 percent of the time
- Pacing of the lesson appropriate to the students' ability level

Once I started writing clear content and language objectives and really thinking about what I wanted students to learn, it became much easier for me to make sure that my teaching, guided practice, and application met the objectives. If you are not meeting your objectives through your lessons, and you don't realize it, the students will tell you: "We didn't do that, Ms. Warner!!" We need to remember that everything we do in a lesson should support our objectives that day!

I always tell teachers that either you engage them in learning or they will engage themselves and it *may not be* learning! Think about it! Have you ever brought a Sudoku puzzle book or papers to grade to a workshop, "Just in *case* the speaker is not good?" We should remember that student engagement is very different from students being "busy." When we talk about the value of student engagement, we mean being engaged in the content and learning. When we talk about English learners, we need to think about how to engage them in the content when language is a roadblock to engagement.

(Continued)

FIGURE 6.8 *SIOP® Component #7: Lesson Delivery* *(Continued)*

Pacing of the lesson is so important. When they start drooling on the desk, it's time to pick up the pace! Or if you feel yourself saying, "We need to finish this today!" you may need to actually slow down and teach for understanding instead of covering material.

Here are some pacing ideas to think about while delivering your next lesson:

1. Well-planned lessons—Think about how long each part of your lesson will take. Is there time allotted for students to move between groups or to get out their materials during your lesson?

2. Clear explanation of academic tasks or instruction—Give instructions in small, bite-size pieces. Use visuals and display written directions for multistepped instructions.

3. Appropriate amount of time spent on an academic task. Not too much, and just enough! I read somewhere that if you take the age of your students and add 1, that is about the length of time they can attend to one thing without needing a change. In other words, the kindergarten teacher needs to think about making a change in activity about every six to seven minutes while a high school chemistry teacher can expect to need a change every nineteen to twenty minutes in class.

4. Strong classroom management skills—Think about what could possibly go wrong and plan how to avoid it! How will you pass out materials, assign roles, or move to the next part of your lesson?

Liz Warner
ESL Program Coordinator

FIGURE 6.9 *SIOP® Component #8: Review and Assessment*

While Review and Assessment is the last of the eight components of the SIOP® Model, it by no means should be done only at the end of a lesson. Review and assessment should be ongoing. The features are as follows:

- Comprehensive review of key vocabulary
- Key concepts review
- Regular feedback on student output
- Assessment of objectives throughout the lesson

One of my favorite review activities is loved by kids from kindergarten all the way to graduate students. It is called Relay Review, and it is just that . . . a relay race to review terms and key concepts. It is great for facilitating the use of academic language and a great way to finish up the day!

To get ready for this review, set up a piece of chart paper for each team of four to six. Use a *big* vocabulary word as your acrostic. Write the word or words down the side of each chart paper, like so:

```
S           I
H           N
E           S
L           T
T           R
E           U
R           C
E           T
D           I
            O
            N
```

The teams line up equal distance from their poster with the person in the front holding the marker. The teacher begins some music as a signal to start the relay. Person #1 in each team runs to the poster, writes something he or she learned, beginning with one of the letters in the large key concept on the chart, runs back, and passes the pen off to Person #2. Person #1 goes to the back of the team lineup. Play continues until the team fills up their chart. The team hurries back to their seats and sits, and participates in a team cheer.

(Continued)

I know you and your class will enjoy this activity. It is fun to watch kids in the line feverishly searching notes and to hear kids using academic language to help the next writer! You will love to see your students actively engaged in this review!

Liz Warner
ESL Program Coordinator

After each of the components was covered in a monthly installment, Liz Warner began providing a monthly technique or idea that could be used in future SIOP® lessons. For example, "I Can" sentences used with objectives (see Figure 6.10) are ideal to distribute in September when most schools begin their academic year. Teachers are provided with a way to make their objectives "kid-friendly," and the e-newsletter serves as a reminder that content and language objectives are part of every SIOP® lesson. Other ideas such as cooperative learning structures (see Figure 6.11) provide teachers with fresh ideas for encouraging interaction among students and offer several effective practice opportunities for students.

As you can see, an e-newsletter may be brief or lengthy, but the idea is to provide regular communication with teachers who have been trained in the SIOP® Model to encourage implementation of the thirty features to a high degree.

FIGURE 6.10 *September Technique of the Month: Sharing "I Can" Objectives*

"I Can" objectives are kid-friendly ways of sharing a focus for lessons you teach with students. Asking students to *do* something with the "I Can" objectives can help them internalize the reasons for the lesson and can help them develop a personal learning objective in their minds. This focus is especially helpful for English language learners. It allows them to formulate questions when they are not understanding a part of the lesson and allows them to celebrate themselves and their learning when they "Get It!"

According to the SIOP® Model, objectives should be posted and discussed with students. It is not enough to simply write the "I Can" statement in kid-friendly, grade- and age-appropriate terms and post it on your bulletin board or white board. Kids have to be involved and engaged in the sharing of the objective. That objective should be introduced, revisited during the lesson, and then again at the end of the lesson to allow students to self-assess their learning. Objectives should be specific and explicit for each lesson you teach.

Sharing "I Can" Objectives
So you have written your objectives for your lesson on the board or on chart paper for your students to see. If you never do anything more, if you *ask* a student what she is learning in the lesson, can she verbalize her learning? Most likely the answers you get may be spotty. But if we devise ways of helping students internalize the purpose for the lesson, they will be better able to tell their parents something other than, "nothing" when they are asked what they learned in math, reading, or science that day. They will begin to take learning as their responsibility, too, as opposed to all your responsibility to get it in their brains.

Before the Lesson
1. Read the objectives as a shared reading piece with your entire class.
2. Then ask students to paraphrase the objective with a partner, each taking a turn.
3. Ask students to read the objectives on the board and to add them to their learning notebooks in a paraphrased form. Then have them read them to each other. This could be done while you are taking roll!

(Continued)

FIGURE 6.10 *September Technique of the Month: Sharing "I Can" Objectives* *(Continued)*

4. Present the "I Can" statement and then do a Timed Pair Share (Kagan, 2004), asking students to predict some of the things they think they will be doing in class that day.

5. Ask students to do a RallyRobin (taking turns) (Kagan, 2004), naming things they will be asked to do that day in that particular class.

6. Ask students to pick out important words from the objectives and highlight them, such as the action words or nouns.

During the Lesson

1. Give students important words to watch for during the lesson and to call attention to that part of the objective when you mention the academic vocabulary in the words.

2. Reread the objectives using shared reading during the lesson to focus your students.

3. Ask students to rate themselves with how well they are understanding and meeting the objective using finger symbols that can be shown in class or hidden under the desk.

> Thumbs up—I got it!!
> Thumbs down—I am completely lost!
> Flat hand tilted back and forth—I understand some of it but I'm a bit fuzzy.

NOTE: If they are showing themselves as lost or fuzzy, ask them, "What is it that is confusing you?" "What part *do* you understand?" "Where does your confusion start?" *Don't* just let them say, "I don't get it!"

After the Lesson

1. "Rate yourself 1 to 3, how well did you meet our objectives today?"

2. Ask students to write one or two sentences explaining what they learned in class today and to show an example. This can be in a learning log or on a Post-It note left on the desk.

3. Round robin (taking turns talking in a group of four) (Kagan, 2004), reviewing what they learned in class.

4. Timed Pair Share (taking turns talking for a specified time with a partner) (Kagan, 2004) about how they can prove they met their learning objectives for the day.

5. Tickets out: Students write a note to the teacher (or a letter to the parent at the end of each day) telling them what was learned and asking any clarifying questions they need.

(Kagan Structures can be found in *Cooperative Learning* by Dr. Spencer Kagan.)

Liz Warner
ESL Program Coordinator

FIGURE 6.11 *May Technique of the Month: Quiz-Quiz-Trade*

Learning from Liz, ESL Program Coordinator

I have heard so many positive comments about my little once-a-month e-mail newsletter. I am glad that some of these ideas are being implemented and that teachers are finding them to be so helpful.

As you implement Quiz-Quiz-Trade, watch the interaction of your students. You will see students helping each other as they read, listen, and answer content questions in a safe learning environment. It is perfect for all students, but especially good for our English language learners. Talk about comprehensibe input!!! When you see them laughing, you know you have provided a stress-free environment, which not only promotes learning but promotes language acquisition. If students make their own matching cards, you implement reading, writing, speaking, and listening all in one activity!

Practice can be boring, but we must give students the opportunity to practice. In the SIOP® Model (Sheltered Instruction Observation Protocol), this one structure incorporates both the Interaction and Practice/Application components. Quiz-Quiz-Trade implements the research based on basic principles of cooperative learning proven in hundreds of controlled studies to produce academic achievement gains for students

(Continued)

of all races, ages, and ability levels—especially the lowest-achieving students who most need gains. Quiz-Quiz-Trade is a structure that helps learners of all ages retain more in any subject area.

Quiz-Quiz-Trade (Kagan, 2004)
Steps: Students quiz a partner, get quizzed by a partner, and then trade cards to repeat the process with a new partner.

Setup: The teacher or class creates a set of cards based on the content to master. Each card has a matching card. For example, to learn vocabulary, one card would be the word and the matching card would be the definition. Each student receives one card.

1. Stand Up-Hand Up-Pair Up. With cards in hand, all students stand up, put a hand up, and find a partner.
2. Partner A Quizzes. Partner A quizzes Partner B. For example, if Partner A has a vocabulary word, he/she asks his/her partner to define the word. If Partner A has a definition, he/she reads the definition and asks his/her partner to identify the word defined.
3. Partner B Answers.
4. Partner A Praises or Coaches. If Partner B is correct, Partner A shares a compliment. If Partner B is incorrect or doesn't know, Partner A offers help, if possible.
5. Switch Roles. Partner B now takes a turn quizzing Partner A. Partner B then praises or coaches.
6. Partners Trade Cards. When done, partners trade cards and get ready for another round of Quiz-Quiz-Trade.

Repeat Steps 1 through 6 a number of times.

Management Ideas

- If students make cards, check them for accuracy.
- If there is an odd number, teacher can play to get class started.
- If needed, assign who goes first each time.
- Remind students to keep a hand up when looking for a partner. This makes it easier to see at a glance who still needs a partner.
- Identify a location in the room to wait with hand up.
- Monitor to assess and help.
- Put answers on back of cards if needed.
- Color-code cards by levels of difficulty—students find someone with same-color card to quiz.
- Use pictures instead of words.

Social Skills

- Asking questions
- Greeting
- Departing
- Coaching
- Praising
- Tolerance
- Asking for help

Ideas for your class

- Favorites
- Vocabulary and definition
- Elements and symbols
- Patterns—what comes next
- Coins and values
- Synonyms/antonyms
- How did you feel when . . .
- Geography terms and definitions
- Important events—Treaty of Paris
- Identify instruments
- Clap this pattern
- Practice greetings
- What is the artist trying to convey?
- About you
- Animals and baby names
- Parts of plants
- Telling time
- Multiplication facts
- Spelling words
- Fact/opinion
- Map-reading skills
- Famous athletes
- Musical notes
- Singers and songs
- Famous pictures/artists
- Identify art tools
- Vacations
- Animals and species
- Conversation questions
- Fractions and equivalents
- Initial letter identification
- Story words
- Famous people—known for
- Bill of Rights
- Rules
- Read notes—name that tune
- Pictures and words
- What time period is this painting from

Liz Warner
ESL Program Coordinator

A Pocket Full of Protocols

In one of the elementary schools, the SIOP® Coach mounted a manila envelope full of copies of the SIOP® protocol in an area visited by staff on a daily basis—the mail room near the copy machine. Having the protocols in a visible place reminded teachers to take copies of the protocol and use them for planning and reflection. It also helped the coach gauge interest. If few teachers took the protocols after a week or so, she realized that she needed to do something to get them thinking about SIOP® lesson planning and implementation again.

SIOP® Bookmarks

One district (Dearborn, Michigan) developed a SIOP® resource for teachers that kept the eight SIOP® components visible as a reminder about SIOP® techniques and practices. The copies seen in Figure 6.12 through 6.20 were printed on the front and back to form a bookmark. Many teachers have laminated them and put them on a ring for quick reference.

The first one (see Figure 6.12) shows all the components and features of the SIOP® Model. The others each reflect one component and its features, and provide examples of ways to implement each feature.

The staff uses the bookmarks in district trainings and distributes them at conference presentations as well. Many teachers in the district and in other districts use this resource since it is a way to have a summary of the SIOP® Model readily accessible.

Resource Book of SIOP® Lesson Plans

In a few settings, the trainer, coach, or lead teacher collected lesson plans (and typed them, if necessary). The lesson plans were compiled into a book so that teachers had many sample lesson plans from which to choose.

Sharing of Professional Resources

Ongoing contact with teachers, coaches, and district support personnel helped keep SIOP® implementation on their radar. As mentioned earlier, this was done through newsletters or during meetings. Melissa Castillo of the Oxford schools used meetings to distribute an educational article or other materials to maintain interest. She said,

> Whenever we found articles we would use them to work with our curriculum coaches. We met as a team I think once every three weeks but we'd always have a piece and talk about what was new and what was going on. I also had a monthly meeting . . . with my ELL facilitators where I would do mini workshops so our meeting would always start with an hour and fifteen minutes of SIOP® training, and I would always do a piece on building background or vocabulary or a minilesson on strategies, something that they could always take back to their schools.

Also, meetings provided an opportunity for refresher activities. Wanda Holbrook and Kendra Moreno, trainers at Lela Alston Elementary School, used a handout to get

(Continued on p. 116)

FIGURE 6.12 *Making Content Comprehensible for English Language Learners—SIOP® Model*

Components—of the SIOP® Model:

Preparation
- Clearly define content objectives—write on the board, state orally
- Clearly define language objectives—write on the board, state orally
- Choose content concepts for age appropriateness and "fit" with educational background of students
- Use supplementary materials to make lessons clear and meaningful
- Adapt content to all levels of student proficiency—use graphic organizers, study guides, taped texts, jigsaw reading . . .
- Provide meaningful and authentic activities that integrate lesson concepts with language practice opportunities—surveys, letter writing, making models, plays, games . . .

Building Background
- Explicitly link concepts to students' background experience
- Make clear links between students' past learning and new concepts
- Emphasize key vocabulary

Comprehensible Input
- Speak appropriately to accommodate students' proficiency level
- Clearly explain academic tasks
- Use a variety of techniques to make content concepts clear—modeling, hands-on materials, visuals, demos, gestures, film clips . . .

Strategies
- Provide ample opportunities for students to use strategies—GIST, SQP2R, Reciprocal Teaching, mnemonics, 12-minute research paper, 2-column notes, repeated readings, . . .
- Consistently use scaffolding techniques throughout lesson—think-alouds, paraphrasing, partnering . . .
- Employ a variety of question types—use Question Cube, Thinking Cube, Bloom's Taxonomy . . .

Interaction
- Provide frequent opportunities for interaction and discussion—supplies much-needed "oral rehearsal"
- Group students to support language and content objectives—use at least 2 different structures during a lesson—pairs, triads, teams, varied by language proficiency or interest
- Consistently afford sufficient wait time—let other students write down answers while waiting for one student to respond
- Give ample opportunities for clarification for concepts in L_1—use bilingual paraprofessionals, native language materials, notes by students . . .

Practice/Application
- Supply lots of hands-on materials
- Provide activities for students to apply content/language knowledge—discussing and doing make abstract concepts concrete; allow students to work in partners before working alone
- Integrate all language skills into each lesson—listening, speaking, reading, writing

Lesson Delivery
- Clearly support content objectives—objectives apparent throughout lesson; no "bird-walks"
- "Clearly support language objectives—students given ample opportunities to "show off" their language capabilities in speaking, reading, writing
- Engage students 90–100% of the lesson—less "teacher talk," no "down-time," students are actively working in whole groups, small groups, individually . . .
- Appropriately pace the lesson to students' ability level

Review/Assessment
- Provide comprehensive review of key vocabulary—teach, review, assess, teach . . . ; use word study books, Content Word Wall, . . .
- Supply comprehensive review of key content concepts—review content directly related to objectives throughout lesson; use graphic organizers as review
- Regularly give feedback to students on their output—clarify, discuss, correct responses
- Conduct assessment of student comprehension and learning—use a variety of quick reviews: thumbs up-down, numbered wheels, small dry-erase boards; include student self-assessment . . .

Adapted from *Making Content Comprehensible for English Language Learners*, Echevarria, Vogt, Short, 2nd Edition, 2004.
Compiled by the Bilingual and Compensatory Education Resource Team, Dearborn Public Schools, Michigan, revised 2005.

FIGURE 6.13 *Making Content Comprehensible—
1. Lesson Preparation*

Comprehensible and Thoughtful Lesson Design
- Base lessons on **grade-level** appropriate **curriculum**
- **Share** content and language objectives with EL students—take from **Grade-Level Content**

Expectations
- Start with **"jump-start" minilessons** that develop context and access to background knowledge

A. Adapting Content Will Provide Support
- By modifying dense and difficult text
- By using before, during, after reading/writing scaffolds
- By making texts accessible to all students without "watering down" text

1. Graphic Organizers
Schematic visuals that assist students in grasping the "wholeness and parts" of a concept. Use to supplement written or spoken words.

- Before reading or writing: as a guide and supplement to build background for difficult or dense text and an aid to help organize writing
- During reading: to focus students' attention and make connections, help with taking notes, and assist with understanding text structure
- After reading or writing: to assist in recording personal understandings and responses; double-checks organization

Examples: "I Wonder," Venn Diagrams, Timelines, Discussion webs, Thinking maps . . .

Tip: With English language learners, it is helpful to actually **construct the graphic organizer step-by-step** in front of the students on chart paper or transparency for deeper understanding

2. Outlines
Teacher-prepared outlines that help students take notes in an organized manner

Tip: T-charts are useful outlines to begin organizing

Tip: Some students need picture support, or need to see the completed outline first

3. Leveled Study Guides
Teacher composes guides to accompany students' textbook—may include: Summary of text, Questions, Statements of learning, Definitions. Teacher can designate questions for different levels by marking with * (easiest), ** (moderately challenging), and *** (most challenging)

4 Highlighted Text
For newcomers: highlight (using blue highlighter) key concepts, important vocabulary, and summary statements in students' textbooks. Newcomers only read highlighted sections. This reduces stress yet maintains key concepts.

5. Taped Text
Teacher, paraprofessional, or older student tapes textbook for newcomers. This allows for multiple exposures to text and should improve reading fluency and understanding. Students can take text and tape home for homework.

6. Adapted Text
Sometimes it is necessary to rewrite dense text in order for ELs to comprehend content. **Short, simpler sentences are easier** for newcomers to understand. Format: topic sentence + several supporting detail sentences—relevant to the content. Maintaining consistent format = easier reading, more connections to prior knowledge. Including definitions of key vocabulary will further comprehension.

7. Jigsaw Text Reading
One or two members of each cooperative team are chosen by the teacher to form an "expert" team. Each "expert team" is responsible for one section of assigned text. Text sections are read aloud, discussed and reviewed for essential information, key vocabulary, and better collective understanding. When clear understanding is reached, "expert team" members return to their original cooperative teams to teach their teammates—demonstrating **peer modeling**. ELs benefit greatly because they are learning from others while not burdened with reading the whole text.

8. Marginal Notes
Like highlighted text, teacher notes in the margins of a newcomer's textbook assist in focusing attention on important ideas, key concepts, and key words and their definitions, or draw attention to important supporting facts for "why" or "how." The Teacher's Edition marginal notes may help in choosing key facts, etc. Parent volunteers could assist in putting marginal notes in multiple textbooks. If you didn't want to write in actual student textbooks, you could use sticky notes that are removable.

9. Native Language Texts and Web sites
Texts written in students' native language may supplement or clarify key concepts for literate students. Appropriate Web sites may provide translations of key words or concepts.

B. Appropriate Supplementary Materials
- Hands-on manipulatives and realia: connects abstract concepts with concrete experiences and student's own life
- Pictures, Photos, Visuals: provide visual support to harder concepts. Include models, charts, overheads, maps, timelines as you are presenting concepts
- Multimedia: film clips, songs and chants, posters, computer games, etc.—related to concept solidify key concepts into the deep memory
- Demonstrations: Model step-by-step completion of tasks, or model language to use with presentations. This scaffolds and enhances learning.
- Related Material: Most schools have a multitude of leveled books—both fiction and non-fiction—that supplement science and social studies concepts. Check your school's resource room for materials.

C. Meaningful Activities: real-life activities
- Plan activities to promote language
- Relate authentic activities to students' lives
- Apply to grade level content standards
- Involve students in reading, writing, discussion of important concepts and ideas

Adapted from *Making Content Comprehensible for English Language Learners*, Echevarria, Vogt, Short, 2nd Edition, 2004. Compiled by the Bilingual and Compensatory Education Resource Team, Dearborn Public Schools, Michigan, revised April 2004.

FIGURE 6.14 *Making Content Comprehensible—2. Building Background*

- Links Concepts to Students' Background
- Provides Links between Past Learning and New Concepts—Effective teaching takes students from where they are and leads them to a higher level of understanding
- Develops Key Vocabulary—There is a strong correlation between vocabulary knowledge and student achievement

3 Major Instructional Interventions
- Preteach vocabulary
- Provide experiences (ex: showing video <u>before</u> lesson)
- Introduce conceptual framework (ex: graphic organizers)

Principles That Guide Instruction: Students should
- be **active** in developing understanding
- **personalize** word learning
- be **immersed** in words
- **build** on **multiple sources** of information—repeat exposures (Recommended 25 times for word ownership)

1. Contextualizing Key Vocabulary
Review content and select **key terms that are critical** to understanding the lesson's most important concepts.

- Introduce and define terms simply and concretely
- Demonstrate how terms are used in context
- Explain use of synonyms or cognates to convey meaning; clarify multiple-meaning words

2. Vocabulary Self-Selection
After reading a content text, students **self-select vocabulary** they think is essential to understanding the content concepts.

- Words are selected by individuals, partners, or teams
- Shared, discussed, and agreed upon by whole class
- Strategy empowers students in choosing the most appropriate key vocabulary
- Works as a good strategy for vocabulary review

3. Personal Dictionaries
Personal dictionaries are created as an individual vocabulary and spelling resource for students.

- Students read text with partners or teams and select unknown words
- Teacher works with teams to review each student's personal dictionary and provide clarifications where needed
- Words can be arranged alphabetically, by concept, or by structure

4. Content Word Wall
This is a Content Word Wall specific to one content area, reserved for key vocabulary that relates to that content.

- Display key words alphabetically
- Revisit frequently during lessons
- Have students use words throughout unit of study
- Remove some words regularly in order to keep words displayed to a reasonable number

Ex: Social Studies Word Wall: *Revolutionary War*

A	Battle	Constitution concede		decide Declaration
E	flag	G	H	Independence
J	**K**	liberty	**M**	notify...

5. Concept Definition Map
A simple graphic system used to discuss complex concepts and clarify the meaning of a concept.

Ex: Concept Definition Map—*Revolution*

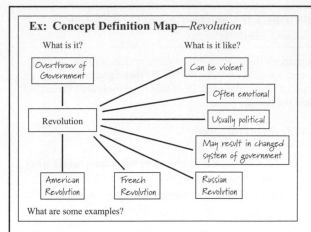

6. Cloze Sentences
Used to teach and review content vocabulary in context.

- Teacher chooses a sentence that has a strong contextual support for the vocabulary focus word
- Possible replacement words are brainstormed
- Teacher assists students in choosing correct word

7. Word Sorts
Students categorize words or phrases (previously introduced) and sort them according to meaning, structure, word endings, or sounds. This reinforces word relationships, spelling, and word structure. Use List-Group-Label as one technique.

Ex: Word sort by endings—*American Revolution*

–tion	–sion	–tation
revolution	tension	
		representation
taxation	passion	
plantation		
frustration	mission	
participation	vision	

8. Word Generation
This is a review of new content vocabulary through analogy. Students brainstorm words that contain a "chunk" of a word.
Ex: *port* "to carry"—portable, export, transport, deport . . .

9. Word Study Books
Help students group words by structure or meaning. Aid in the study of high-frequency words.

10. Vocabulary Games
Use commercial word games to practice words—Pictionary, Scrabble, Word Search (use only for beginners, with only 5 or 6 words, all going left to right), Crossword Puzzles—work with a partner or in teams

11. Visual Vocabulary
English language learners benefit from a "picture" of a term added to a definition of the word. Use stick figures, a picture-dictionary format, or a photograph.

12. Vocabulary through Songs
Use the "Jim Walters Approach"—"Science through Song CD" for teaching difficult concepts through a song format. Concepts and relationships are explained and remembered more easily for some students through this multiple intelligence medium.

Adapted from *Making Content Comprehensible for English Language Learners*, Echevarria, Vogt, Short, 2nd Edition, 2004. Compiled by the Bilingual and Compensatory Education Resource Team, Dearborn Public Schools, Michigan, revised April 2004.

FIGURE 6.15 *Making Content Comprehensible—3. Comprehensible Input*

Comprehensible Input makes verbal communication more understandable for English learners by making adjustments to speech. Comprehensible input should be **measured throughout the lesson**.

A. Appropriate Speech
How said and what is said

1. Use speech that is **appropriate to students' proficiency level**—slow down and enunciate where applicable

2. **Avoid jargon** and idiomatic speech as much as possible

3. Use **paraphrasing** and **repetition**

4. Use **simple sentence structure**

B. Explanation of Academic Tasks

1. Present instructions in **a step-by-step manner** and/or with demonstrations. Write oral directions on board—ask students to reexplain

2. Use **peer modeling**—Focus attention on one group that is functioning well on activity. Let those students explain step-by-step instructions to whole class using an overhead transparency

C. Use of a Variety of Techniques
Allow sufficient planning time to incorporate appropriate techniques for EL students

1. Adapt content to ELs' proficiency levels
   - Use **graphic organizers** before, during, and after lessons
   - Use **leveled study guides**

2. Highlight key vocabulary by **preteaching key words**

3. Ensure **multiple exposures** to new terminology
   - Use multiple modalities to remember words
   - Have students use individual Word Study Books for personal reference—grouping words by structure (*-tion, -sion, -ation*, etc.)
   - Have students "buddy study" words

4. Use **scaffolding techniques** routinely

Verbal Scaffolding
   Paraphrasing—restating student's response to model correct English
   Think-Alouds—saying out loud what you are doing as you try to use a strategy
   Reinforcing contextual definitions—restating a term by giving a context or definition: Ex. Aborigines, *the native people of Australia*, were being driven from their homes.

Procedural Scaffolding

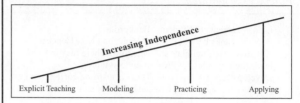

Small group instruction with less experienced students practicing with experienced students
Partnering students for practice

5. **Model** techniques for students several times

6. **Use gestures** when presenting lessons

7. Whenever possible employ **hands-on activities** at least once during a lesson

8. Use **demonstrations** of techniques, experiments

9. Use activities that apply new content and language knowledge
   - **Discussing and doing** make abstract concepts concrete, therefore projects, discussion teams, oral reports lend themselves to true comprehension
   - Including opportunities for students to practice English solidifies comprehension:
     Let students **report out orally and in writing daily**; let them **work in teams and with partners routinely**

10. **Sentence strips** that are cut apart and reassembled in order give ELs practice with sentence structure in a hands-on manner. Students could challenge each other by exchanging their "cut-up" sentences with each other

11. Include **multimedia and other technologies** in daily lessons
    - **Overhead transparencies** are excellent tools to involve students in the content presented. Students can underline key words, draw lines to connect concepts, correct English sentence structure . . .
      Students can also **make their own** overheads for presentations to their peers. Routinely use this medium with students for greater "comprehensible input"
    - Use **PowerPoint presentations** to highlight key points and present visuals—students can then **revisit information** on their own computers
    - Visit **relevant Web sites** to enhance content. Bookmark appropriate ones for students.

Adapted from *Making Content Comprehensible for English Language Learners*, Echevarria, Vogt, Short, 2nd Edition, 2004. Compiled by the Bilingual and Compensatory Education Resource Team, Dearborn Public Schools, Michigan, revised April 2004.

FIGURE 6.16 *Making Content Comprehensible— 4. Strategies*

A. Learning Strategies

Help ELs **comprehend, integrate**, and **retain** new information. Carefully designed lessons incorporate **metacognitive** (ways of monitoring our thinking—ex: self-questioning), **cognitive** (ways of organizing information—ex: previewing a story or word-splash), and **social-affective strategies** (ways of enhancing learning—ex: working with a partner or group discussions)

- *Mentally active learners **are** better learners*
- **Strategies** can be **taught**
- Learning strategies **transfer** to new tasks
- **Discussing and doing** make abstract concepts concrete
- Academic language learning **is more effective** with learning strategies

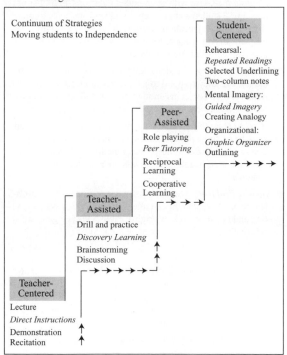

A Variety of Strategies

Use at least one or two every day

1. **Mnemonics**—using acronyms to memorize terms or concepts, ex: HOMES—each letter stands for one of the Great Lakes

2. **"I Wonder"**—brainstorming about book, topic, theme— should be in the form of questions (who, what, when, what if, why . . .) or "I wonder if . . . "

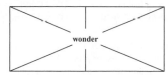

3. **GIST Summarizing Strategy—7 minutes:** 3 minutes–After reading a passage or section of text, teacher and students underline or pick out 10 words and concepts that are "most important" to understanding text.

   3 minutes—Teacher and students write 1 or 2 summary statements using as many of the listed words as possible. Could be partner work. Post on board.

   2 minutes—Repeat process through subsequent text. When finished, add a topic sentence to precede summary sentences—a summary paragraph!

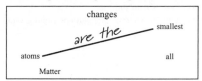

1 minute — Write 10 words on the board.	
matter	forms
changes	gas
solid	living things
liquid	space
states of matter	atoms

4. Make a ***Word Splash*** using the important words in a text:

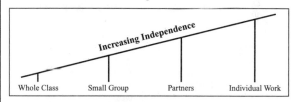

5. ***Illustrate*** new learning on a poster including appropriate captions and details.

6. ***Create a poem, chant, song, or play*** demonstrating new learning.

7. **Graffiti Write**—represents students' learning: Each team has chart paper; each team member has a marker. A topic or question is posed. At the start signal, each person writes a personal comment about the topic or question on the chart paper—*at the same time*. 2 minutes

   When time is called, teams rotate to next table, read comments, and add their own—may be same topic/question or another question or focus. 2 minutes
   Rotate again, either to another table or back to own table. Post results.

B. Scaffolding Techniques

1. Use think-alouds—say out loud what you are thinking as you try to use a strategy

2. Construct a graphic organizer (T-list, Venn Diagram, etc.) depicting the highlights of a reading selection.

3. Use Procedural scaffolding

Increasing Independence

| Whole Class | Small Group | Partners | Individual Work |

C. Questioning Techniques

Ask questions that promote critical and strategic thinking

1. Use a ***Thinking Cube*** to generate at least 6 higher-order thinking questions about text. Ex: <u>How</u> can you measure matter?

2. Use a ***Question Cube*** as a question starter to stimulate a variety of questions after a passage is read. Roll the cube and one student asks the question—who, what, when, where, why, how—another student answers.

3. **QAR (Question-Answer Relationships)**—helps students distinguish between "Right Here" (literal) questions, "Author and Me" (inferential), and "On My Own" (from experience) questions and know where to find the answers.

4. **QtA (Questioning the Author)**—this technique assists students in developing a deep comprehension of the reading material.

Adapted from *Making Content Comprehensible for English Language Learners*, Echevarria, Vogt, Short, 2nd Edition, 2004. Compiled by the Bilingual and Compensatory Education Resource Team, Dearborn Public Schools, Michigan, revised February 2005.

FIGURE 6.17 *Making Content Comprehensible—5. Interaction*

A. Opportunities for Interaction
- Learning is more effective when students have an opportunity to **participate fully**—**discussing** ideas and information
- Effective teachers strive to provide a more **balanced** linguistic exchange between themselves and their students—ELL students need the practice in speaking!
- Interaction **accesses** the thought processes of another and **solidifies** one's own thinking
- Talking with others, either in pairs or small groups allows for **oral rehearsal** of learning
  - Encouraging more elaborate responses
  - going beyond "yes" and "no" answers
  - "Tell me more about that"
  - "What do you mean by . . . ?"
  - "What else . . . ?"
  - "How do you know?"
  - "Why is that important?"
  - "What does that remind you of?"
    or teacher restates student's answer
  - "In other words. . . . Is that accurate?"
    or teacher allows **wait time** for student to formulate answer or teacher calls on another student to extend classmate's response
  - **Fostering student-student interaction**
    - Putting students in pairs, triads, or small groups
    - Types of activities that encourage "table talk": Literature circles, think-pair-share, jigsaw readings, debates, science or math experiments
    - Other ways: dialogue journals, e-mail, pen pals, research files

B. Grouping Configurations
- All students, including English language learners, benefit from instruction that frequently includes a variety of grouping configurations
- It is recommended that at least 2 different grouping structures be used during a lesson
- Variety
  - **Whole class**
    To develop classroom community
    To provide a shared experience for everyone
  - **Flexible small groups**
    To promote multiple perspectives
    To encourage collaboration
  - **Partnering**
    To provide practice opportunities
    To scaffold instruction
    To give assistance before independent practice
  - **Homogenous or Heterogeneous Grouping**
    - By gender, language proficiency, language background, and/or ability
    - Variety maintains students' interest
    - Movement from whole class, to partners, to small group increases student involvement
    - Varying group structures increases the preferred mode of instruction for students

C. Cooperative Learning Activities
1. *Information Gap Activities*—Each student in a group has only one or two pieces of information needed to solve the puzzle or problem. Students must work together, sharing information while practicing their language, and using critical thinking skills.
2. *Jigsaw*—Jigsaw reading task by chunking text into manageable parts (1 or 2 pages). Number students in each group (1 or 4 or

5). All #1s read the first 2 pages, #2s read the second 2 pages, etc. These expert groups then discuss their reading and share ideas. The original groups reconvene, discuss the whole text, and share their expertise. Students pool their information.
3. *Numbered Heads Together*—Similar to Jigsaw without forming expert groups. Each student works on one portion of assignment and then students share.
4. *Four Corners*—Great activity to introduce a topic or chapter of study. Write one question or idea on each chart paper. Divide class into 4 groups; each group has a different color marker. Students move to one corner of the chart paper and designated student begins writing their ideas on chart. Time activity 2–4 minutes. Students move clockwise to next corner, read responses, and add their comments.
5. *Roundtable*—Use with open-ended questions, grammar practice. 4 or 5 students are grouped at tables, one sheet of paper, and one pencil. Question or grammar point is given by teacher, students pass paper around table, each writing their own response. Teacher circulates room.
6. *3-Step Interview*—Students are paired. Each student listens to the other as they respond to a topic question. At the end of 3 minutes, each pair joins another pair of students and shares what their partners said. Good way to practice language.
7. *Writing Headlines*—Good way to practice summarizing an activity, story, or project. Provide models of headlines. Students work in pairs writing a headline for an activity. Pairs share out their headlines and class votes on most effective headline.
8. *Send a Problem*—One table team sends a question or problem to another table. Each table team solves or answers question and passes it back to original table. This is a good way to review for a test.

D. Wait Time
- **Wait time varies by culture:** The average length of wait time in U.S. classrooms is clearly not sufficient—give students at least 20 seconds wait time
- Effective teachers **allow students to express their thoughts fully** without interruption

TIP: Allow students to practice their answer with a partner before calling on them to speak out before the whole class.

TIP: Have more advanced students write down their responses while waiting, and then check their answers against the final answer.

TIP: If students cannot answer right away let them answer from a list of choices or "phone" (ask) a friend for help.

E. Clarify Key Concepts in L₁
- Best practice indicates that ELLs benefit from opportunities to clarify concepts in their native language (L₁) with a peer, a paraprofessional, or the teacher
  - Use bilingual paraprofessionals, teachers, peers as clarifiers for vocabulary, concepts, or procedures
  - Use native language texts, dictionaries as tools to illuminate or illustrate topic
  - Use bilingual Web sites and bilingual dictionaries in text and software formats to clarify words and concepts

Adapted from *Making Content Comprehensible for English Language Learners,* Echevarria, Vogt, Short, 2nd Edition, 2004.
Compiled by the Bilingual and Compensatory Education Resource Team, Dearborn Public Schools, Michigan, revised April 2004.

FIGURE 6.18 *Making Content Comprehensible—6. Practice and Application*

1. Hands-on Materials and/or Manipulatives for Practice

- Students have a greater chance of mastering content concepts and skills when:
  - given multiple opportunities to practice
  - practice is in relevant, meaningful ways
  - practice includes "hands-on" experiences
- Planning for hands-on practice:
  - Divide content into meaningful short chunks— chunk by <u>meaning, not just length</u>
  - Time for practice should be short—10–15 minutes
  - New learning should have several short practices <u>close together</u>
  - Older learning should be practices <u>distributed</u> further apart—review material periodically
  - Give students immediate feedback on how well they have done
- ELL students need to **connect abstract concepts with concrete experiences**: Material can be organized, created (chart learning), counted, classified (concept mapping), stacked (index card review), rearranged, dismantled . . .

2. Application of Content and Language Knowledge

- Abstract concepts and new information need to be applied in a **personally relevant way**
  - Writing in a diary format through a character
  - Making and playing a game for content review (Jeopardy, Bingo, Wheel of Fortune . . .)
  - Creating a semantic map
  - Writing test questions to ask another student
  - Teaching concepts to another student
- **Discussing and "doing"** make abstract concepts concrete
  - Clustering
  - Making and using graphic organizers
  - Solving problems in cooperative groups
  - Engaging in discussion circles
  - Partnering students in a project before independent work
- Opportunities for **social interaction** promote language development
  - Small group discussions
  - Working with partners
  - Reporting out information orally and in writing
- **Modeling correct English** after a student has made a pronunciation or grammar error can **gently but effectively** instill appropriate usage

3. Integration of Language Skills

- Reading, writing, listening, and speaking are **interrelated and integrated naturally**—we read when we write, we listen when we are talking with someone, etc.
- Most young children become grammatically competent in their home language by age 5—for ELL students, the teacher needs to **develop language skills in a holistic manner**
- **Practice** in any one area (listening, speaking, reading, and writing) **promotes development** in the others
- **Connections** between abstract and concrete concepts are best accomplished **when all language processes**—reading, writing, listening, and speaking— **are incorporated during practice and application**
- When teachers **teach through different modalities** and students practice and apply their new learning through **multiple language processes**, their content and language development needs are better met

What does a Classroom That Incorporates Listening, Speaking, Reading and Writing . . .

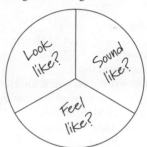

Examples and ideas: _____

_____

_____

_____

_____

Does your classroom incorporate a variety of Listening, Speaking, Reading, and Writing activities during Practice and Application?

Adapted from: *Making Content Comprehensible for English Language Learners,* Echevarria, Vogt, Short. 2nd Edition, 2004.
Compiled by the Bilingual and Compensatory Education Resource Team, Dearborn Public Schools, Michigan, 2005.

FIGURE 6.19 *Making Content Comprehensible—7. Lesson Delivery*

A. Plan Lessons That Support:

1. Content Objectives
- Content objectives must be **clearly supported** by lesson delivery
- Should be **stated orally**
- Should be **written on board for all to see**—preferably in a designated space every time
- Purpose
  - Reminds us of lesson focus
  - Provides a structure to classroom procedures—before, during, after
  - Allows students to know direction of the lesson
  - Supplies way for students and teacher to evaluate lesson in light of content objectives
- Limit content objectives to one or two per lesson
- "When teachers spend their time and energy teaching students the content the students need to learn, students learn the material . . . "

2. Language Objectives
- Language objectives must be **clearly supported** by lesson delivery
  - Should be **stated orally**
  - Should be **written on board for all to see**—preferably in a designated space every time
  - Can **relate to ESL Standards** from TESOL
  - Can be from State Language Arts **Grade Level Content Expectations**
  - Can be **specific to book language** studied (certain verb form, word endings, vocabulary, punctuation, summarizing, active discussion . . .)
  - Need to be **recognizable in lesson's delivery**

B. Promote Student Engagement

Engaged Time
- Students should be **engaged 90–100%** of the period for lesson delivery to be effective

Academic Learning Time
- When students spend their time **actively engaged in activities that relate strongly to the materials they will be tested on**, they learn MORE of the material." (Leinhart, Bickel & Pallay)

- The most effective teachers **minimize** boredom, off-task behaviors, making announcements, passing out papers, etc.
- Aspects of student engagement to consider
  - **Allocated Time**—decisions teachers make regarding amount of time spent on topic and each academic task (reading, word study, writing . . .)
  - There is a balance between teacher presentation and opportunities for students to apply information
  - **Engaged Time**—Time students are actively participating during allocated time: *The more **actively students** participate in the instructional process the more they achieve.*
  - Students **learn more** when they are **attending to the learning tasks** that are the focus of instruction
  - **Academic Learning Time**—Students' time-on-task, when the task is related to the materials on which they will be tested—not just-for-fun activities!
  - Class time needs to be **planned efficiently**—and therefore effective use of time and resources
- Factors that contribute to high levels of student engagement
  1. *Well-planned* lessons
  2. *Clear explanation* of academic tasks or instructions
  3. *Appropriate amount of time* spend on an academic task
  4. *Strong classroom management* skills
  5. *Opportunities* for students to *apply learning* in meaningful ways
  6. *Active* student *involvement*
  7. Lesson design *meets the language and learning needs* of students

C. Pace Lessons Appropriately
Pacing refers to the **rate** at which information is presented during a lesson.
- Rate for ELL students must be **brisk enough** to maintain students' interest **but not too quick** to lose their understanding
- Pace depends on lesson content, proficiency level of EL student's and students prior knowledge of content
- *Appropriate pace* comes with practice
- **Ask** for student's feedback: How am I doing—going too fast . . . too slow . . . just right?

Adapted from *Making Content Comprehensible for English Language Learners,* Echevarria, Vogt, Short, 2nd Edition, 2004.
Compiled by the Bilingual and Compensatory Education Resource Team, Dearborn Public Schools, Michigan, revised April 2004.

FIGURE 6.20 *Making Content Comprehensible—8. Review and Assessment*

A. Review Lesson Objectives

At the end of each lesson return to the lesson's content and language objectives and affirm that the objectives have been accomplished.

- Highlight and review key information
- Explicitly indicate what students should focus on and learn
- Summarize important items throughout the lesson

1. Review of Key Vocabulary

Review of vocabulary needs to include attention to word and sentence structure:

- Key vocabulary can be developed through <u>analogy</u>
  - Relating newly learned words to other **words with the same structure or pattern** (ex: Photosynthesis ↔ photography)
  - Drawing students' attention to **tense, parts of speech, and sentence structure**
  - Repeating and **reinforcing language patterns** for words to become automatic
- Ways to <u>scaffold</u>
  - **Paraphrasing**—oral rehearsal of what student is going to say with group before saying it to the whole class or saying the definition of a word right after the word
  - Systematic Study—remember, research says isolated word lists and dictionary definitions alone do not promote vocabulary and language development. **Words should be studied through multiple modalities**—see them, say them, write them many times in different ways, act them out, sing them, draw them, and find them in context
  - **Word Study Books**—This is a student-made personal notebook in which the student includes frequently used words and concepts. Book can be organized by language structure: -tion, -sion, -tation and/or alphabetical, and/or by topic of study (ex: Revolution words)
    <u>One way to enter words</u>: **Write the word**, include a **personal definition**, use the word in a **sentence**, and add a **memorable symbol** or drawing that will trigger the word from memory.
  - **Non-print Ways to Review**—use "acting out words," Pictionary, Charades
  - **"School Talk" Sessions**—Teach discussion circle protocol: taking turns, polite disagreement words, how to ask and answer questions. Do a practice session with a fun topic of students' interest like movie stars, cars . . . Teach test-taking "talk"—how questions are worded on a test

2. Review of Key Content Concepts

- Review key concepts during and at the end of a lesson and link to content objectives:
  - **Informal Summarizing Review**—ex: "Up to this point. . . . Discuss in your groups the 3 important things we have learned so far."
  - **Periodic review** (chunking) leads into next section to be studied
  - **Link Review** to content objectives—ensures focus on essential concepts
  - **Final Review**—allows students to assess their own understandings and clarify misunderstandings
  - **Outcome Sentences**—is another wrap-up technique. Students respond to one of the following sentence starters: I wonder . . . , I discovered . . . , I still want to know . . . , I learned . . . , I still don't understand

  - **Structured** Review—summarizing with partners, listing key points on board. Always link to content objectives

3. Providing Feedback on Student Output

- Periodic review
  - Clarifies and corrects misconceptions
  - Develops students' proficiency in English
  - Allows for paraphrasing students' responses in correct English and complete sentences
- Feedback can be given orally or in writing, supported by facial expressions and body language—nod, smile, encouraging look . . .
- Peer feedback benefits all students by allowing them to evaluate their own and their peers' language production and content understanding

B. Assessment of Lesson Objectives

- **Assessment** is *"the gathering and synthesizing* of information concerning students' learning"
- **Evaluation is** *"making judgments about students' learning." Assessment comes first, then evaluation*
- **Gathering baseline data before** instruction occurs helps teachers know students' growth over time
- **Plan multiple assessments** in order to truly assess students' content and language learning
- **Informal Assessment**
  - On-the-spot, ongoing opportunities to determine the extent of students' learning.
  - Includes teacher observations, anecdotal reports, informal conversations with students, quick-writes
- **Authentic Assessment**
  - Application to real life—real-life contexts
  - Multidimensional—ex: students' writing, taped pieces, interviews, videotapes, observations, projects, discussion, performances, portfolios, journals, group responses . . .
  - Includes multiple indicators to show competency of a content objective. Use of a rubric defines level of learning and is shared with students and parents
  - Group response activities quickly gauge students' level of understanding:
    - **Agree/Disagree, True/False, Yes/No**—index cards that students or groups of students could use to quickly give their answers to questions. Teacher can quickly see responses.
    - **Thumbs Up/Thumbs Down**—Like the index cards, students can quickly respond to questions. For "I don't know," students can make a fist. Teacher gets a feel for whole class understanding or agreement.
    - **Numbered Wheels**—Tag board strips (5" × 1"). Each strip is numbered 0–5 or 0–10. This allows students to answer multiple-choice questions quickly by holding up appropriate number. O is a "Don't know" response. These are great for review before a written test.
    - **Response Boards**—Small chalk or white boards, or even plastic plates, can be used for group responses. Use dry-erase markers, chalk, or crayons that can be erased for next question.

Adapted from *Making Content Comprehensible for English Language Learners*, Echevarria, Vogt, Short, 2nd Edition, 2004.
Compiled by the Bilingual and Compensatory Education Resource Team, Dearborn Public Schools, Michigan, revised April 2004.

During SIOP® training, two teachers focus on successes and challenges for Review/Assessment.

teachers to reflect on their practice, then share with one another. Figure 6.21 is an example of the type of handout they used. Creating a staff culture where reflection, sharing, and professional growth are valued goes a long way in maintaining teachers' interest in being consistent, effective SIOP® teachers.

Web site Information

Some districts created SIOP® Web sites or SIOP® links on district Web sites to announce trainings and provide resources. For example, in Charlotte-Mecklenburg, the district has

FIGURE 6.21 *Handout for Teacher Reflection*

What have you done recently in each of these areas to make lessons better for English language learners? Please be prepared to share your answers.

1. Supplemental Materials

_____

_____

_____

Supplemental Materials	
• Hands-on manipulatives	• Multimedia
• Realia	• Demonstrations
• Pictures	• Related literature
• Visuals	• Adapted text

2. Adaption of Content

_____

_____

_____

Adaption of Content	
• Graphic Organizers	• Audiotaped text
• Outlines	• Jigsaw text reading
• Leveled study guides	• Marginal notes
• Highlighted text	• Native language texts

3. Meaningful Activities

_____

_____

_____

high regard for the SIOP® Model and has created a special section on the Web site to inform staff and support teachers during the implementation process (http://documents.cms.k12.nc .us/dsweb/View/Collection-831). The materials on the site include teacher lesson plans, presentation PowerPoint slides, summaries of classroom observations, training resources, and more.

Chapter Summary

In this chapter, we discussed ways that SIOP® Model professional development has been successfully enhanced and sustained. Perhaps the most critical issue is getting buy-in from teachers and administrators. If individuals aren't sold on the professional development program, it won't take root and change instructional practice. The goal is to improve instruction for students through effective teaching that meets their needs. We presented ways to facilitate the process as well as experiences in dealing with resistant teachers.

Once there is buy-in, even the most committed teachers are distracted by the multiple and varied demands associated with teaching. We presented a number of ideas for sustaining programs as well as ideas that have been used successfully to maintain interest in and enthusiasm for the SIOP® Model. They include newsletters, keeping copies of the SIOP® protocol visible and usable for teachers, creating bookmarks representing each of the SIOP® components, a compilation of lesson plans, SIOP® Model Web sites, and ways to use materials for reflection or to extend learning.

We hope you will find the experiences of others useful in sustaining SIOP® implementation in your school or district.

Questions for Reflection and Discussion

1. In your school or district, who will take leadership for introducing and promoting the SIOP® Model? What will be each person's responsibilities? (See Chapter 3, Figure 3.2 as an example)

2. How might you and your colleagues who are committed to the SIOP® Model introduce it to your colleagues? What do you think is the most effective way to maximize initial buy-in?

3. Based on what you have read in this chapter, what types of support materials do you think would be most effective with the elementary teachers? With the secondary teachers? What other types of information and materials might teachers need?

4. As you think of the teachers who will be implementing the SIOP® Model, can you identify any who may have resistance to the process? How might you plan beforehand to bring them around?

Classroom Implementation of the SIOP® Model

With the SIOP®, my students are working at a much higher level even though they are English language learners. They are using a lot more higher-level thinking and are interacting with one another, practicing academic English. They have to negotiate meaning with one another, there's a lot of debate and compromise. So it has really benefited them. They're not just giving a yes or no answer; they have to explain their thinking so it's taking learning to a higher level.

Kendra Moreno, SIOP® lead teacher

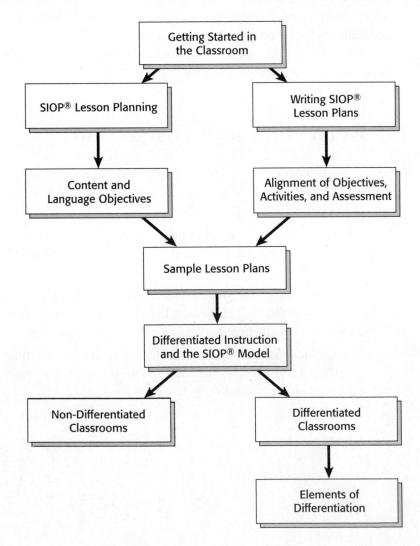

Reflect on three different students that you are currently teaching. Do the following descriptions apply to any of them?

1. Student #1 makes you, the teacher, look and feel good. He or she pays attention, completes work on time, is an eager, optimistic learner, reads and writes well, and appears to complete high-quality classroom assignments almost effortlessly.

2. Student #2 makes you, the teacher, feel inadequate sometimes. He or she struggles with nearly every assignment, rarely completes or turns in homework, has negative feelings about school, has difficulties with reading and writing, and despite your help, fails to make academic gains.

3. Student #3 is an English learner who makes you, the teacher, feel accomplished and satisfied with your teaching on some days—and inadequate and frustrated on others. He or she may share characteristics with both students #1 and #2: eagerness, attention during class, difficulty with reading and writing English, hope for academic success in English, problems with assignments, frustration . . .

The SIOP® Model has provided thousands of pre-K, elementary, and secondary teachers with a structured, organized, systematic approach to teaching English learners, whatever their talents, ages, needs, and language proficiencies. Many teachers have reported, as Kendra does above, that with the SIOP® their ELs begin to look and sound like other high-performing students.

We are frequently asked, "Isn't the SIOP® Model just good instruction for all kids?" After thinking about each of the features of the model, it's easy to respond with, "Yes, all students need this type of instruction." However, while the SIOP® Model may be good for all students, its implementation is critical for English learners because of the focus on English language teaching and learning. Mark Crossman explains,

> . . . [It's] a double-edged sword when a teacher says, "This is good teaching—this is good for all students and not just my ELL students will benefit from this." The flip side is always, "Okay, but are you truly getting the language pieces that your ELL students need at the same time?" Are we coming to that understanding without diminishing the distinction of unique learner needs and characteristics of ELLs?

As teachers begin the process of implementing the SIOP® Model, they all have questions about how to start, how to plan, what to teach, and so forth. We have attempted to answer these questions and more in the following sections.

Getting Started in the Classroom

At first glance, many teachers' reaction to the SIOP® Model's thirty features is that it seems overwhelming to implement the entire model. We suggest that teachers take the protocol and as they read through each feature, mark the ones that they already include in their lessons. For example, most teachers ask some higher-order questions and plan their lessons according to content standards. But these same teachers may infrequently or never post and explain language objectives for their English learners. As teachers complete this exercise of reflecting on each feature, they realize that many of the good practices reflected in the SIOP® Model are already part of their teaching repertoire, even though the features' inclusion in lessons may not be as consistent or systematic as is necessary for English learners. Therefore, implementing the SIOP® features becomes a matter of increasing consistency with some features, while adding other new features to teachers' daily practice.

One of the strengths of the SIOP® Model is that it is a framework for teachers to organize their instruction. They understand that it is not necessary to discontinue use of ideas and activities that are familiar and effective. In fact, the model encourages the incorporation of meaningful activities and organizes them in a way so that instruction is understandable for English learners, as well as for all students (Vogt & Echevarria, 2008).

Display created to provide information about the SIOP® Model of sheltered instruction for teachers, administrators, and students.
Used with permission of Charlotte-Mecklenburg Schools, North Carolina.

Some schools and districts require teachers to follow a particular plan for implementing the components, while others allow them, individually, as a grade-level group or department, to start with components with which they feel most comfortable. We do not have strong preferences, as long as teachers begin incorporating English language instruction and practice early in the process. Therefore, many teachers begin with the Preparation component, practicing those features for several weeks or months, writing and delivering content and language objectives, and then adding other components, one by one. As you have previously read, some schools and districts add a new component each month, while others choose to implement one each quarter. Whatever your choice, it is important that teachers have the opportunity to discuss, share, and collaborate with each other about particular SIOP® components that they are implementing.

Ivanna Mann Thrower of Charlotte-Mecklenburg School District reported that her district developed some resources to help facilitate classroom implementation of the SIOP® components. For example, the district prepared posters listing the thirty features of the SIOP® Model and gave one to each teacher to hang in his or her classroom for ready reference. Coordinators of the SIOP® project in Dearborn, Michigan, distributed to teachers colorful bookmarks as a similar resource (see Chapter 6 for copies of the bookmarks).

SIOP® Lesson Planning in Different Contexts

Elementary teachers frequently ask, "How do I possibly plan for SIOP® implementation for every subject with the SIOP® Model?" Secondary teachers are puzzled by how to plan for five or six different periods each day, even if they're teaching the same content

During SIOP® training two teachers focus on successes and challenges for Lesson Delivery.

several times—students differ from period to period, so it is often necessary to vary lesson plans.

When implementing the SIOP® Model in their classrooms, teachers generally begin by focusing their efforts on one content area (elementary teachers) or one period (secondary teachers). In this way, writing content and language objectives becomes part of the instructional routine for a specific part of the day, until the teacher is comfortable adding more subjects or periods. It is important to allay teachers' concerns early in the implementation process about the amount of planning that is necessary when implementing the SIOP® Model. We have found repeatedly that when teachers implement a component for one subject or one period, then later add another component for that subject area or period, and so forth, the teaching practices advocated within the model begin to infiltrate other subjects and/or periods. Also, teachers have reported that because student response to their SIOP® instruction is positive, they become motivated to begin implementing the other components in more subjects and/or periods. In fact, Marilyn Sanchez from Creighton School District reported, "One teacher told us, 'I can't believe it! The kids are actually listening!'" Obviously, the ultimate goal is that teachers will eventually implement all thirty features for all subjects and/or periods, but realistically, this will likely occur over one to two years.

As an example of how one district decided which subject area to begin with, Charlotte-Mecklenburg School District paid teachers for eight weeks of curriculum development work. The participating teachers worked in teams by grade level and content area, designing their own project for SIOP® implementation. The middle school teachers focused on sixth grade social studies and developed SIOP® lessons for each of the North Carolina state standards. The high school group decided to enhance an existing World History unit. These teachers collected pictures and other visuals to support the topics covered in the unit and also created image-word-definition tables that were differentiated for students by their English language proficiency levels.

Ivanna Mann Thrower stated that her main goal in her first year as a SIOP® Coach was "to make the SIOP® concrete." For example, the district supports classroom implementation of the SIOP® Model on their Web site. On the ESL/Second Language Department's Web page, "The SIOP® Model" is a direct link. From there, teachers can access SIOP® lesson plans, summaries of classroom observations, PowerPoint slides of district trainings, photos of SIOP®-related scenes from pilot schools (such as Word Walls and decorated hallways).

When There Are Few English Learners in a Classroom

All teachers in this age of standards and accountability face the issue of content coverage versus ensuring students' deep understandings of key content concepts. Some perceive that implementing the features of the SIOP® Model will result in a slower pace and less content coverage. The concerns about pacing occur most frequently in classrooms where there are few English learners and a heterogeneous mix of native English speakers.

We handle these valid concerns by asking teachers to look at a copy of the SIOP® protocol. We ask them to identify those features that would *not* be necessary to include in a content lesson for native English speakers. Usually they respond by identifying a few of the features, such as clarifying in the student's L1 or perhaps including language objectives (for the native English speakers). However, there are always students, especially in urban settings, who benefit from an emphasis on academic English. So some teachers will argue that the language objectives will benefit these students as well as the ELs.

The point here is that the implementation of the SIOP® components is not deleterious to other students, and teachers readily acknowledge this as they become familiar with the features. With appropriate pacing (not too fast and not too slow), and effective differentiated instruction, heterogeneous groups of students benefit from the quality of effective teaching with the SIOP® Model. Even if teachers have very few English learners in their classes, it is still necessary and equitable to meet the students' needs through the SIOP® Model.

Writing SIOP® Lessons

Most teachers learn how to write lesson plans during university teacher preparation courses. The formats that are learned serve teachers well, and eventually the move to the small boxes in planning books is a welcome relief for most. With the SIOP® Model, however, there is frequently a need to revert to more detailed lesson planning, to ensure that the eight components of the model are considered when writing each lesson plan. As with the beginning stages of learning to be a teacher, eventually SIOP® lesson planning becomes more automatic, though it still must be thoughtful and purposeful.

It is important to remember that even veteran, capable teachers come to realize they have areas to improve when working with English learners, and this realization often surfaces as they begin to write SIOP® lesson plans and deliver SIOP® lessons. Laurie Beebe, a reading specialist, said,

> I can't believe I used to teach the way I taught. . . one of the things that I was not aware of was the implication of developing a second language. . . . At a parent-teacher conference, one of my little ESL gals, whose family speaks only Spanish, said, "You know, sometimes I don't understand what you're saying," and I'm

thinking, "Oh, great. I'm a SIOP® teacher and I'm supposed to be comprehensible and I'm not doing a very good job of that." To hear her say that to me made me really aware of how conscientious you have to be in instructing. I don't try to get through twenty-nine things in an afternoon now. I try to get through a language lesson and a science lesson . . . So, hopefully, they're deepening their knowledge, which is what I was trying to teach before [but not achieving.] All of us are learning all the time, I guess.

As teachers begin the lesson planning process by incorporating one component at a time, they may choose to use their own or the district's lesson plan format. As subsequent components are added, they may find that another type of lesson plan will better focus attention on the SIOP® components. Eventually, experienced SIOP® teachers may choose to write less detailed lesson plans once they are familiar with the model. What is important is that all teachers who are implementing the SIOP® Model strive to incorporate all of the eight components and thirty features into lesson planning and delivery.

Lesson Plan Formats

Over the years, teachers and administrators have shared a variety of SIOP® lesson plans, and we've created a few of our own. We do not endorse one format over another, but encourage you to find the one that works best for you. We include several plans in this section that have been used by teachers throughout the country; a few are district recommended while others have been created by individual teachers. Some educators feel there are advantages to having a uniform plan in a school or district because teachers can learn how to write SIOP® lessons together in like-grade levels or departments.

In Figure 7.1, you will see the "8-Step Lesson Plan Guide" created by Stefan de Vries from Boise, Idaho. He created this as a reminder of the SIOP® components and features, and he describes the Lesson Plan Guide in the following way:

> When I first started training in SIOP®, I was always a bit confused with all the different parts and pieces and did not see the whole picture. Using the [protocol] . . . assumes a lot of prior knowledge of SIOP®. . . . I would like to bypass the intimidation factor when teaching it to new hires and our staff and give them something that provides a methodical overview . . . this will allow us to present it as 'refining their existing skills'. . . One side of the template allows for planning notes and ensures consideration of all eight [components] in a lesson plan. The flip side of the template has notes . . . that serve as reminders or clarification of each section.

Those of you who have read the core SIOP® text (Echevarria, Vogt, & Short, 2008), are familiar with "Ms. Chen's" lesson plan format. What follows are two lesson plans written for grade 4, one in science and one in English, using this format (see Figures 7.2 and 7.3, pages 127–128).

An eighth grade teacher of Language Arts created a two-day plan for a Historical Fiction unit (see Figures 7.4 and 7.5, pages 129–132). Note the well-written journal entries submitted by two students; both are English learners (see Figures 7.6 and 7.7, pages 132–133).

In Figure 7.8 on page 134, you see another lesson plan format and a detailed lesson plan on the geologic time scale.

. . . . •

125

FIGURE 7.1

SIOP® Lesson Plan 1

Date: _____

Class: _____

Grade: _____

Unit: _____

1) Preparation

Content Objective	
Language Objective	

2) Building Background	3) Comprehensible Input

4) Strategies	5) Interaction

6) Practice and Application	7) Lesson Delivery

8) Review and Assessment	Lesson Sequence & Reflections

FIGURE 7.1 *(Continued)*

SIOP®: 8-Step Lesson Plan Guide

Preparation

a) Clearly defined **Content Objective**

b) Clearly defined **Language Objective**

c) Ability level appropriate

d) Supplementary materials

e) Adaptation of content

f) Meaningful activities that integrate content with language practice

Building Background

a) Link concepts to students PAST

b) A learner's schemata is their base for their understanding

c) Activate their prior knowledge

d) Build a common background

Comprehensible Input

a) Speech equal to proficiency level

b) Clear explanation of academic task

c) Written, not just oral, directions

d) Variety of techniques (realia)

e) Interesting and relevant lessons

f) Follow natural language patterns

g) Input provided in sufficient quantity

h) Approprite monitoring of errors

Strategies

a) Ample opportunity to use strategies

b) Consistent use of scaffolding

c) Variety of questioning levels (Bloom)

d) Metacognitve: awareness, reflection, interaction

e) Cognitive: mentally/physically manipulate material/apply

f) Others: graphic organizers, PENS, mnemonics, SQP2RS, rehearsal, GIST, paraphrasing, "think-alouds," etc...

Interaction

a) Wait Time!

b) Language is primary vehicle for intellectual development

c) Talking helps learning. Plan to facilitate academic conversation

d) Organize activities that require kids to speak in complete sentences

e) Direct instruction = convergent thought

Practice/Application

a) Use manipulatives to practice new knowledge

b) Plan activities that apply content & language knowledge

c) Utilize: Read/Write/Speak/Listen

d) New knowledge must be practiced!

e) Practice is linked to objectives

Lesson Delivery

a) Content objectives are supported

b) Language objectives are supported

c) Students task engaged: 90% of time

d) Pacing appropriate

Review/Assessment

a) Key vocab review (protected time)

b) Key concept review (protected time)

c) Review daily objectives

d) Ongoing assessment

e) Individual, group, written, oral

Created by Stefan deVries, Boise School District

FIGURE 7.2

SIOP® Lesson Plan 2

Date: 11-18-05   *Grade/Subject:* 4th ESL Science
Unit/Theme: THE EYE   *Standards:* _____
Content Objective(s): Students will review the parts of the eye & how we see, predict, and explore whether it is possible to look at something and not see it.
Language Objective(s): SW review by writing, speaking, and talking. SW predict & explore by speaking, reading, and listening.
Key Vocabulary: Peripheral vision, optical illusions   parts of the eye: iris, pupil, cornea, schlera, retina, lens, optic nerve
Supplementary Materials: Eye chart, ball, magnifying glasses, copy of blk white pic.

SIOP® Features

Preparation	*Scaffolding*	*Grouping Options*
— Adaptation of content	— Modeling	✓ Whole class
— Links to background	— Guided practice	— Small groups
✓ Links to past learning	— Independent practice	✓ Partners
— Strategies Incorporated	✓ Comprehensible input	— Independent

Integration of Processes	*Application*	*Assessment*
— Reading	✓ Hands-on	— Individual
— Writing	✓ Meaningful	✓ Group
✓ Speaking	✓ Linked to objectives	— Written
✓ Listening	✓ Promotes engagement	— Oral

Lesson Sequence:

1] Review Parts of the eye — Add to kwl chart (use eye parts) (5 min)

2] Review light & your eye (5 min)

3] Making pictures from light — Activity (5 min)

Experiments

1] Blk & White picture (5 min)

2] Flower hearts (5 min)

Peripheral Vision

3] Behind your teacher (5 min)

? Is it possible to look at something & not see it? (5 min)

Answer ? (5min)
ADD to KWL

Reflections:

I need to watch time/speech delivery. Sometimes I talk too fast & forget to pause for wait time.

FIGURE 7.3

SIOP® Lesson Plan 3

Date: _12-2-05_   Grade/Class/Subject: _4th grade English_

Unit/Theme: _Verbs_   Standards: _____

Content Objective(s): _Students will be able to name the main verb and helping verb in a sentence._

Language Objective(s): _Students will discuss the practice sentences with a partner and with the whole group. They will write practice sentences and identify the main and helping verbs._

Key Vocabulary	Supplementary Materials
Helping verb	
Main Verb	

SIOP® Features

Preparation	Scaffolding	Grouping Options
— Adaptation of content	✓ Modeling	✓ Whole class
— Links to background	✓ Guided practice	— Small groups
✓ Links to past learning	✓ Independent practice	✓ Partners
✓ Strategies Incorporated	✓ Comprehensible input	✓ Independent

Integration of Processes	Application	Assessment
✓ Reading	— Hands-on	✓ Individual
✓ Writing	— Meaningful	✓ Group
✓ Speaking	✓ Links to objectives	✓ Written
✓ Listening	— Promotes engagement	✓ Oral

Lesson Sequence:

Intro Verbs, Review Vocabulary.
Review Predicates and show connection to verbs. Model-Write sentence on board and identify Helping verb and verb. Do the first sentence of the guided practice together. Do the rest of guided practice with partner and share with class. Review the individual assignments and get started.

Reflections:

Lesson went well, but as I corrected the written assignment I found that a number of students didn't get it. So next time I will work on a little more modeling and practice before I make the assignment.

FIGURE 7.4

SIOP® Lesson Plan 4

Date: Day One of Historical Fiction   *Grade/Class/Subject:* 8th Language Arts
Unit/Theme: Historical fiction   *Standards:* MO GLEE H 1.6, 3.5
Content Objective(s): We will discover that historical fiction pieces contain true historical facts and information that is not true.
Language Objective(s): We will read a historical fiction piece and sort facts and fiction. We will discuss this piece with our partners. We will write a list of facts that we learned in Social Studies that we could use in our historical fiction pieces.

Key Vocabulary	**Supplementary Materials**
Historical fiction	A Ballad of the Civil War by Mary Stolz
Fact	Photocopies of the first two chapters of the book
	Highlighters
	Writer's notebooks

SIOP® Features

Preparation	*Scaffolding*	*Grouping Options*
X Adaptation of content	X Modeling	X Whole class
__ Links to background	X Guided practice	X Small groups
X Links to past learning	X Independent practice	X Partners
X Strategies incorporated	X Comprehensible input	X Independent
Integration of Processes	*Application*	*Assessment*
X Reading	X Hands-on	X Individual
X Writing	X Meaningful	X Group
X Speaking	X Linked to objectives	X Written
X Listening	X Promotes engagement	X Oral

Lesson Sequence

Motivation

The students have previously studied fiction. Ask each table to decide on a definition for the word *fiction*. They may flip back into their notebooks to reference notes from earlier in the year. Once they've agreed on a definition, the teacher asks, what do you think historical fiction means? What could we add to the definition of fiction to make it historical fiction? Think about what the word "historical" means. The definition the class compiles should be similar to this definition: historical fiction is a story that is not true but includes true historical information and facts.

Presentation

Now that the definition for Historical fiction has been established, the book A Ballad of the Civil War should be introduced. The book is leveled at a 3.9 reading level but it is still a challenging text. However, the students have been studying the Civil War in Social Studies and

(Continued)

FIGURE 7.4 *SIOP® Lesson Plan 4* *(Continued)*

should be able to follow the story. The teacher will read the story to the students but they will follow along with their copy of the text. As the teacher reads, the students will use their highlighters to highlight information they believe is true. Before the reading begins the class will discuss the definition of a fact.

After the first two chapters of the book have been read, the students will compare their text with a partner. Did they highlight the same things? If not, they must explain to the other person why they chose to highlight the text that they selected. After they have compared their responses, they will create a T-chart in their writer's notebook that looks like this:

Fact	Fiction

All of the information they highlighted should go into the fact category on the chart. For example: the Civil War, the North fought the South, people in the South owned slaves, etc. To make sure everyone really understood the activity after everyone has attempted the chart, each person will write down one fact they highlighted on a sentence strip and place it on a class chart that is displayed on the board. If any student is missing a fact from the board, they must place it into the chart in their notebook.

After the fact side of the chart has been completed, the students will complete the fiction side of the chart. What are some elements of the story that may not be true? Follow the same whole-class procedures as the fact side of the chart. Is this piece of text historical fiction? How can you tell? How does this piece fit our definition of historical fiction?

Practice/Application

Now that the students have completed a T-chart about the text, they will make another T-chart in their notebooks that looks exactly like the other T-chart. On the fact section of the chart they will write information that they learned about the Civil War during Social Studies. They may work as a table to come up with information. After they have completed the fact section they will write ideas under the fiction section. What kind of character would they like to create? Is it a man or woman? What age? What do they look like? And other information that they would like to make up.

Review

Review objectives. Why was the piece that we read together historical fiction? How do you know? Why is the brainstorming you did for your piece historical fiction? How do you know?

FIGURE 7.5

SIOP® Lesson Plan 5

Date: Day Two of Historical fiction   *Grade/Class/Subject:* 8th Language Arts
Writing

Unit/Theme: Historical Fiction   *Standards:* MO GLEE F 1.6

Content Objective(s): Using the charts we completed yesterday, we will create historical fiction stories that incorporate facts and fiction.

Language Objective(s): We will write a one-page historical fiction piece as a class and a one-page historical fiction piece as individuals. We will discuss the ideas for our characters with our partners.

Key Vocabulary	Supplementary Materials
Historical fiction	Writer's notebook
Fact	Chart from the day before
	Overhead

SIOP® Features

Preparation	Scaffolding	Grouping Options
X Adaptation of content	X Modeling	X Whole class
___ Links to background	X Guided practice	___ Small groups
X Links to past learning	X Independent practice	X Partners
___ Strategies incorporated	X Comprehensible input	X Independent

Integration of Processes	Application	Assessment
X Reading	X Hands-on	X Individual
X Writing	X Meaningful	___ Group
X Speaking	X Linked to objectives	X Written
X Listening	X Promotes engagement	___ Oral

Lesson Sequence

Motivation

Yesterday the students created charts of facts about the Civil War and fictional elements that they would like to include in their historical fiction pieces. They will begin by telling their partner what sort of character they created.

Presentation

Begin by placing a chart that the teacher created on the overhead like this:

(Continued)

FIGURE 7.5   *SIOP® Lesson Plan 5*   *(Continued)*

Facts	Fiction
People in the South owned slaves during the Civil War Slaves were treated poorly Slave families were often separated	A slave girl named Miriam Her brother was just sold She heard about the war and hopes the North will win

The class will now work together to turn the information included in the chart into a journal entry. The teacher will write the story on the overhead and think out loud as he/she writes. The students may contribute but the teacher will start the piece.

Dear Diary,
Today was a sad day. I was working in the kitchen in the Master's house when I heard the news: my brother Moses had been sold.

As the teacher writes the students will put the chart and the piece in their notebooks as well so that they have an example they can refer to later.

Practice/Application

After the example has been completed, the students will work independently to create a journal entry with the information they compiled in their charts. The teacher will circulate during this time and offer help where needed and read the pieces the students are creating. Before coming back to the entire class, ask students to share what they've written so far with their partner.

Review

Ask if any students would like to share their pieces. After a student has shared ask the class, how do you know this is a historical fiction piece? Revisit objectives.

FIGURE 7.6   *Student Journal Entry 1, Historical Fiction Unit*

Dear: Mom

I am Thanh I go to fight and I unhurt. We fight very hard and sometime I think about home. I feeling the war have people die I don't want it. Some time I scare about it and some time I think about people stop fighting. And I think why you not my friend I think we well good friends.

FIGURE 7.7   *Student Journal Entry 2, Historical Fiction Unit*

March 9, 1860

Dear family

Hi! Family I am sorry that I had to leave the house. But I had no other choice I want to set slaves free. I came to the war because I thought that it was going to be easy and end fast. But now that I know that it's going to take a long time.

I think that I should have never come. Every day I see my friends lying down on the floor almost dying. I get sad because I just can't stop thinking about when I will die. I want to let you know that if I die I will be happy at least because I let the slaves be free.

Take care my family and remember that I love you guys with all my heart. Also remember that after all I hated this war.

Your loved one,

Miguel Valasquez

SIOP® Lesson Plan 6 (Earth Science)

Topic: Geologic time scale	Class: Earth Science	Date: 10/30/06

Content Objectives	Language Objectives
Students will be able to organize five periods of the geologic time scale in order from oldest to most recent. Students will be able to link specific events in Earth's history to the geologic time scale.	Students will form a chronological line of events based on cards they will each have. Students will read their card orally. Students will create a table of the information they read in groups of two. Students will complete a homework assignment based on a Fresno Bee article discussing an event which happened during one of the geologic time periods mentioned in today's lesson.

California Earth Science Standard

1f: Students know the dramatic effects that asteroid impacts have had in shaping the surface of planets and their moons and in mass **extinctions** of life on Earth.
8b: Students know how the composition of Earth's atmosphere has evolved over **geologic time**.

Key Vocabulary	Materials
Precambrian, Paleozoic, Mesozoic, Cenozoic Quaternary Defining events Geologic events Extinction	Defining events cards Geologic time scale table Overhead of geologic time scale table Overhead of geologic time scale Scrambled sheet of events, glue, scissors Homework worksheet ("footprints")

Higher-Order Questions

What is the difference between the start of complex animal life and the start of life?
Why are significant events in life measured in millions of years when the age of the Earth is measured in billions of years?

Time	Activities
	Building Background

2 min.
 	
1 min.
	Links to experience:
	    Discuss movies the students may have seen about significant past events like *Ice Age, Jurassic Park, The Day After Tomorrow.*
	Links to learning:
	    From our Astronomy Unit, students know the Earth formed 4.6 billion years ago.
	Key vocabulary:
	    The students will help each other when forming the chronological line. The students will read the cards to recall words that are familiar.

	Student Activities

5 min.
 	
10 min.
 	
20 min.
	Students will copy the Review and Preview question from the board. It will prompt them to copy the writing on a card they receive and discuss the meaning with their neighbor.
	    Students will stand up and arrange themselves in a chronological line from oldest events to most recent. Students will read their card out loud.
	    Students will return to their seats. They will create a table of the geologic time scale of events with a partner. They will cut the scrambled components of the table and paste them in the blank table.

	Review and Assessment
5 min. at home	When the students have completed the table, I will ask questions to the class using an overhead of the table. Students will answer by raising their hand. Students will complete the homework assignment about a specific event framed in the time periods of the geologic time scale.

Created by Anne Ybarra, Fresno Unified School District

Additional examples of blank SIOP® lesson plan formats follow. Perhaps you can find one that best matches your teaching style (see Figures 7.9–7.13, pages 137–145).

The last SIOP® lesson plan format included here is one that incorporates specific guidance for teachers throughout the plan. For teachers new to the SIOP® Model and perhaps unaccustomed to detailed lesson planning, this format provides a great deal of support (see Figure 7.14, pages 146–147).

For additional SIOP® lesson planning ideas in a variety of content areas and for varied grade levels at the elementary and secondary levels, see Echevarria, Vogt, & Short, 2008; and Vogt & Echevarria, 2008.

Content and Language Objectives

Most teachers in this standards-based era are required to design content lessons according to district and/or state standards. Using the standards as a guide for writing lesson-specific content objectives may be somewhat taxing for teachers new to the SIOP® Model. Learning to write (and orally deliver) objectives for students' English language development, however, may be one of the most challenging tasks for any teacher, experienced or not, when beginning to implement the SIOP® Model.

However, once teachers have become more comfortable in writing language objectives for their English learners, they find their teaching is more focused. An elementary SIOP® teacher in the Northwest explains,

> What's happened is [that] having to write a language objective focused my approach to teaching kids and now I'm very focused. Sometimes I get into that classroom at the same time that the kids are coming back from lunch. The kids expect it [objectives written on the board]. They even say, "Where are the objectives? What are we doing today?" I'll say, "Just give me a few minutes and I'll get them written down."

District personnel involved with the implementation of the SIOP® Model have done a variety of things to assist teachers in learning how to write content and language objectives in different content areas. For example, Wanda Holbrook and Kendra Moreno, from Lela Alston Elementary School, created a list of phrases that could be used for writing language objectives for elementary subject areas (see Figure 7.15, page 148). These were enlarged as posters so that teachers could highlight the day's language objective without having to write it on the board.

Charlotte Daniels, from Kansas City, Missouri, distributed to high school teachers examples of content objectives in American History that were closely matched with language objectives (see Figure 7.16, page 149). As you review these, note how the language objectives include relevant American History content, but their focus is primarily on developing ELs' language proficiency through reading, writing, listening, speaking, viewing, and vocabulary development.

Elizabeth Fralicks from Fresno Unified School District shared a number of resources for helping teachers develop English learners' academic language. In Figures 7.17 and 7.18, on page 150 you see words that identify language-related tasks found in the state science and social science standards.

In Figure 7.19, on page 151 you see a chart that includes academic language from the state social science standards across a continuum of language functions from "specific example" to "process." The initials at the top of the chart represent levels of English proficiency necessary for understanding: EI = Early Intermediate; I = Intermediate; EA = Early Advanced; A = Advanced. Students who do not have the designated level of proficiency would require differentiated instruction. All students will benefit from instruction in academic language found in standards, but matching students' level of proficiency to the task [teaching them and providing practice in what they mean] is critical for English learners. This chart can serve as a focus for language objectives related to academic language development in the social sciences.

Teachers often ask if it is necessary to have different content and language objectives for each subject or period during the day. As mentioned previously, we advocate that SIOP® teachers new to the model start with one subject area or period to begin with. Therefore, content and language objectives are posted and explained orally for that subject area or period. Eventually, of course, the goal is to have both content and language objectives posted for every lesson where English learners are present.

Not surprisingly, very young children and perhaps older ELs will not be able to understand most content and language objectives if they are written in "teacher-talk." Therefore, teachers have created a variety of ways to write and explain objectives, including phrases, pictures (e.g., as rebus illustrations), and more relevant "kid-talk." Liz Warner, from Washoe County Schools, suggested,

> The 'I Can' statement is something that we developed in our district. . . because I was going into classrooms and everybody had their objectives written on the board. And nobody was doing anything with them, and at the kindergarten-first-second grade levels, the kids couldn't even read what was up there . . . .We just turned it into kid-friendly language and what we're working on with teachers is . . . when you're presenting your objective . . . use it as a shared reading . . . so that kids have a focus in their mind of, "Oh, this is what I'm supposed to do." And then . . . we're asking them [teachers] to come back at the end of the lesson and have kids do a kind of self-evaluation: "Have I got this? Am I clear on it? Could I teach it to someone else? Am I kind of iffy on this?". . . It's especially important that our ELLs know what the heck is going on.

Liz continued by describing an activity in an elementary school classroom where students were working on a portfolio folder about a story they had read. The children were writing "I can" statements on the insides of the folders, listing the things they could do.

> [The teacher related] that she had a parent come in and that she [the teacher] had the child do the conference. The parent was concerned about her child's reading and so she [the teacher] pulled out these portfolios and the child starts, "Oh, this is the one that shows that I can find adjectives in a sentence, and this is the one that shows that I can write a friendly letter." The kid just knows!

Another question about objectives that often arises is how and where to post them. The answer differs a bit depending on whether a teacher is at the elementary or secondary level. We have seen elementary teachers post their objectives on their white boards near

FIGURE 7.9

SIOP® Lesson Plan 7

Topic:	Class:	Date:

Content Objectives:	Language Objectives:

Key Vocabulary:	Materials (including supplementary and adapted):

Higher-Order Questions:

Time:	Activities:
	Building Background
	Links to Experience:
	Links to Learning:
	Key Vocabulary:

(continued on next page)

Writing SIOP® Lessons

FIGURE 7.9   *SIOP® Lesson Plan 7   (Continued)*

Time:	**Student Activities** (Check all that apply for activities throughout lesson):
	Scaffolding: ❏ Modeling ❏ Guided ❏ Independent
	Grouping: ❏ Whole Class ❏ Small Group ❏ Partners ❏ Independent
	Processing: ❏ Reading ❏ Writing ❏ Listening ❏ Speaking
	Strategies: ❏ Hands-on ❏ Meaningful ❏ Linked to Objectives
	Review and Assessment (Check all that apply):
	❏ Individual ❏ Group ❏ Written ❏ Oral
	Review Key Vocabulary:
	Review Key Content Concepts:

Developed by John Seidlitz, SIOP® National Faculty, Pearson Achievement Solutions

FIGURE 7.10

SIOP® Lesson Plan 8

Key: SW = Students will; TW = teacher will; SWBAT = Students will be able to...; HOTS = Higher-Order Thinking Skills

SIOP® Lesson:

Grade:

Content Standards:

Key Vocabulary:

Visuals / Resources:

HOTS:

Connections to Prior Knowledge / Building Background Information:

Content Objectives:	Meaningful Activities:	Review / Assessment:
1.	1.1	1.1
	1.2	
	2.1	2.1
2.	2.2	2.2

(continued on next page)

FIGURE 7.10 *SIOP® Lesson Plan 8* *(Continued)*

3.

3.1

3.2

Language Objectives:

1.

1.1

1.2

2.

2.1

3.1

3.2

1.2

2.2

Wrap-up:

Created by Melissa Castillo & Nicole Teyechea, SIOP® National Faculty, Pearson Achievement Solutions

FIGURE 7.11

SIOP® Lesson Plan 9

Subject: _____ Unit: _____

Content Objective:

Language Objective:

Building Background: Activate prior knowledge

Key Vocabulary:

Comprehensible Input:

Teaching Strategies and Sequence:

Instruction:

Guided Practice:

Extention Activities or Independent Practice:

Review / Assessment:

Created by Laurie Beebe, American Falls, Idaho

SIOP® Lesson Plan 10

Teacher: _____   ELD Level: _____ Number

Class: _____   Lesson: Multiday or Single Day (circle one)

Unit: _____

Content Objectives:	Language Objectives:

Content Objectives *Kidspeak:*	Language Objectives *Kidspeak:*

Vocabulary:	Building Background:

Regular Materials:	Supplementary Materials:

Strategies:	Activity/Application:

FIGURE 7.12 *SIOP® Lesson Plan 10* *(Continued)*

Lesson Delivery:

- ○

- ○

- ○

- ○

- ○

- ○

- ○

Review/Assessment:

Students Are Ready To Move On: _____ YES   _____ NO

Notes (what worked/what didn't work):

Format adapted by Davia Irwin, SIOP® National Faculty, Pearson Achievement Solutions

SIOP® Lesson Plan 11

Class Level

Class Periods

Subject

Topic:	
MO Content Standard:	
GLE:	
Content Objective:	
Language Objectives:	
Key Vocabulary:	

SIOP® Features

Preparation	Scaffolding	Grouping Options
— Adaptation of content	— Modeling	— Whole class
— Links to background	— Guided practice	— Small groups
— Links to past learning	— Independent practice	— Partners
— Strategies incorporated	— Comprehensible input	— Independent

Integration of Processes	Application	Assessment
— Reading	— Hands-on	— Individual
— Writing	— Meaningful	— Group
— Speaking	— Linked to objectives	— Written
— Listening	— Promotes engagement	— Oral

<u>Language Skills:</u>	**Beginning**	**Intermediate**	**Advanced**
Content:			
Speaking:			
Reading and Writing:			
Language Structures:			
Thinking			

<u>Resources</u>	
Materials:	

Motivation/Preparation:	
Presentation:	
Practice/Application:	
Review/Evaluation	

Created by Charlotte Daniel, Kansas City, Missouri

FIGURE 7.13 *SIOP® Lesson Plan 11* *(Continued)*

Lesson Sequence:	

FIGURE 7.14   *Essential Elements of Immersion Teaching (Guide for an Immersion Lesson Plan)*

Teacher: Bilger   *Date:* 9/13/05
Grade: 3
Language of Lesson: ENGLISH

Arizona State Standards:
<u>Power Standard 10</u> Students will use the writing process including prewriting, drafting, revising, editing, and publishing when composing written pieces across a variety of writing tasks with emphasis on revising and editing by writing a narrative based on real events.

Content/Skill Objective:
(What will they know at the end of the lesson? What will they be able to do?) <u>Write on board or chart paper to use during Intro and End</u>

"Students will demonstrate synthesis of revision strategies **(Bloom's Taxonomy)** by asking and processing clarifying questions to improve pieces of writing **(student behavior)**."

Expected Prior Knowledge:

(Identify what they need to know before proceeding with lesson. Ask yourself if they are ready for this lesson.)

Language Objectives:
(What language will they know or be able to use at the end of the lesson? Write on board or chart paper to refer to during the Introduction and <u>during</u> the lesson.)

"Students will demonstrate application of key vocabulary and questions in the form of complete sentences by recording a question on a Post-it Note and by asking questions about another student's story."

"Students will demonstrate application of key vocabulary and questions with correct singular/plural verb agreement by using either 'are there' or 'is there' in a question stated as a complete sentence."

Content Obligatory Language:

(Language required for comprehension and mastery of concept in content objective. May focus on vocabulary, function, and/or grammar. Content Objective determines this language.)

Vocabulary	**Function**	**Grammar**
Why	Questions in the form of complete sentences	
What	Singular/plural verb agreement	
When		
Who		
Are there		
Is there		
What if		

Content Compatible Language:

(Language that gives students opportunities to expand language skills. May focus on vocabulary, function, and/or grammar. Oral language levels, Scope & Sequence, IDEA Profile Card determine this language.)

   • **Teacher attention to language objectives and opportunities for student practice are <u>woven throughout the lesson.</u>**

Materials
   1. Teaching Supplies: large Post-it Notes, revision strategy cards, poster with question sentence starters
   2. Student Supplies: Post-it Notes, revision strategy cards for questioning, key rings with sentence starters

(Continued)

FIGURE 7.14 *Essential Elements of Immersion Teaching (Guide for an Immersion Lesson Plan)* *(Continued)*

Immersion Teaching Techniques and Student Strategies:
(What are you going to do to make sure the information presented will be understood by the students?)

- Voice modulation and pace
- Linguistic encoding and scaffolding
- Sufficient wait time
- Grouping for student interaction
- Think-pair-share
- Natural approach
- Integration of read/write/listening/speaking
- Supplementary materials (realia, visuals, manipulatives)
- Linking past to present
- Written instructions w/graphics
- Teacher/student interaction
- Writing/drawing while talking
- Total physical response
- Adaptation of text/assignment
- Variety of question types
- Activities to practice language

Procedures
[Each step involves <u>content and language</u> that students need to learn.]:

- **Anticipatory Set:** *(attention grabber, immersion experience with realia, visualization, drama, role playing, video, virtual field trip—try to involve a minimum of three senses)*
  - Teacher presents a written piece on the board with certain elements missing.

- **Introduction:** *(explain both content and language objectives, i.e., "at the end of today's lesson you will know . . . or be able to . . ." and refer to objectives written on board)*
  - Teacher introduces objective and the "questioning card."

- **Teacher Demonstration:** *(think-aloud—show them what you expect them to do as you are doing it)* **and checking for understanding**
  - Teacher will present clarifying questions on large Post-its that "Mr. Brotherton asked."

- **Guided Practice:** (individuals, pairs, and/or groups practice activity similar to teacher's demonstration) **and checking for understanding throughout**
  - The students will then write questions on Post-it Notes about the piece written on the board.

- **Independent Practice:** *(students do actual project or activity to demonstrate understanding and/or mastery of objectives— although called "independent practice," this may be done in pairs and/or groups)* **Checking for understanding—major evaluation/assessment takes place here.**
  - Teacher will review the "status of the class" and students will share what they are going to be working on during the workshop time.
  - Students will work independently on the writing process and will apply the questioning revision strategy when they get to that stage in their writing process.

- **Ending the Lesson—Closure/Reflection:** (refer back to objectives, sum up, reflect, i.e., "How did we discover this, what did we find out?") **Involves active student participation and checking for understanding**
  - Selected students will share a rough draft and others will be encouraged to ask revising questions.

- **Remediation:** *(what are you going to do for or with students who do not understand concepts or the language and/or are unable to complete the task)*
  - Students will learn the same skill in the Spanish component of the dual language model so they will have the chance to process in their first language.

- **Enrichment:** *(what will you do for advanced students who immediately grasp the concept and/or who finish quickly)*
  - Students will be encouraged to explain to the class which questions helped them make their piece better and which questions they chose not to use.

- **Evaluation:**
  Content Objective: *(how will you know if the student understands the concept and/or how will you measure whether the student accomplishes the objective)*
  - Students need to show the teacher questions that they wrote on Post-its about another student's story in order to receive the "questioning strategy" card for their toolbox.

  Language Objectives: *(how will you know if the student is adopting the desired language ability)*
  - Students will have to write questions in complete sentences, using proper grammar, on their Post-its.

Adapted from *Mastery Teaching* by Madeline Hunter, *What It Means to be an Immersion Teacher* by Myriam Met, and *Making Content Comprehensible for English Language Learners: The SIOP® Model* by Echevarria, Vogt, & Short for Creighton School District Title VII by Penny Reuben, 2001.

FIGURE 7.15 *Phrases for Writing Language Objectives*

Language Objectives
- Ask and answer questions
- Practice agreeing/disagreeing
- Make comparisons
- Express interest and preferences
- Give descriptions using precise vocabulary
- Comprehend multiple-step directions
- Issue multiple-step directions
- Relate personal experience
- Use correct grammar
- Take notes/complete graphic organizer
- Record observations
- Use knowledge of base words
- Read abbreviations
- Comprehend content vocabulary words
- Recognize the meaning of prefixes and suffixes
- Participate in choral reading
- Use clue words to identify sequence
- Use clue words to identify cause and effect
- Ask and answer cause and effect questions
- State author's purpose
- Write a paragraph in 1st person
- Identify main idea
- Read/perform poetry
- Paraphrase/summarize
- Orally defend position

Created by Wanda Holbrook and Kendra Moreno, Isaac School District

their daily schedules; pocket charts with sentence strips that can be kept and reused; a chart pad located close to "the rug" where the objectives will be shared with students; a bulletin board used exclusively for posting content and language objectives; and so forth.

In secondary classrooms, where objectives must be changed for each period, teachers use transparencies for use with an overhead projector; a mounted computer monitor (up near the ceiling), with a computer on the teacher's desk so objectives can be written and saved for repeated use; a pocket chart (not often found in secondary classrooms); the white board (probably most time consuming); PowerPoint slides, and so forth. There is no one spot for objectives or one way to post them. What is most important is that the content and language objectives be observable by all students.

Some teachers, especially at the secondary level, require students to record the content and language objectives in a content-specific notebook, but this may be perceived by some as consuming too much instructional time. Both elementary and secondary students regularly read aloud the objectives, sometimes chorally. It is critical that all students understand the meaning of the content and language objectives for any lesson, so that they can determine the degree to which they have met them at the conclusion of the lesson.

FIGURE 7.16 *Content Objectives Matched with Language Objectives, American History ESL*

Content Objective	Language Objective
We will explore the materials we will be using this summer to learn about American History.	We will discuss and write features of the textbook. We will begin to create a timeline of American History.
We will begin the study of the causes and outcomes of the conflict in Vietnam. We will watch an excerpt of *Forrest Gump* to learn more about the country of Vietnam.	We will answer questions about the Vietnam conflict. We will discuss our opinions about the Vietnam conflict and war in general. We will compare the conflict in Vietnam to what we know about war.
We will continue our study of the conflict in Vietnam and its impact on the United States. We will compare communism to capitalism.	We will define communism and capitalism. We will write and answer questions that we have. We will discuss our opinions about communism and capitalism.
We will complete our study of the conflict in Vietnam and begin to explore the conflict in Korea. We will compare and contrast the conflict in Korea with Vietnam.	We will read and answer questions about the conflict in Korea. We will discuss similarities and differences between the two conflicts. We will create a chart to compare and contrast the conflicts in Vietnam and Korea. We will write in complete sentences.
We will contrast differences between the United States and the Soviet Union that led to the Cold War.	We will listen to Donald Fagan sing "New Frontier." We will discuss the lyrics and how they relate to the Cold War. We will make a list of what we would need in the "New Frontier." We will write and answer questions about the Cold War.
We will continue our study of the Cold War, focusing on how the changes in the attitude of the people affected politics and policies.	We will read an article and write and answer questions that relate to attitudes on the Cold War. We will define the vocabulary in context of the article.
We will begin our study of World War II, focusing on events in Pearl Harbor, Hawaii, Hiroshima, Japan, and during the Holocaust.	We will view and then discuss the film *One Survivor Remembers*. We will read sections of the text about the events leading to the Holocaust. We will look at artifacts from Holocaust survivors. We will discuss the significance of the artifacts.
We will continue our study of the Holocaust and the U.S. involvement in World War II.	We will read about World War II and answer questions. We will watch excerpts from the film *The Pianist* to build background on what life was like during the Holocaust and the liberation.
We will study the major battles in Europe during World War II.	We will work in small groups to create posters that portray important events in Europe during World War II. We will use the posters in a gallery walk.

Created by Charlotte Daniel, Kansas City, Missouri

Aligning Content and Language Objectives with Meaningful Activities and Assessment

Go back and take another look at Figure 7.10, a lesson plan created by SIOP® National Faculty members, Melissa Castillo and Nicole Teyechea. This format encourages teachers

Figure 7.17 *Language-Related Tasks of the Social Science Standards*

Study	List	Detect
Discuss	Name	Judge
Describe	Use	Pose
Identify	Relate	Locate
Trace	Distinguish	Recite
Explain	Test	Label
Understand	Construct	Research
Analyze	Connect	Determine
Study	Simplify	Select
Demonstrate	Conduct	Recognize
Know	Apply	Read
Map	Consider	Write
Detail	Present	Illustrate
Examine	Discuss	Organize
Evaluate	Cite	Investigate
Enumerate	State	Develop
Outline	Frame	Ask
Compare	Interpret	Display
Contrast	Assess	Indicate

Created by Elizabeth Fralicks, Title III, Fresno Unified School District

to carefully and thoughtfully align a lesson's content and language objectives with assigned activities and assessment opportunities that occur throughout the lesson. Teachers frequently ask, "Does implementing the SIOP® Model mean that I can't use what I know works with my students (including English learners)? Do I have to use all new activities?"

FIGURE 7.18 *Language-Related Tasks of the Science Standards*

Know	Observe	Collect
Use	Collect	Perform
Select	Repeat	Display
Communicate	Differentiate	Label
Construct	Formulate	List
Plan	Draw conclusions	Apply
Conduct	Estimate	Solve
Distinguish	Guess	Investigate
Recognize	Classify	Analyze
Evaluate	Develop	Demonstrate
Apply	Select	Interpret
Interpret	Read	Check
Predict	Write	Relate
Draw	Discuss	Indicate
Record	Plan	Develop
Make	Explain	Organize
Measure	Communicate	Prove
Use	Ask	Derive
Sort	Pose	Explain

Created by Elizabeth Fralicks, Title III, Fresno Unified School District

FIGURE 7.19 *The Academic Language of the Social Science Standards*

Language Functions	Specific Examples	Features	Importance	Sources & Causes	Consequences and Effects	Relationships	Process
English	*All Levels*	*All Levels*	*I, EA, A**	*EI, I, EA, A**	*I, EA, A**	*I, EA, A**	*I, EA, A**
Primary language	*All Levels*	*All Levels*	*All Levels***	*All Levels***	*All Levels***	*All Levels***	*All Levels***
	the location of . . .	the features of . . .	the significance of . . .	the cause of . . .	the effect of/on . . .	the connections between . . .	the development of . . .
	the policy of . . .	the components of . . .	the importance of . . .	the reasons for . . .	the result of . . .	the influence of . . .	the evolution of . . .
	the borders of . . .	the characteristics of . . .	the challenges of . . .	the roots of . . .	the impact of . . .	the relationship between . . .	the transition of/from/to . . .
	the ideas of . . .	the principles of . . .	the contributions of . . .	the origins of . . .	the legacy of . . .	the conflicts between . . .	the rise of . . .
	the teachings of . . .	the ideas of . . .	the purpose of . . .	the source of . . .	the consequences of . . .	the obstacles to . . .	the growth of . . .
	the rivers in . . .	the goals of . . .	the role of . . .	the basis of . . .	the cost of . . .	the pattern of . . .	the spread of . . .
	the capital of . . .	the policy of . . .	the achievements of . . .	the foundations of . . .	the ramification of . . .	the collaboration between . . .	the emergence of . . .
	the birthplace of . . . (timeline)	the similarities to . . .		the grounds for . . .	the toll of . . .	the complexity of . . .	the trends in . . .
	the date of . . . (timeline)	the differences between . . .			the response of . . .	the nature of . . .	the history of . . .
	the life of . . . (timeline)	the advantages of . . .			the outcome of . . .		the establishment of . . .
	the events of . . . (timeline)	the disadvantages of . . .					
	the customs of . . .	the philosophy of . . .					
	the landforms of . . .						
	the plants in the crops of . . .						

Created by Elizabeth Fralicks, Title III, Fresno Unified School District
*Indicates the language level at which EL students may be able to perform this academic task at an independent or almost independent level. Secondary EL students at various levels of language acquisition can learn all levels of knowledge with proper scaffolding; **May depend on level and consistency of background education.
EI = Early Intermediate, I = Intermediate, EA = Early Advanced, A = Advanced

The best way to answer these questions is to suggest that teachers carefully align their lesson activities with their objectives; the activities are the means to the end (meeting objectives), not the end. If the activities are meaningful (not busywork), and they provide practice and application of the content and language described in the objectives, then there is alignment. Assessment of students' progress toward meeting the objectives may occur during the meaningful activities, or additional techniques may need to be employed for adequate review and assessment. Again, alignment of the assessment and the objectives is necessary. Too often, objectives are written, posted, and explained, but there is little alignment among the components of the lesson. If that's the case, then the activities may not be appropriate for the tasks at hand.

Another way to determine whether particular activities are appropriate for a lesson is to use the SIOP® protocol during planning. Teachers might ask themselves while planning a lesson: Will the proposed activity keep students engaged 90 to 100 percent of the time? Is it meaningful and relevant? Does it develop and provide practice in the areas stated in the objectives? Is it interactive? When teachers work together to reflect on their teaching using the SIOP® Model, their insights can be powerful, as Liz Warner illustrated:

> When we're doing trainings . . . in lesson preparation, they bring that piece in and we just have them look at it and say, "How did we do?" Rate yourself [on the protocol] on how you did this month and look at what you would give yourself. What's interesting is you hear teachers [talk while] they are sitting in a team. They're looking over their work from the month before and they'll look at each other and say, "Well, how would you rate this? This is what I did." Then someone will say, "Well, this is what I did. How would you rate that?" So it's interesting that they're using it [the SIOP® protocol] as a reflection tool—as a way of looking at their teaching. I've even heard teachers say, "Oh, you did it that way," so they're getting ideas from each other.

This goes back to earlier discussions of teacher buy-in and how to sustain the SIOP® momentum (see Chapter 6), but it also involves teachers using the SIOP® protocol, with its eight components and thirty features, for lesson planning, self-reflection, renewal, and self-assessment.

Differentiating Instruction to Meet the Needs of All Students

Perhaps the question we are asked by teachers most frequently, throughout the country and from Pre-K to grade 12, is "I have so many different ability and language groups in my classroom. How can I possibly meet their individual needs—without going too fast for some kids and too slowly for others?"

What has become abundantly clear is that the SIOP® Model does not represent "one-size-fits-all" teaching. Instead, SIOP® teachers are learning to differentiate their instruction

Note how the bulletin board display differentiates for English and Spanish speakers, and provides visual support for information students are expected to remember.
Used with permission of Charlotte-Mecklenburg Schools, North Carolina.

for students with varied abilities, cultural backgrounds, and language differences. Liz Warner told a story that may describe an all-too-frequent classroom scenario:

> I went into a middle school for a meeting. . . and a math teacher stood up at this meeting and said, "Out of my twenty-eight students, I have twelve ELLs and eleven of them are flunking. . . one has a D. I said, "There are a couple of things you can do to help them," and it kind of changed his look. And I saw him a couple of months ago and I asked him, "How's it going?". . . And he said, "You know, you taught me a lot. . . the main thing I can say is that we weren't ready for these kids [English learners] and we were doing these kids a disservice . . . that's it. We've got to be ready . . . the problem with our school district is that we were not ready." This is a big jump for this guy.

According to the *The Literacy Dictionary* (Harris & Hodges, 1995), differentiation is defined as "The provision of varied learning situations, as whole-class, small-group, or individual instruction, to meet the needs of students at different levels of reading competence (p. 60)." We also add, ". . . to meet the needs of students at different levels of *academic competence and language proficiency. . . .* "

While the term *differentiated instruction* means different things to educators depending on their educational role and context, most agree that it has something to do with providing appropriate instruction for students with diverse needs, strengths, and abilities. What is challenging is determining what this looks like and how it works. One ESL coordinator explained,

Being able to understand our students, and meeting them where they are, rather than expecting them to come up to where we are . . . I think that's been a huge epiphany for all of us because we get so bogged down with what the state expects us to do that we lose sight of the kids sitting in their seats and what they really need us to do [for them] . . . That's always been a struggle for us because we have state expectations, but many of our kids haven't reached that place yet . . .

Non-Differentiated and Differentiated Classrooms

So what distinguishes a differentiated classroom from a non-differentiated classroom? Perhaps this question can best be answered by using the SIOP® Model as a lens through which you can compare and contrast these two classrooms. As you read and reflect on each of the following descriptions, you may wish to have a copy of the SIOP® protocol, with the eight components and thirty features, before you.

In Typical Non-Differentiated Classrooms, you are likely to see:

- Assessment is used to see "who got it." The teacher assesses at the end of a lesson (or perhaps a unit) to determine who "passes" and who "fails."

- Student differences and interests are not particularly relevant during lesson planning. Teachers plan lessons based on the curriculum, and what has been taught in past semesters or years.

- Whole-class teaching prevails. Teachers use whole-class teaching to convey key concepts through lecture, and to maintain classroom control.

- Instructional goals focus on content coverage. Teachers are cognizant of the need to complete the textbook, cover the material, and teach to all content standards. Doing so is a top priority.

- Assignments, texts, and tasks are the same for all students. There is one class textbook for all students and a common set of assignments and expectations.

- The daily schedule and time allotments are relatively inflexible. Because of the need to cover content, it is impractical to adjust daily and weekly schedules.

- Individual desks placed in rows, represent the predominant organizational structure for the classroom.

- A search for one correct answer and/or single interpretation is the norm.

- The preponderance of talk is the teacher's. There are few opportunities for discussion and interaction among students.

- Teacher-directed questioning is common with the question-evaluation-response pattern dominating. The teacher asks frequent questions, students respond (one at a time), and the teacher evaluates the correctness of the response.

- High-level thinking questions/tasks are reserved for the highest-achieving students. Low-performing students are involved in more structured, less generative tasks.

- The same assessment is used for all students with a single standard for grading.

- The teacher is the one who knows the objectives for the lesson.
- Teacher expectations for success vary according to students' academic performance levels.

Whereas the preceding may seem unfamiliar based on your own teaching experiences, the reality is that the non-differentiated classroom has been the predominant organizational structure and set of teaching practices in the United States for over one hundred years (Vogt, 1989). However, it is no longer acceptable to have some students succeed in school while others struggle and/or fail. In order to fully implement the SIOP® Model, we encourage teachers to create a differentiated classroom. For those who are already implementing the SIOP® Model, we hope this list of what you will see in such a classroom is much more familiar.

In Typical Differentiated Classrooms, you will see:

- <u>Student differences, interests, and needs guide lesson planning</u>. Teachers use assessment data, interest inventories, student needs, strengths, and interests to guide their lesson planning.

- <u>Assessment is ongoing, continuous, and includes multiple indicators</u>. Teachers conduct informal assessment before, during, and after lessons, in addition to more formal measures.

- <u>A variety of texts, tasks, and options is evident</u>. Leveled texts, adapted texts, student choice of tasks and products are the norm, along with required assignments that are designed to accommodate diverse needs and abilities.

- <u>Grouping of students for instruction is frequent and flexible</u>.

- <u>Multiple perspectives are routinely sought</u>. Teachers acknowledge that students from diverse backgrounds must be encouraged to activate and use their prior knowledge; diverse perspectives often result.

- <u>Time is used flexibly based on student attainment of objectives</u>. Although teachers recognize the need for a schedule and for meeting content and language objectives, there are times when extra time is needed for all students to accomplish goals.

- <u>Talk is shared between students and teacher</u>. Structured discussion is the norm and student-to-student interaction is strongly encouraged through the careful selection of meaningful activites.

- <u>High-level thinking questions and tasks are the norm for all students</u>.

- <u>Students know and follow classroom routines</u>. In order for flexible grouping to occur, teachers teach and provide practice in how to work alone and in groups.

- <u>Both the teacher and students know the content (and language) objectives for each lesson</u>. The objectives are posted for each lesson, explained to students, and assessed with students at the end of each lesson.

- <u>All students are believed capable of achieving learning goals and standards</u>.

You may be thinking, "This sounds like a list of many of the SIOP® features." You're right—many are included here because that's what a differentiated classroom involves. Few, if any, effective teachers would choose to have a non-differentiated classroom. However, creating a differentiated environment can be challenging. As John Seidlitz has observed,

> Teachers need more training and practice with differentiated instruction and cooperative learning. We need to add more staff development so teachers will be able to implement [these techniques] in the classroom.

How have schools and districts helped teachers to bring about effective differentiated instruction while implementing the SIOP® Model? What kind of support do teachers need to learn about differentiated instruction so they can implement the SIOP® Model to a high degree?

District and School Support for Differentiating SIOP® Classrooms

One district used the work of Carolyn Weiner (2001) to differentiate for language levels. Her book, *Preparing for Success*, provides very practical ways for assessing and developing language with children of poverty. In particular, the district has found that work designed for kindergarteners is useful since many of their students enter kindergarten at the preproduction level of English proficiency. Children at this level are provided with "encoding" or rich language interactions where teachers narrate the child's thoughts or actions, much like the "motherese" that parents practice as children develop language.

An example of the way that Weiner's work interfaces with the SIOP® Model is with the Practice and Application component. Children use manipulatives or go to high interest centers and as they work at the centers, the teacher circulates and encodes or narrates. This is done by directly telling a child what he is doing and why it is important. In this process, the teacher moves from child to child, narrating and developing language that is attached to the child's own actions. Marilyn Sanchez, Director of Language Acquisition in Creighton Schools, explains,

> And it's all also about developing behaviors as a central piece so that by second quarter you can start sitting in groups and then start the reading process with key words and language experience. At the first level you work with encoding like a mother would do with a toddler; that's how they develop the language because it's so meaningful. Once the children are speaking then . . . teachers . . . scaffold and extend their expressions.

Another wonderful resource that demonstrates differentiated instruction was created by Elizabeth Fralicks from Fresno Unified School District. It is the Content-Based Language Objectives chart (see Figure 7.20). The three columns represent levels of English proficiency, and the content objectives are based upon the state standards in social science. Elizabeth explained that Fresno Unified describes three levels of language development (rather than five or more used by districts and states) because of ease of use, even though teachers are well aware that English learners don't neatly fall into the three

FIGURE 7.20 *Content-based Language Objectives*

Goal: To use English to achieve academically in Social Science
Standard 3: Students will use learning strategies to construct and apply academic knowledge

Beginning	Intermediate	Advanced
Students will be able to:		
• Use simple graphic organizers, maps, tables, and timelines to process information	• Construct and present various graphic organizer, maps, tables and timelines to organize ideas and process information	• Construct, interpret and present various graphic organizers, maps, tables and timelines to organize ideas and process information
• Use prewriting and drafting to produce selected content-related responses	• Use the writing processes of prewriting, drafting, and editing for basic conventions and spelling to produce content-related responses to selected assignments	• Use the writing processes of prewriting, drafting, editing and revising to produce content-related responses to selected assignments
• Begin to apply cognitive strategies of skimming, scanning, highlighting, and margins notes to a learning task with assistance	• Apply cognitive strategies such as skimming, summarizing, scanning, highlighting, making margin notes, note-taking, outlining, etc. to a learning task	• Apply cognitive strategies such as skimming, summarizing, scanning, highlighting, margin notes, note-taking, outlining, etc. to a learning task
• Use a journal or interactive notebooks to process content information using teacher-made prompts, frames, vocabulary lists, graphic representations, etc.	• Use a journal or interactive notebook to process content information with prompts, response frames, vocabulary and graphics	• Use a journal or interactive notebook to process content information
• Connect new information to previously learned information	• Connect new information to previously learned information	• Actively connect and apply previously learned information to newly-acquired knowledge
• Use cognates to access and define new content-related vocabulary	• Use cognates to access and define new content-related vocabulary	• Use cognates to access and define new content-related vocabulary
• Use a dictionary, word list, glossary, pictures, journal, etc. to discover the meaning of unknown vocabulary	• Use a dictionary, word list, glossary, pictures, journal, context clues, peers, and teacher to access the meaning of unknown vocabulary	• Use a dictionary, word list, glossary, pictures, journal, context clues, peers, and teachers to access the meaning of unknown vocabulary
• Use primary language for clarification and to access and acquire higher level concepts	• Use some primary language for clarification and to access and acquire higher level concepts	• Use primary language periodically for clarification and to access and acquire
• Use simple summaries and outline to identify key information	• Create simple summaries and outlines to detail key information	• Create complete summaries and outlines to process and explore content information
• With teacher assistance identify and define key words from content text	• Identify and define key words in content text with context clues and some teacher/peer assistance	• Identify and define key words in content clues, previously learned vocabulary, dictionaries etc.
• Use one or two methods of research and investigation (e.i. library use, Internet) with teacher assistance	• Use a variety of methods of research and investigation (e.i. library use, Internet, surveys, interviews) with some assistance to deepen knowledge gained in classroom activities	• Use a variety of methods of research and investigation (e.i. library use, Internet, surveys, interviews) to deepen knowledge gained in classroom activities
• Recognize the need for assistance and begin to use assistance-seeking strategies (teacher, peers, reference sources, "question-box," etc.	• Seek assistance when appropriate with a variety of strategies (teacher, peers, reference sources, question box, etc.)	• Seek assistance independent from the teacher as needed through a variety of strategies

(Continued)

FIGURE 7.20   *Content-based Language Objectives*   *(Continued)*

Beginning	Intermediate	Advanced
Students will be able to:		
• Begin to self-monitor and self-correct some basic content and language errors	• Self monitor and self-correct content and language errors at the appropriate level	• Self-monitor and self-correct content and language errors
• Begin to evaluate one's own success on a completed assignment, activity or project with assistance from peers, teacher and others	• Evaluate one's own success on a completed assignment, activity or project	• Use text features such as unit, chapter and section titles and headings; bold print, table of contents, glossary, appendix index, etc. to locate and apply information
• Notice and imitate the behavior of native/proficient English speakers to complete tasks successfully	• Imitate the behavior of native/proficient English speakers to complete tasks successfully	• Imitate the behavior of native/proficient English speakers to complete tasks successfully
• Point out text features such as unit, chapter, and section titles and headings; bold print table of contents, glossary, appendix , index, etc.	• Use text features such as unit, chapter and section titles and headings; table of contents, glossary, appendix, index, etc. to locate information	• Use text features such as unit, chapter and section titles and headings; bold print, table of contents, glossary, appendix, index, etc. to locate and apply information

Created by Elizabeth Fralicks, Title III, Fresno Unified Schoool District

classifications. Note in the examples how all students are expected to meet the standard, but their anticipated responses and products are differentiated according to their level of English. As you follow the chart from left to right, notice how even beginning speakers are expected to fully participate in activities and instruction that will promote their social science knowledge acquisition.

Teaching for Independence and Small Group Work

Another way that schools and district personnel can help teachers effectively differentiate instruction is by sharing a set of steps for teaching students to work independently—a necessity if students' academic needs are to be met. Too often, teachers assign students to groups and tell them, "Get to work!" However, many students, ELs and others, have not learned how to work well independently, or in groups, because no one has ever taught and modeled for them how to do so. Therefore, it is important that elementary and secondary teachers alike spend time at the beginning of the year, and thereafter as needed, to do the following:

- Teach students to work on their own
- Teach students to work with others

- Teach students appropriate behavior while working in groups
- Teach students the value of working with others
- Teach students to appreciate the contributions of others

These important social skills can be taught through a series of steps that once initially learned will need to be reviewed frequently, depending on the students' age. These steps include the following:

1. Organize the classroom for effective partner, small group, and independent work. This doesn't mean completely redoing the classroom, but rather it involves considering where the teacher will teach a small group; where partners will work; where small groups will work; and where students will work independently. What will not be effective is if students are just all over the place completing assignments, because most likely the teacher will have multiple interruptions. If the small groups are working across the room from the teacher's table, and they know what to do and necessary materials are close by, the groups can learn to work together. Students working in pairs or independently can sit nearby, closer to the teacher, so there is a noise buffer between the working groups and the small group the teacher is teaching. This doesn't require reorganizing the room; just moving the kids around temporarily to accomplish your goals.

2. Determine who will work with whom in instructional (teacher-student) and interactive (student-students) groups. This should be a systematic task in which the teacher uses assessment data, observation, and intuition about which students will work well with others, and which may need some help in learning to work well with others. As students learn the social skills necessary for working in groups, their membership in several groups will be possible. That's the "flexible group" part.

3. Teach students how to work with others and in groups. This step is critical to the process. Have students brainstorm the answer to this question: "When you're working with a partner or in a small group, how do you know that you're working well together?" Even very young children can answer this question (adapt the language in your question appropriately). The students' list will look something like "We listen to each other; we get along; we take turns; everyone participates; we finish what we start," etc. Take any relevant items on the list and complete a T-chart (Looks Like, Sounds Like) with the students' ideas about each social skill that they need to work on (e.g., listening, sharing, taking turns, etc.). For secondary students, the T-chart can deal with more sophisticated group dynamic skills (e.g., one person not dominating, everyone pulling their weight, etc.). These T-charts can be posted throughout the room and referred to as needed.

4. Model how to work independently. Provide students with small group tasks that can be completed in fifteen to twenty minutes—the time needed for you to work with a small group (less time for grades K-2). These should not require a great deal of preparation or clean-up, and should be routines, if possible. For example, upper elementary, middle, and high school students can engage in a Written Conversation, during which they write to a partner about an appropriate topic, switching papers

every few sentences or paragraphs. This isn't busywork—students are required to communicate complete thoughts through writing, write legibly, perhaps discuss a particular content topic, etc. A Written Conversation is always completed the same way, so it becomes a routine. Younger children can work with a partner to find words they can read in a picture; they can list them on paper and read them to each other. It only takes a bit of imagination to come up with other "independent routines" that students can complete with others in partners and small groups (think "interaction") while the teacher is teaching a small group. Of course, this small group time can be used for other activities, such as completing assignments, reading, doing research, participating in centers, and so forth. The most important point is that students are taught how to work *independently*—depending on the students, this may take considerable modeling and practice.

5. <u>Assess the effectiveness of the groups.</u> With your students, debrief how well small groups are working, referring back to the posted T-charts, discussing how students' social skills are developing, and candidly talking about what's working and what's not. Some teachers regularly ask students to complete a half-page group evaluation sheet on which they determine how well the group members worked together to complete a lesson's tasks.

Elementary and secondary teachers all over the country have followed these steps to create a classroom environment in which students know the routines and can work with each other independently so that their teacher can teach. In these classrooms, students are learning to get along with each other while they are working toward meeting standards and objectives. Are these steps for teaching independence a "must" for implementing the SIOP® Model? Probably not—but they certainly will help teachers to effectively differentiate instruction for the students in their charge.

Elements of Differentiation

Another way that schools and district personnel can assist teachers in learning how to appropriately differentiate their instruction is to demystify what differentiation is. Some teachers think they need to individualize instruction, others think that they need to continually run "groups," with a great deal of preparation and grading. Others think it's something that university types dream up and that in reality, it's impossible to really differentiate. However, the following elements of differentiation are practical, doable, and congruent with the SIOP® Model.

1. <u>How instructional tasks are designed.</u> This includes the number of tasks occurring at once (e.g., some students are working on the computer, others may be writing in their journals, while a third group is working with the teacher); the diverse products students may produce (see Figure 7.20 for examples); the sequencing and pacing of tasks (e.g., some students may be able to accomplish a task in three steps, while other students may need modeling and guidance in five or more steps); the difficulty of tasks (again, see Figure 7.20); and the amount of material covered. For

example, for some English learners (and other students, as well), independently reading an entire chapter is an impossibility. However, if the key concepts, critical explanations, and key vocabulary are highlighted, and the ELs are expected to only read the highlighted sections, they may cover less material but develop greater understanding.

2. <u>How instructional materials are used.</u> Certainly all students, including ELs, must have opportunities to read independent-level materials, but for many students (and as mentioned in #1), grade-level texts can be very frustrating. Therefore, some students may need significant scaffolding (e.g., taped texts, reading with a partner or small group, etc.). The same can be said for carrying out experiments, creating a research project, completing math assignments, and so forth. A key feature of the SIOP® Model is the use of supplementary materials just for this purpose.

3. <u>How students are grouped for instruction and practice.</u> In differentiated classrooms, students work with partners, small groups, independently, and as part of the whole class. In order to promote interaction, teachers need to consider how they will group students during each and every lesson, and most important, for what purpose. "Instructional groups" are small (approximately three to seven students), where the teacher is providing instruction. They include guided reading groups, "jump-start" (or preteaching) groups, acceleration groups, reteach/review groups, and minilessons. "Interactive groups" are those where students are expected to work on their own while the teacher is working with another small group. They include partners, triads, small groups (4–5 students) discussion circles (once students have been taught how to participate), cooperative/jigsaw groups, research groups, and centers.

4. <u>How teachers provide feedback and ask questions.</u> There has been considerable evidence over the years about how teachers ask questions in elementary and secondary classrooms. We know that higher-performing students generally are on the receiving end of high-order thinking questions; lower-performing students are asked lower-level questions. In differentiated (and SIOP®) classrooms, teachers ask higher-order questions of all students, and provide helpful, academic feedback, differentiating only for English learners in how questions and feedback are worded.

5. <u>How teachers hold expectations for student success and achievement.</u> In differentiated, SIOP® classrooms, teachers hold high academic expectations for all students, even though this may feel difficult at times.

Special Education

Unfortunately, special education programs are often treated as separate entities or a school-within-a-school. Perhaps it is because of different funding sources, the laws for individuals with disabilities, and/or the specialized certification that special education teachers must have. Whatever the reason, the students are as much a part of the student body as any other student and should be treated as such. Special education teachers need to be part of the professional development in which the rest of the staff participates, including the SIOP® Model. Such participation is important for a number of reasons.

- Special education is a service, not a place. Students identified as having special needs receive support and instruction from teachers with specialized training as needed.

- One goal of special education services reflected in the federal law is to include children with disabilities in the general education program to the greatest extent possible. In the vast majority of the cases, this means that students with disabilities are with their grade-level peers in general education most of the day. The specialist working with that student on his or her IEP goals needs to know the curriculum and methods being used in the general education classroom to be able to adequately support the student.

- Students in special education reflect the same ethnic demographics of the United States as do students in general education. That means that in some districts with high numbers of English learners, many children with disabilities are also ELs. In other districts, the numbers may be smaller, but appropriate services are just as important. Special education teachers should know best practices for working with ELs, as well as best practices for educating students with disabilities. (For additional information about the SIOP® Model and Special Education, See Echevarria, Vogt, & Short, 2008).

Through all of this discussion about classroom implementation of the SIOP® Model, one thing has not been mentioned, and that is the joy that teachers have reported when they realize that their content and language instruction is making a difference with their students who are English learners. In the opening quote by Kendra Moreno, she expresses the delight she feels when ELs begin to see themselves as capable learners. As all teachers know, that's just about the best feeling an educator can have.

Chapter Summary

This chapter may be the most important one in this book because it is in the classroom where the SIOP® Model must be implemented well if the academic achievement of English learners is to improve. Therefore, the chapter has focused on how to get started as a SIOP® teacher, how to plan for different classroom contexts, and how SIOP® lessons are designed. A variety of lesson plan formats are included to assist teachers in learning how include the SIOP® components and features in a lesson plan. Examples of content and language objectives are included along with suggestions for how to include them during lesson delivery. Differentiated classrooms are described and compared to non-differentiated classrooms. Suggestions are given for how to teach students to work on their own so that teachers can provide appropriate differentiated instruction to small groups of students, including English learners. Finally, issues related to the SIOP® Model and special education students are discussed.

Questions for Reflection and Discussion

1. Why do you suppose that many teachers find writing language objectives to be so challenging? What would you suggest to teachers new to the SIOP® Model to help them overcome their concerns about language objectives?

2. If you are a SIOP® trainer in your school or district, teach a group of students the steps for working independently. Model the steps and provide the students with practice in completing several independent routines. What is the students' reaction? How long do you think it will take this group of students to be able to work independently? Some experts predict that it might take as long as six weeks at the beginning of a school year for students to develop the social skills for independent work. What might teachers do to move this process along so that effective differentiated instruction is possible? Share the steps to independence with your collagues.

3. Discuss with the special educators in your school and district the percentage of English learners who have been referred for services. Does this number reflect the native-English-speaking population of special education students? How might the SIOP® Model stem the tide of overrepresentation (and sometime underrepresentation) of English learners in special education programs?

The Impact of the SIOP® Model on Students and Teachers

Research reviewed here has identified a number of instructional characteristics that are influential in promoting the academic success of ELLs. . . . What distinguishes research on ELLs from that on mainstream students is the importance of making the curriculum accessible to students who are not fully proficient in English. Indeed, research indicates the importance of incorporating language-development components and sheltering techniques into content instruction.

Lindholm-Leary & Borsato, 2006, p. 203

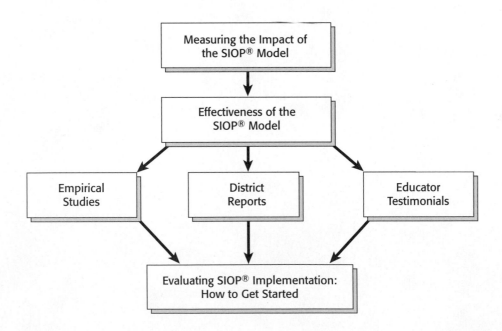

Educators who have been learning and practicing the SIOP® Model have consistently reported positive, observable changes in classroom practice. This impact on classroom practice is important because our ultimate goal is increasing student content knowledge and academic English proficiency, particularly for English learners. We want teachers to incorporate research-based practices shown to be effective with ELs, but having teachers know the SIOP® Model is not sufficient if the result is not a marked difference in the students' academic achievement. As the National Reading Panel (National Institute of Child Health and Human Development, 2000) concluded, inservice professional development that leads to improved teacher knowledge and practice can result in improved student achievement. As educators we want to know for certain that changes we make to classroom practices are beneficial for students.

Measuring the Impact of the SIOP® Model

One issue with the SIOP® Model is that significant change may not occur after a few weeks or even months of implementation. It is a process that takes time, as is true of most professional development. (See Chapter 2 for a discussion of the process of teacher change.) Teachers need to learn about the model, understand it, and spend time learning how best to implement it with their students. In SIOP® research to date (described in more detail later in this chapter), districts have found that most teachers take one to two years to implement the SIOP® Model consistently and to a high degree. The effect on student performance would take at least that long, most likely longer. It is important, therefore, to view SIOP® implementation as a long-term professional development program, perhaps even a school reform endeavor.

Many schools and districts began SIOP® implementation without planning to collect student data. As several of the teachers and district coordinators told us during these interviews, the focus was on improving teaching practices, not on collecting student achievement data. That direction usually shifted after one or two years of implementation, especially as SIOP® implementation became more widespread, either throughout one school (as at Lela Alston) or across many schools (as in Charlotte-Mecklenburg). Often the collection of student data was tied to program evaluation and in some cases, school boards were interested in results that would show they should continue to fund the SIOP® Model, especially if support came from local sources rather than federal funds. The teachers indicated that once SIOP® lesson planning became second nature, they were more focused on collecting evidence of the impact on the students.

Effectiveness of the SIOP® Model

We present three types of evidence for the effectiveness of the SIOP® Model in this chapter. First, we report the findings of several empirical studies already conducted and several that are in process. Second, we share evaluation and achievement results from a number of districts with improved student performance after implementation of the SIOP® Model. Third, we offer qualitative evidence from teachers, coaches, and administrators regarding positive changes in teacher practice as well as student performance.

Empirical Studies

Since we conducted the original SIOP® research for CREDE (Echevarria, Short, & Powers, 2006), some additional large-scale quasi-experimental and experimental studies have been taking place. These studies have involved SIOP® professional development along with analysis of student achievement and included not only the teachers and students where the SIOP® intervention occurs but also either matched comparison subjects (teachers and students) or randomly assigned treatment and control subjects (likewise, teachers and students). In addition, unlike during the original CREDE research when

Some members of the SIOP® research team: Jana Echevarria, Rebecca Canges, Dina Cassidy, and Cara Richards.

most of the students were exempted from state standardized testing, the more recent SIOP® studies are examining student performance on state exams and other measures. For example, in the Texas project below, the students are at primary grades and not yet subject to state testing. We describe these studies here but encourage you to look at www.cal.org and www.siopinstitute.net for updates and final results.

Academic Literacy through Sheltered Instruction for Secondary English Language Learners

- This study incorporates a quasi-experimental research design. It was conducted in two districts in New Jersey. Funded by the Carnegie Corporation of New York and the Rockefeller Foundation from 2004–2007, researchers from the Center for Applied Linguistics (CAL) have been collecting and analyzing data to investigate the relationship between professional development in the SIOP® Model and the academic achievement of secondary English language learners. One school district has received the SIOP® Model as the professional development treatment; the other was a comparison site. Both school districts have two middle schools and one high school with similar multilingual English learner populations. More than 500 ELs were in the treatment district and approximately 200 were in the comparison site both years, 2004–2006. Each district follows an ESL program design in grades 6–12 with some designated sheltered courses.

- In the treatment site, math, science, social studies, language arts, ESL, and technology teachers participated in ongoing SIOP® Model training. Approximately thirty-five teachers formed Cohort 1 in August 2004 and received intensive training and occasional coaching for the first year with follow-up training and more coaching the second. An additional twenty-five teachers formed Cohort 2 in the 2005–2006 school year and participated in the intensive training and some coaching for one year. Each cohort had seven days for workshops spread throughout the intensive year and Cohort 1 had three follow-up days their second year. The district supported three part-time, on-site coaches in the first year and added two more in the second year to accommodate the increased size of the teacher group. The coaches primarily facilitated after-school meetings and offered guidance in lesson design and material resources. Some coaches were able to make classroom visits. Ongoing support by CAL researchers was also provided via closed Listserv, a project-dedicated Web site, and online chats.

- The teachers in the comparison site did not receive any SIOP® Model training, but they continued with their regular district staff development. A total of twenty-two teachers participated at the comparison site for the two years.

- CAL researchers collected teacher implementation data (two classroom observations each year, one in the fall, the other in the spring) using the SIOP® protocol at both sites. Even though the comparison teachers were not trained in the SIOP® Model, the SIOP® protocol was used to evaluate the level of sheltered instruction they provided in their lessons so their overall teaching could be compared to the SIOP® teachers in the treatment site. In addition, pre- and post-SIOP® lesson plans have been collected at the treatment site to measure how well teachers incorporate SIOP® Model components in their preparation.

- Preliminary findings have shown that the SIOP® Model Cohort 1 teachers, on average, increased their level of SIOP® implementation from fall 2004 to fall 2005 as measured by the protocol almost 20 percent (Short & Bauder, 2006). The growth was nearly the same by school level: middle school teachers improved by 20 percent on average and high school teachers by 18 percent. Per SIOP® component, the range of the average percentage growth gain was from 12 percent (for Comprehensible Input) to 39 percent (for Lesson Delivery). The incorporation of SIOP® features in the teachers' lesson plans improved by more than 50 percent during the first year.

- Furthermore, the number of high implementers of the SIOP® Model increased to a greater extent in the treatment district than in the comparison district. High implementation was determined by a score of 75 percent or higher on the SIOP® protocol's rating scale. Low implementation was 50 percent or below. After one year of SIOP® professional development, 56 percent of Cohort 1 and 74 percent of Cohort 2 teachers in the treatment district implemented the model to a high degree. After two years, 71 percent of Cohort 1 reached a high level (Cohort 2 did not participate for a second year). In contrast, only 5 percent of the teachers reached a high level of implementation after one year at the comparison site and only 17 percent after two years (Center for Applied Linguistics, 2006).

- The researchers also collected student data: New Jersey state test results in reading, math, social studies, and science for grades 6 and 7, reading, math, and science for grade 8, and reading and math for grade 11 (or grade 12 for some ELs), and scores on the state-approved English language proficiency assessment, the IPT (Idea

Proficiency Test), for all ELs in grades 6–12. From the baseline year of 2003–2004 to Year 1 in 2004–2005, preliminary analyses showed that students who had SIOP®-trained teachers in the treatment site had a statistically significant percentage growth in their average IPT scores for the oral, reading, and writing subtests. By the second year (2005–2006), the treatment students out-performed the comparison students on these IPT tests (Center for Applied Linguistics, 2006).

- The final results for this study should be available in the fall of 2007.

Optimizing Educational Outcomes for English Language Learners

- This is a five-year experimental study conducted by the University of Houston, the University of Texas at Austin, the Center for Applied Linguistics, and the University of Miami (2003–2008). It is supported by the U.S. Department of Education, Institute of Education Sciences. Within this research project, the SIOP® Model is part of a larger intervention design to enhance academic language/literacy development and content knowledge in elementary school students in ESL and bilingual programs.

- The project follows a longitudinal, experimental design in order to evaluate traditional and enhanced models of ESL and bilingual programs in grades K–3. Approximately twelve schools in one district are participating. Some offer an early-exit bilingual (Spanish-English) program model; others, an ESL program. At the start, students and their grade-level classroom teachers were randomly assigned to a traditional or intervention kindergarten class within a program type. As the students progress up the grades, they stay in the traditional or intervention cohort, with new teachers assigned each year. The study thus follows the same students over four years as they are promoted from kindergarten to grade 3.

- The intervention consists of the following elements:
  - Tier I (core instruction)
    - Enhanced language enrichment in English and/or Spanish for phonics and reading (grades 1–3)
    - SIOP® Model instruction with a focus on mathematics classes (English or Spanish depending on the program) (grades K–3)
    - Additional language development using authentic text and focusing on vocabulary in English and/or Spanish (grades K–3)
  - Tier II
    - Classroom-based supplemental reading instruction (offered in small groups to students identified as not making expected progress) (grades K–3)
  - Tier III
    - Intensive small-group, pull-out intervention for reading instruction for students at risk of not learning to read (Grades 2–3)

- Data collection consists of classroom observations using the SIOP® protocol and other researcher-developed measures to determine the teachers' level of implementation of the several interventions. In addition, student data are collected in various ways. For treatment and control students from kindergarten through grade 3, the researchers gather results from pre- and post-assessments for literacy/language development in both English and Spanish. These outcome measures include the Woodcock Language Proficiency Battery (picture vocabulary, letter-word identification, listening comprehension) and other measures of early reading (letter names, letter sounds, phonological awareness, vocabulary, and word reading). When students reach grade 3, they will also be assessed with the Texas reading and mathematics tests.

- Findings from this study should be available in 2009.

The Impact of the SIOP® Model on Middle School Science and Language Learning

- This is the third large-scale study of the SIOP® Model to date. Like the Optimizing study, it is a five-year study funded by the U.S. Department of Education, Institute of Education Sciences (2005–2010). In this case, however, it is one of several studies in the national research center devoted to ELs known as CREATE (Center for Research on the Educational Achievement and Teaching of English Language Learners). The SIOP® research is conducted by researchers at California State University Long Beach, the Center for Applied Linguistics, and the University of Houston. This study uses a randomized experimental design to investigate the impact of the SIOP® Model on student academic achievement in middle school science. Researchers are developing science curriculum units with SIOP® lesson plans and science language assessments that focus on the acquisition of science concepts and academic literacy among English learners.

- The study is being conducted in phases. Phase 1 in 2005–2006 was a pilot study designed to 1) develop and refine science curriculum lessons that incorporate the SIOP® Model features and 2) field-test academic science language assessments. The four curriculum units and language assessments were revised as a result of the pilot study in two districts. Phase 2 (2006–2008) involves two one-year studies. In the first year, eight schools participated as treatment or control sites. Treatment teachers received SIOP® training, the SIOP® science lessons organized around four seventh-grade curriculum units, and coaching. In the second year, approximately twelve schools in another district will participate as Treatment 1, Treatment 2, or Control sites. Treatment 1 teachers will receive SIOP® training, the SIOP® science lessons, and coaching. Treatment 2 teachers will receive SIOP® training and coaching alone. The analyses will examine if SIOP® lessons help teachers learn the SIOP® Model faster or better. Student performance on science content and language assessments will also be analyzed. Phase 3 will occur in the final two years of the research center (2008–2010). At this time, the SIOP® science data results from Years 1–3 will be combined with the research findings from other CREATE research studies to form a school reform model. This new blended intervention for English learners will be evaluated in several sites across the United States.

- Data collection and analyses for Phases 2 and 3 will be of teacher implementation ratings using the SIOP® protocol and student state test results in reading, science, and English language proficiency. In addition, the researchers are collecting data from local district content tests and the project-developed science language assessments. Moreover, in order to compare student performance across all major CREATE studies, researchers will collect data on a norm-referenced, commercial test of reading and vocabulary.

- Findings from this study should be available in 2011.

District Reports

As mentioned at the beginning of this chapter, many districts have not collected data on the impact of the SIOP® Model. For those that have begun looking at their students' performance, the examination has rarely been done using a carefully controlled research design. Because many variables can have an impact on student performance, a carefully designed study would be needed to isolate the SIOP® Model intervention and determine its influence. Nonetheless, we can look at some of the reports from districts as adding to our body of knowledge on the SIOP® Model and as a first step to future, more rigorous investigations.

Lela Alston Elementary School, Phoenix, Arizona. Some districts have considered their students' performance over time on state tests and looked for improvement. Lela Alston, which initiated SIOP® professional development schoolwide in 2001, was a new school in a low-performing district. However, the administrators' concerted effort to train and coach all the teachers and work on grade-level lessons, as described in Chapters 4 and 5, led to remarkable growth in student achievement. The SIOP® Model was the only staff development initiative at the school for three years. Figure 8.1 below shows

FIGURE 8.1 *Lela Alston's Average Student Performance on State Tests, 2002–2004*

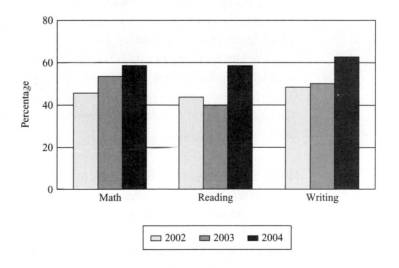

FIGURE 8.2 *Arizona's Instrument to Measure Standards, Spring 2004 Grade 3—Alston School*

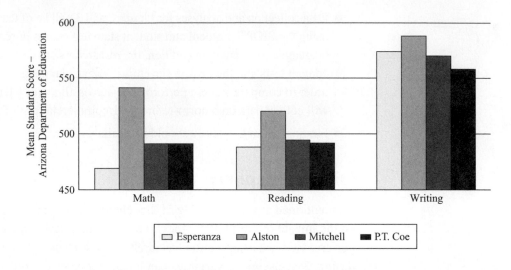

the student performance on the state standardized assessment, the Arizona Instrument to Measure Standards (AIMS), over three years in reading, mathematics, and writing. The progress shown is noteworthy. The 2002 student cohort averaged below 50 percent on all measures while the 2004 cohort reached close to 60 percent or above.

Alston staff also compared their school's results to similar schools in the Isaac School District. At the start of SIOP® implementation, Alston students performed on par or below the students in these three schools of similar socioeconomic status and performance. By the end of three years, Figure 8.2 shows how Alston outperformed the other schools. In fact, by 2004 Alston staff members were being asked to provide professional development to other elementary schools in the district and opened its doors to observations by teachers from these other schools.

Alston is located in a poor neighborhood with high levels of transience which leads to high levels of student mobility. Hence, many of the Alston students do not remain at the school for all four years. In 2004, the staff examined the achievement of those students who had started at Alston in kindergarten and continued through third grade. Figure 8.3 shows that 86 percent of those students had met or exceeded grade-level standards, which is noteworthy for any school, especially for one with Alston Elementary School's demographics.

Hillcrest Elementary School, Lawrence, Kansas. At the time of this writing, Hillcrest teachers had been implementing the SIOP® Model for more than two years. The average performance of ELs in the school was better than the average performance of ELs in the state for the state reading test in both the 2004 and 2005 school years. When the percentages are combined, more ELs at Hillcrest scored at the proficient, advanced,

FIGURE 8.3   *Off To A Good Start*

86% of third grade students who began in Alston's full-day kindergarten program are currently performing at or above grade level.

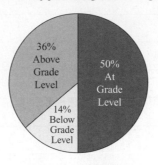

36%
Above
Grade
Level

50%
At
Grade
Level

14%
Below
Grade
Level

This graph represents the third grade students who began kindergarten at Alston Elementary in the fall of 2001.

and exemplary levels than ELs statewide as shown in Table 8.1 and Figure 8.4. Sixty-two percent for Hillcrest v. fifty-two percent for the state in 2004; eighty-three percent for Hillcrest v. sixty-seven percent for the state in 2005. The results for the statewide mathematics test in the two years were similar.

Tammy Becker, the principal at the elementary school, informed us that

Hillcrest continues to make AYP [adequate yearly progress, the benchmark set by the state to meet NCLB requirements] each year. We have been awarded the state's Standard of Excellence recognition in either Reading, Math, or both since 2000. Math in 2000, 2001, 2002, 2004, 2005, and 2006. Reading in 2002, 2003, and 2005.

Lewisville I.S.D., Lewisville, Texas.   As mentioned earlier, Alvaro Hernandez, Amy Washam, and Pam Creed developed districtwide training on the SIOP® Model for teachers

TABLE 8.1   *Kansas State Test Scores, Grade 5 Reading, 2004 and 2005, Hillcrest Elementary School*

	Exemplary		Advanced		Proficient		Basic		Unsatisfactory		Not Tested
	2004	2005	2004	2005	2004	2005	2004	2005	2004	2005	2005
All Students											
Building	14.6%	33.3%	46.3%	39.6%	9.8%	19.0%	19.5%	7.9%	9.8%	0.0%	1.5%
District	25.1%	29.1%	29.3%	28.7%	20.4%	20.0%	17.4%	15.7%	7.7%	6.3%	0.4%
State	20.7%	24.1%	28.9%	31.6%	22.5%	21.9%	20.3%	17.4%	7.5%	4.7%	0.1%
ELL											
Building	4.8%	41.6%	42.9%	33.3%	14.3%	8.3%	19.0%	16.6%	19.0%	0.0%	7.6%
District	13.5%	41.6%	32.4%	33.3%	16.2%	8.3%	18.9%	16.6%	18.9%	0.0%	7.6%
State	7.9%	17.7%	22.2%	27.4%	22.7%	21.7%	30.5%	25.2%	16.6%	7.8%	0.2%

FIGURE 8.4   *Project New Horizons: Reading Accomplishments: Lawrence, KS*

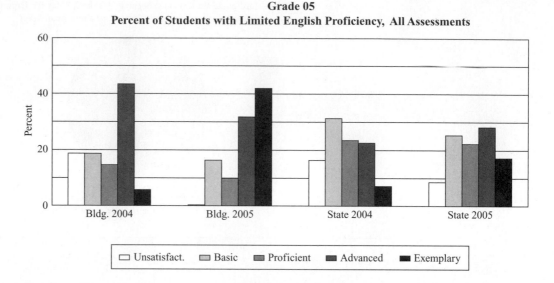

Grade 05
Percent of Students with Limited English Proficiency, All Assessments

Note: Bldg = Hillcrest Elementary School, Lawrence, Kansas

Socorro Herrara, Project New Horizons at the University of Kansas. Used with permission.

in the Lewisville Independent School District in Texas. Alvaro switched positions in the district and as assistant principal of Peters Colony Elementary School, he has led staff development on the SIOP® Model schoolwide since August 2005. He reported the following about English learner performance on Texas state exams:

> Student test scores went up in the first year of implementing the model, 2005–2006. We moved from an acceptable to a recognized campus [according to the Texas Education Agency's accountability scale].

He explained that "We have a vested interest in student achievement. . . . Holding teachers accountable makes a difference." The school also experienced a 50 to 79 percent increase in science test scores across the grade levels.

Charlotte-Mecklenburg Schools, North Carolina. The SIOP® Coach, Ivanna Mann Thrower, reported that six of the seven elementary school sites that were implementing the SIOP® Model in the 2005–2006 school year made the AYP benchmark set by the state to meet NCLB requirements. This was a significant finding because these schools had not made AYP the previous year.

CMS hired the Praxis Research group to perform a formative evaluation of SIOP® implementation in the 2005–2006 school year. As part of that effort, the researchers observed SIOP® and non-SIOP® teachers and rated their lessons using the SIOP® protocol. They also examined student performance on state end-of-grade reading and mathematics tests (for grades 3–8) and end-of-course exams in Algebra 1, Geometry,

English 1, U.S. History, and Biology (for grades 9–12). In addition, they gathered information about teacher professional development in the SIOP® Model and in other areas.

The results found that in terms of SIOP® lesson implementation, SIOP® teachers scored higher on the protocol than non-SIOP® teachers but not to a statistically significant level. Part of the interpretation for this had to consider the fact that some designated SIOP® teachers had been participating in SIOP® professional development for two years, others for one year, and two had not had any formal SIOP® training despite being labeled as SIOP® teachers.

Student performance was promising, according to the Praxis Research report (2006):

> The strongest findings supporting the positive effects of the model are found at the high school level, where student testing outcomes indicate statistically higher scores for students in SIOP® classrooms in Algebra I, Geometry, and English I when controlling for previous achievement and teacher experience. While the analysis fell just short of statistical significance at the middle school level, the trend data indicates greater gains in reading by students in SIOP® versus non-SIOP® classrooms.

There were no significant differences in scores for high school biology or U.S. history.

The elementary results were less conclusive. Although the non-SIOP® students outperformed the SIOP®-trained students on the reading assessment, the Praxis researchers pointed out that two of the SIOP® elementary reading teachers were the teachers with zero hours of formal SIOP® training. This fact may have had an effect on the results.

Educator Testimonials

The following are changes that have been observed in SIOP® classrooms across the country.

Positive Changes in Instructional Practice According to the interviewees, a good deal of the impact of the SIOP® Model was on teaching practice. Many teachers were able to become high implementers of the SIOP® Model with one year of sustained professional development. The teachers and their supervisors and coaches noticed the changes in practice, even if they did not rate the lessons using the SIOP® protocol.

Debbie Hutson, the Lela Alston Elementary School principal in Arizona, observed that her teachers were planning more effectively and actually engaged in the act of teaching more often than before SIOP® implementation.

> Improvement has been seen . . . with them teaching more, I mean, like up on their feet teaching more and working really hard to keep students engaged. I think their planning is much more effective. I think, too, with all of the training and all the different components that we've done, the teachers are so much more aware.

Tammy Becker, principal of Hillcrest Elementary School (Kansas), echoed this sentiment:

A very basic observation of that would be about five years ago, my first year here, if ELLs were in the classroom, which they would periodically be for an hour or so, I would see them and it was not unusual to see them sitting in the back of the room, often not engaged, scribbling on a paper. . . . I never see that today in any of our classrooms. So just that piece about the constant dialogue with the kids is huge. And I honestly think that we have a much better appreciation of all of our cultures and teachers are constantly working. In probably every one of my classrooms, there are probably five to seven ethnic groups represented, so it's a challenge, but it also has allowed teachers to branch out and get to know our families better.

The formative evaluation conducted by Praxis Research in Charlotte-Mecklenburg schools revealed that the teachers who were implementing the SIOP® Model had high levels of satisfaction. The teachers were particularly pleased with the flexibility for instruction that was embedded in the model. The coach, Ivanna Mann Thrower, told us that by the second year of staff development and coaching, many of the teachers "get it." In other words, they understand the features of the model and how to plan and deliver successful SIOP® lessons.

Nicole Teyechea, SIOP® National Faculty, gave an example of how changes in teacher practice led to improved student outcomes.

You see a teacher who is doing the SIOP® Model next to a teacher who's [not and] the scores are completely different. We had a teacher who was doing a lot of the SIOP® Model, and her ninth and tenth graders took the same test as her eleventh and twelfth graders in English and did better than the eleventh and twelfth graders.

The Effect of Language and Content Objectives. It would be expected that the posting of objectives—especially language objectives—would be something new and different in most classrooms. However, it is the effect of the objectives that makes the difference. Some teachers reported that they didn't have a specific content objective in mind for all their lessons previously, which led to unfocused instruction. Once they posted language and content objectives in the classroom and discussed them during lessons, lessons were more focused and effective, and students noticed the difference. Teachers and SIOP® trainers made the following comments about the impact of objectives on teacher practice and student learning during exchanges on the SIOP Institute's® electronic Listserv. (They are identified by their geographic location.)

- Teachers who took our SIOP®-based course last year commented most on the benefits of writing and stating the content and language objectives before a lesson. They help the teacher stay focused and at the end of the lesson give the teacher and students a sense of accomplishment when they go back and check off what they learned. (Alaska)

- I saw one teacher get a lesson back on track by pointing to the objectives and stating that they had a lot to cover so they needed to stay focused. (Arizona)

- It's also a basic learning styles issue. Some students are more visual learners so seeing the objectives will register with them when hearing the objectives may not. (Arkansas)

- One of our model teachers here says she feels posting the objective is important to keep herself on track! (Oklahoma)

- I am a classroom teacher. My students appreciate having the objectives up and often times they add to the objectives after class. They also write the objectives in their agendas at the beginning of each class. (Texas)

- Not only does it help the students, but when the teacher has to write out the objectives, s/he can be sure that lesson activities do in fact lead towards meeting them. (Arkansas)

- This does not really take that much time once put into practice. It's like writing the date on the board. Plus, look at the advantage of writing complete sentences on the board—students get a spelling lesson, a sentence lesson, and a strategy to help them as adults: that is, to write things down. (Nevada)

- For ELs, objectives provide the much-needed context that helps them put the individual lessons into their "what is this for, what does this mean to me?" schema. (California)

Remarkably, the impact of language and content objectives has also been expressed by students, as this account describes. A second grade class had been reading "how-to" books and students were told to create their own, by writing about something they knew how to do. Figure 8.5 shows that one student wrote about how to make popcorn. Notice that on her own initiative she wrote a content and language objective for her directions; it was not part of the teacher's instructions for the assignment!

Evaluating SIOP® Implementation: How to Get Started

Because many districts are eager to provide widespread staff development on the SIOP® Model and thus direct resources to that goal, they may wait several years before they collect data on the effectiveness of the model. To help with this situation, we offer formative evaluation guidelines that might jump-start the process.

1. Decide on a means for comparing student achievement without SIOP® implementation and with it. Some options include
   - Historical tracking: collect, organize, and compare data to show how similar students had been performing on assessment measures, such as state tests within the

(Continued on p. 179)

FIGURE 8.5 *Student-Made Booklet*

How To Make Popcorn.

Written By Angelica
Illustrated By Angelica

Content Objective:
You will Pop
a bag of Popcorn
Without burning.

· Popcorn
· Microwave
· Bowl

Language Objective:
You will read
a how to Book.

Step 1
You will
need a bag of
Popcorn.

Step 2
Next You will
put it in the
Microwave and wart
1 minute.

Step 3
Then You stop
the Microwave and get
it out.

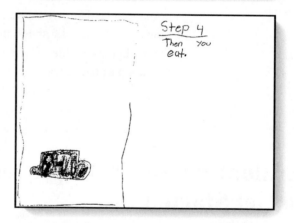

Step 4
Then you
eat.

Step 5
You will wash
your bowl and
hands.

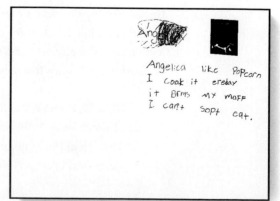

Angelica like Popcorn
I cook it ereday
it Brms my moff
I cant sopt eat.

district (or the school if implementation is schoolwide), for a few years before SIOP® implementation began, and a few years afterward.

- Comparisons to state average performance for ELs: collect student performance on state measures during SIOP® implementation and compare to EL performance statewide.

- Comparisons to other districts in the state that are not implementing the SIOP® Model: compare student performance on state tests in the SIOP® district with performance in a non-SIOP® district. Try to find a comparable district in demographic and socioeconomic terms.

- Matched comparisons with other schools in the district: if the SIOP® Model is being implemented widely in one school but not in others of similar backgrounds (in terms of student population, language background, socioeconomic status, teacher experience, etc.), student performance can be compared.

- Matched comparison groups within the school: if one group of students would receive SIOP® Model instruction and another group of similar students would not, then comparisons at the school level are possible. Caution must be taken to avoid cross-fertilization of SIOP® practices as can happen when a SIOP® teacher inadvertently shares SIOP® techniques with a non-SIOP® teacher and that teacher begins to implement aspects of the SIOP® Model.

2. <u>Determine who the student subjects will be.</u> A district or school may want to track the same students over time as they receive SIOP® Model teaching as they move up the grade levels, or the district or school may want to compare cohorts at a particular grade level.

3. <u>Choose assessment measures and collect baseline data.</u> No matter which type of comparison is selected, it is important to gather and organize the baseline data to show how students were performing prior to SIOP® implementation. If, for example, teachers begin learning the SIOP® Model at a summer institute for implementation the following school year, collect test scores (e.g., state tests, district exams, end-of-course assessments), portfolio entries (or other student work samples that are required of the treatment and comparison students), or other benchmark measures from the previous spring. When choosing an assessment measure, look for one that will endure. States often change their tests, as do schools, so if you want longitudinal data, it is useful to invest in an assessment that will last throughout the time of the evaluation.

4. <u>Support a sustained implementation process.</u> We know that for the SIOP® Model to be effective teachers must be engaged in ongoing staff development. One three-day summer workshop will not be sufficient without follow-up. It is not worth conducting a formative evaluation without a sustained plan designed to help teachers implement the model fully in their classrooms.

5. <u>Document the implementation activities and additional professional development initiatives.</u> Record what supports have been offered to teachers to implement the SIOP® Model well and which teachers partook of the activities. If additional initiatives are taking place at the same time in the school or district (e.g., staff development on a new mathematics textbook series, curriculum development

for language arts), keep track of those efforts and the participation of SIOP® teachers too.

6. <u>To the extent possible, document professional development activities and other initiatives at the comparison site, if there is one.</u> Although another district might not be implementing the SIOP® Model, it might have different initiatives or school reform models in place. It is important to record this information to help in the data analysis and interpretation later.

7. <u>Collect data during the implementation process.</u> This step is the crux of the formative evaluation process. Without data, the formative evaluation is pointless. Two kinds of data may be collected:

   - Teacher level of implementation of the SIOP® Model (a strong SIOP® teacher may improve student performance more than a weak SIOP® teacher) using the SIOP® protocol

   - Student performance on the selected measures

     The collection of other information may be informative as well and could help round out the interpretation of the results. For example, changes to teacher attitude and knowledge base could be surveyed, student attendance records could be monitored, and drop-out and graduation rates could be examined.

8. <u>Analyze the results.</u> By analyzing and interpreting the data, the implementers can determine if the goal for student achievement is being met. Further, because it is formative, the process allows for adjustments to the implementation plan in future years.

While these guidelines do not set forth a rigorous, randomized experiment, they will allow a school or district to track change while implementing the SIOP® Model and determine the benefit to students. It is hard in a dynamic system like a school or district to fully attribute the impact of one professional development approach, such as the SIOP® Model, because the implementation rarely takes place in a vacuum. However, by systematically recording what is taking place, by monitoring teacher participation, by collecting data at regular intervals, and by gathering comparison data from a similar group of students, the stakeholders can have a clearer picture of the impact of the SIOP® Model.

Chapter Summary

In this chapter we have shared information on the impact of the SIOP® Model on teachers and students. The results are quite promising, although the large-scale research studies have not yet concluded. Districts and schools are beginning to collect data on SIOP® implementation and student performance, and we encourage more to do so. We have offered some guidelines for getting started with a formative evaluation process at the site level.

Questions for Reflection and Discussion

1. If you are already implementing the SIOP® Model, what would you report as its impact on your teachers and students? How would you know? What evidence could you offer to show that the SIOP® Model is making a difference?

2. Work with other educators involved in SIOP® implementation at your school or district and sketch a plan for a formative evaluation. What measures would you use to determine the effect of SIOP® Model instruction? How would you collect and store the data you need? Over what period of time would you gather information?

Epilogue:
Lessons Learned

If I had to start a SIOP® professional development program again, first I would sit and make a plan with the school and ask, "How do you plan on implementing the SIOP® as part of your instructional program?" Doing a long-term plan would be the first step, including how to pull existing practices into the SIOP® framework—to work smarter instead of harder.

Nicole Teyechea, SIOP® National Faculty

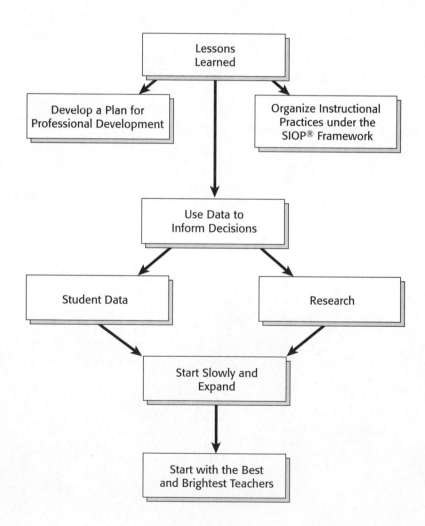

One of the most valuable aspects of interviewing individuals who have implemented the SIOP® Model over time was the insight they provided into how they resolved many of the shared issues that are part of professional development and the culture of our educational system: not enough time, too many demands, limited resources—the list goes on. While there aren't magical solutions contained in this epilogue, there are lessons to be learned.

Taken as a whole, interviewees' reflections coalesced into several general lessons learned. In particular, SIOP® National Faculty have had years of experience using and teaching the SIOP® Model in their own districts and across the country. Our hope is that through the discussion of their experiences presented here, some challenges may be resolved and others avoided.

Lesson 1: Develop a Plan for SIOP® Professional Development

When John Seidlitz, SIOP® National Faculty, begins work with a school district on SIOP® training, he poses the following question to the administrator who has invited him: "How are we going to get teachers to implement the SIOP® in their classroom, know that they are implementing it, and then improve their level of implementation?" By considering this question, John reports, districts can start to develop a systematic plan for effective implementation. He recommends that follow-up sessions be scheduled before the initial SIOP® presentation even takes place. In that way, a comprehensive plan is set up, teachers know the expectations, and the administrative commitment is clear.

Nicole Teyechea, SIOP® National Faculty and former ELL facilitator for Oxford Schools, echoes John's advice. She mentioned the importance of developing a plan based on a school's or district's resources. In her words:

From the very beginning, develop a plan by brainstorming [about resources]: "What days do you have for training?" "What would you want to start with in that training?" "What type of support services do you have?" Also, look at their curriculum, look at their lesson plans and see how it all ties in together to see where [it fits] the SIOP® system.

Lesson 2: Organize Instructional Practices under the SIOP® Framework

Nicole's comment above regarding tying things together was reiterated by many interviewees who talked about the way that they used the SIOP® as a framework for instruction. Educators today are inundated with school reform initiatives, which sometimes create a tension between professional development activities. The SIOP® Model is a framework based on best practice, so virtually any effective method, technique, or instructional approach could align with the SIOP®.

Rosie Santana, a SIOP® professional developer in Idaho, learned the lesson that effective practices don't have to compete with one another. In Figure E.1, you can see how she conceptualized the relationship between the excellent work of the following well-known educators: Gregory & Parry (2003), Marzano, Pickering, & Pollock (2001), Tomlinson (2001), and Payne (2001). While some of the features of these approaches were separated on the chart (e.g., notice Payne's 4a and 4b) to align with the eight SIOP® components, you can see that the essential elements of each is represented. Rosie's creation demonstrates that research-based practices are compatible with one another and the SIOP® Model provides a nice framework around which teachers organize effective practice.

With nearly 80,000 K–12 students, Fresno Unified School District is the fourth largest school district in California. As such, many professional development opportunities are offered. The Title III staff has organized other trainings under the SIOP® umbrella so that all professional development aligns with the SIOP® components, as seen in Figure E.2.

So the lesson learned is that a prudent use of resources is to align them under the SIOP® framework. The SIOP® Model is compatible with, not in competition with, other effective instructional practices.

Lesson 3: Use Student Data to Inform Teachers and Administrators

A number of interviewees talked about the importance of using student achievement data to focus in on areas that need improvement. If students score particularly low in vocabulary, for instance, then lessons may be adjusted accordingly. Some schools used student data to drive the focus of SIOP® professional development or the discussions within learning communities.

FIGURE E.1 *Sheltered Instruction Observation Protocol—SIOP®: An Inclusive Framework*

The following table displays the correlation between the eight components of the SIOP® Model and other research-based instruction. Key areas from the research are placed based on their strongest correlation with the specific SIOP® component(s).

Echevarria, Vogt, & Short (2008). *Making Content Comprehensible for English Learners: The SIOP® Model*	Gregory & Parry (2003). *Designing Brain Compatible Learning*	Marzano, Pickering, & Pollock (2001). *Classroom Instruction That Works*	Tomlinson (2001). *How to Differentiate Instruction in Mixed-Ability Classrooms*	Payne (2001). *A Framework for Understanding Poverty*
*Components**	*Correlation with SIOP® Components*			
Preparation		Setting objectives (2a)*	Whole class preparation Clear criteria	Defining poverty Creating relationships
Building Background	Activating prior learning		Based on readiness, interest, and learning profile	Hidden rules Generational or situational poverty?
Comprehensible Input	Setting the context	Identifying similarities & differences Nonlinguistic representation Advanced organizers (3b)	Organizers, study guides, modeling, clear criteria, student reading levels, tape recorders, manipulatives	The role of language
Strategies	Instructional phase Checking for understanding	Summarizing & note taking		Role models Support systems Discipline Instruction (4a)
Interaction		Cooperative learning	Whole group, small group, individualized, student-teacher sharing	
Practice/Application	Practice & application	Homework & practice Generating & testing hypothesis	Exploration, sense-making, extension, and production Multiple modes	
Lesson Delivery		Reinforcing effort (1a) Questions, cues (3a)		
Review/Assessment	Closure & extension	Providing recognition (1b) Providing feedback (2b)	Reteaching/extended teaching & review	Improving achievement (4b)

*The (1a), (1b), etc., represent a key area that has been split to better match a specific SIOP® component.

Created by Rosie Santana.

In discussing the importance of consistent SIOP® implementation, Wanda Holbrook, SIOP® National Faculty and SIOP® Coach at Alston Elementary School, suggested that using student data is a powerful way of motivating teachers to improve their teaching with English learners. She suggested that the coach or principal talk with the teachers who need assistance (but may not want it) and say, "Okay, let's look at the data. What do you need to do? Why don't you get with the coach and see if you can't work out some things that would make it better."

FIGURE E.2   *What is the CORE Institute?*

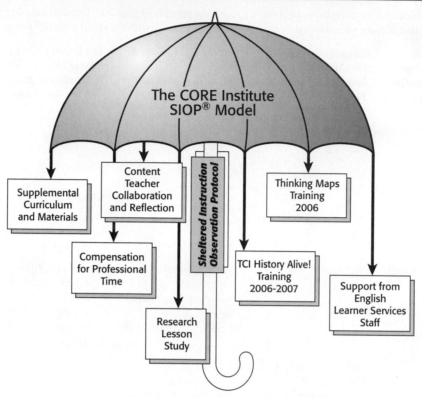

The Features of the CORE Institute

Lesson 4: Use Research to Inform Professional Development Decisions

One of the advantages of NCLB is its emphasis on scientifically validated practices. Educators are more conscientious about approaches that are research based and want to be sure that instructional practices are defensible. The SIOP® Model was developed using research-based practices, and the latest research syntheses on English learners reinforce its validity. Researcher Claude Goldenberg took the findings of the National Literacy Panel on Language Minority Children and Youth along with the research synthesis from Center for Research on Education, Diversity, and Excellence and summarized both reports (Goldenberg, 2006). In Figure E.3, we show how the features of the SIOP® Model align with the current research on instruction for English learners.

This figure may be used when discussing the SIOP® Model with reluctant administrators or teachers. It clearly shows that the SIOP® Model reflects the most cutting-edge research on the education of English learners to date.

Lesson 5: Start Slowly and Expand

This particular lesson applies to the way the SIOP® Model is presented during professional development as well as how quickly capacity is built. With respect to the professional development sessions, John Seidlitz warns,

(Continued on p. 189)

FIGURE E.3 *Alignment of Research with SIOP® Components*

Improving Achievement for English-Learners: What Research Tells Us	SIOP® Components

Improving Achievement for English-Learners: What Research Tells Us

"Ell students benefit from . . ."
- clear goals and objectives.
- predictable, clear, and consistent instructions, expectations and routines.

"Providing English-language development instruction and opportunities to extend oral English skills is critical for ELL students. This places an increased burden on students and teachers alike, since every lesson should target content and English-language development."

"Many educators have also suggested that effective instruction for ELL students must be tailored to the cultures of the students, that is, incorporate the behavioral and interactional patterns rooted in student's cultures."

"What constitutes effective vocabulary instruction for ELLs is not well understood; but there can be little doubt that explicit attention to vocabulary development should be part of English-learner's school programs."

"Their language limitations begin to slow their progress as vocabulary and content knowledge become increasingly important, around the 3rd grade. It is thus critical that, from the very beginning, teachers work to develop these students English-language skills, particularly vocabulary."

"With regard to learning to read, English-learners benefit from instruction that . . ."
- targets vocabulary
- is designed to enhance vocabulary
- builds upon students knowledge and skills in their native language

SIOP® Components

Preparation

1. Content objectives are clearly defined, displayed and reviewed with students

2. Language objectives are clearly defined, displayed and reviewed with students

3. Content concepts appropriate for age and educational background level of students

4. Supplementary materials used to a high degree, making the lesson clear and meaningful (graphs, models, visuals)

5. Adaptation of content (e.g., text, assignment) to all levels of student proficiency

6. Meaningful activities that integrate lesson concepts (e.g., surveys, letter writing, simulations, constructing models) with language practice opportunities for reading, writing, listening, and/or speaking

Building Background

7. Concepts explicitly linked to students' background experiences

8. Links explicitly made between past learning and new concepts

 9. Key vocabulary emphasized (e.g., introduced, written, repeated and highlighted for students to see)

(Continued)

FIGURE E.3   *Alignment of Research with SIOP® Components*   *(Continued)*

Improving Achievement for English-Learners: What Research Tells Us

SIOP® Components

"ELL student benefit from . . ."

- predictable, clear, and consistent instructions, expectations and routines
- physical gestures
- visual cues
- well-designed instructional routines

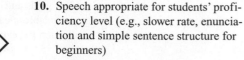

Comprehensible Input

10. Speech appropriate for students' proficiency level (e.g., slower rate, enunciation and simple sentence structure for beginners)

11. Clear explanation of academic tasks

12. A variety of techniques used to make content concepts clear (e.g., modeling, visuals, hands-on activities, demonstrations, gestures, body language)

"An important finding from the NLP was that the impact of instructional interventions is weaker for English-learners then it is for English-speakers, suggesting that additional supports, or accommodations, are needed in order for ELLs to derive as much benefit from effective instructional practices."

"ELL student benefit from . . ."
- Extended explanations
- Redundant information
- Consolidating text knowledge through summarization

Strategies

13. Ample opportunities provided for student to use strategies

14. Scaffolding techniques consistently used throughout lesson, assisting and supporting student understanding such as think-alouds

15. A variety of questions or tasks that promote higher-order thinking skills (e.g., literal, analytical, and interpretive questions)

"Academic instruction in the students' home language should be part of the educational program for English language learners, if at all possible."

"The NLP found that teaching reading skills in the first language is more effective in terms of second language achievement then immersing children in English."

"Primary language instruction can boost student achievement in the second language by about 12 to 15 percentile points."

"Evidence suggests that literacy and other skills and knowledge transfer across languages; if you learn something in one language, you either know it or can easily learn it in a second language."

"ELL students benefit from . . ."
- active engagement and participation
- opportunities to interact with other students
- Strategic use of primary language
- Focusing on the similarities/ differences between English and the native language
- Paraphrasing students remarks and encouraging expansion
- Identifying and clarifying difficult words and passages

Interaction

16. Frequent opportunities for interactions and discussion between teacher/student and among students, which encourage elaborated responses about lesson concepts

17. Grouping configurations support language and content objective of the lesson

18. Sufficient wait time for student responses consistently provided

19. Ample opportunities for students to clarify key concepts in L1

FIGURE E.3 *Alignment of Research with SIOP® Components* *(Continued)*

Improving Achievement for English-Learners: What Research Tells Us	SIOP® Components

Improving Achievement for English-Learners: What Research Tells Us

SIOP® Components

"Writing instruction also makes a contribution to ELLs literacy development."

"Providing English-language development instruction and opportunities to extend oral English skills is critical for ELL students."

"ELL students benefit from . . ."
- providing extra practice in reading words, sentences, and stories
- additional opportunities for practice
- opportunities to practice and apply new learning and transfer it to new situations

"ELL students benefit from . . ."
- Clear goals and objectives
- Predictable, clear, and consistent instructions, expectations and routines
- Active engagement and participation
- Well-designed instructional routines

"ELL students benefit from . . ."
- information feedback
- periodic review and practice
- frequent assessments, and re-teaching as needed
- checking comprehension frequently

Practice and Application

20. Hands-on materials and/or manipulatives provided for students to practice using new content knowledge

21. Activities provided for students to apply content and language knowledge in the classroom

22. Activities integrate all language skills (i.e., reading, writing, listening, and speaking)

Lesson Delivery

23. Content objectives clearly supported by lesson delivery

24. Language objectives clearly supported by lesson delivery

25. Students engaged approximately 90–100% of the period (see Glossary)

26. Pacing of the lesson appropriate to the students' ability level

Review/Assessment

27. Comprehensive review of key vocabulary

28. Comprehensive review of key content concepts

29. Regular feedback provided to students on their output (e.g., language, content, work)

30. Assessment of student comprehension and learning of all lesson objectives (e.g., spot checking, group response) throughout the lesson

C. Goldenberg (July 26, 2006) Education Week Based on NLP (August & Shanahan, 2006) & CREDE synthesis (Genesee, Lindholm-Leary, Saunders & Christian, 2006).

Based on *Making Content Comprehensible for English Learners: The SIOP® Model* (2008). Echevarria, Vogt & Short,

---

Go slowly or you'll scare the teachers on implementation. Go component by component [one per session], although you may speed up over time.

Although many of the features of the SIOP® Model are part of teachers' repertoire, the eight components and thirty features may be overwhelming to implement all at once. As detailed in Chapter 4, most effective programs concentrated on one component, practiced the features of that component, then added the next component.

While best practice may be to focus on one component at a time, Melissa Castillo emphasized the importance of having teachers understand that the components are part of a comprehensive model. She suggested that SIOP® professional development begin with an overview of the whole model so that participants see how the pieces fit together. She said,

> I think it was important that teachers got trained on the whole model along with the [first component of] lesson planning. Now as they started implementing the model in their own classrooms, I can see putting an emphasis on one piece at a time. But I think if teachers don't see how the whole model works, they don't get it as they're implementing a piece at a time.

In terms of building capacity, even districts that had widespread implementation suggested that perhaps beginning more slowly would have been preferable. One school district was concerned about the low achievement of their English learners, so they implemented the SIOP® Model in every one of their seventeen schools at the same time. Their motive was that they wanted every student to have the benefit of SIOP® teaching. However, such an ambitious rollout resulted in inconsistent implementation. The lesson the ELL director came away with was that it may have been more effective to work with a smaller number of teachers and ensure that they had a deep understanding of the model, and then move on to another group. As she explained it,

> I think I would put the focus on a smaller number of schools and try to target them [for intensive training] and then target another group of schools. [I'd] limit the amount of teachers being trained and really add to the follow-through. Then those become your model schools. I would limit my focus and really go in depth. I think when we start to panic is when kids in the meantime are moving through these [non-SIOP®] classes.

Lesson 6: Start with Your Best and Brightest Teachers

Some districts attempted to bring all teachers on board, or those who most "need it." In retrospect, experienced SIOP®ers advise readers to put time and resources into the teachers who are positive and will influence others. As John Seidlitz puts it,

> Choose high fliers to work with first. This is not a remedial teaching program.

Marilyn Sanchez agreed:

> What we've learned is that positives breed other positives, so if you start with someone who really wants to do it and they have a good experience, then that's what spreads it. It never spreads from the top down, it spreads because teachers are empowered.

Final Thoughts

In our observations as authors, we have seen that there is passion and commitment for teaching English learners that is heartening, and one of the most gratifying aspects of our professional lives has been to get to know educators such as those profiled in this book. We appreciate their dedication and the lessons they have learned while implementing the SIOP® Model. Our lesson learned is that educators who strive to improve instruction for English learners do so not out of obligation, but out of dedication to their well-being and future prosperity.

appendix a: historical overview of the SIOP® Model and the SIOP Institute®

In the mid-1990s, as increasing numbers of English learners (ELs) were entering public schools in the United States, educators (particularly ESL, bilingual teachers, and selected classroom teachers) received professional development in how to teach recently arrived immigrant students whose home language was not English. The techniques and methods that were shared during inservices, workshops, and university classes consisted primarily of a range of ESL (English as a Second Language) instructional strategies and sheltered instruction, an approach that extends the time students have for receiving English language support while they learn content subjects. The ultimate goal of sheltered instruction is to provide access for ELs to grade-level content standards and concepts while they continue to improve their English language proficiency (Echevarria, Vogt, & Short, 2008). Generally, sheltered content classes (such as math, science, and social studies) have enrolled English learners with varying levels of English proficiency, and in some cases, a mix of both native English speakers and ELs. In sheltered classes, the language of instruction is English.[1]

In a few states, legislation was enacted that required teachers to receive professional development in how to teach English learners. However, when we (Jana Echevarria and MaryEllen Vogt on the West Coast and Deborah Short on the East Coast) visited classrooms and observed subject area lessons taught by these newly prepared teachers, we did not see many who were implementing effective sheltered lessons for English learners. After discussions among ourselves and with colleagues across the country, we realized that even though instructional techniques were recommended in the ESL literature, in reality there was little agreement about what effective sheltered instruction was and how it should "look" during lessons. Definitions and descriptions varied widely across the country, with most including a list of activities and techniques, few of which had been empirically validated with English learners. To further compound the problem, most school administrators were not receiving professional development in the unique learning and language needs of ELs, and were therefore unable to provide their teachers with instructional assistance after lesson observations, and during conferences about the needs of English learners.

In 1995, we began the process of creating an observation protocol that could be used by researchers, administrators, university supervisors, coaches, and teachers to conference and discuss sheltered lessons for English learners. Our goal was to operationalize sheltered instruction so that educators would have a common language to use when discussing appropriate content instruction for ELs. We also were convinced that English learners do not have the luxury of waiting to learn content until they have mastered English. Instead, they must be able to develop English language proficiency and content knowledge concurrently. Therefore, all teachers who have ELs in their classrooms must know how to implement effective sheltered instruction consistently and systematically. A common definition and instructional framework for this important instructional approach was needed.

---

[1]Note that as the SIOP® Model is implemented in a variety of settings, including two-way immersion, the language of instruction may vary.

Using research findings on ESL/bilingual methods, articles on best practice, and our own experiences as teachers (elementary, middle, and high school; regular education, ESL/bilingual, special education, and language/literacy specialization), we began to create what ultimately became the Sheltered Instruction Observation Protocol or SIOP® (pronounced *sigh-op*). Through a federally funded grant to CREDE, the Center for Research on Education, Diversity, & Excellence, the SIOP® developmental process occurred over five years. During this process, we collaborated closely with teachers who helped shape our thinking, field-tested the SIOP® Model in their own classrooms, implemented the SIOP® components with their students, and eventually became project teachers for a research study (see Echevarria, Vogt, & Short, 2008 for detailed information about the research project and findings). The teacher-researcher collaboration greatly enhanced the SIOP® as it evolved through twenty-two iterations to its present form with eight components and thirty features.

As you review the components and features of the SIOP® Model, many if not most will be familiar to you. Our original task was to take what we know to be effective instructional techniques (such as increasing wait time after questioning) and determine if they positively impact the student achievement of ELs when they are used in combination and to a high degree. At the conclusion of the research study, the English learners in the classrooms of teachers who implemented the thirty SIOP® features to a high degree outperformed those ELs in classrooms where teachers had received professional development in sheltered instruction, but not specifically in the SIOP® Model (see Echevarria, Short, & Powers, 2006).

What began as an observation protocol has now evolved into an empirically validated model of instruction for English learners, where the focus is on the concurrent teaching and learning of both language and content. While the SIOP® Model was originally substantiated with middle school students, it is now being implemented in pre-K through grade 12 throughout the United States and in other countries. Our research has shown that given sustained professional development (from one to three years), teachers can learn to implement the thirty features consistently and systematically, from lesson to lesson. Current longitudinal research studies are investigating the efficacy of the SIOP® Model with varied student populations over time.

SIOP Institutes® were created by the authors of the SIOP® Model in 2002 as a way of meeting the demand for professional development in the model. The first SIOP I Institute® was held at California State University, Long Beach (Jana Echevarria and MaryEllen's Vogt's university). The Center for Applied Linguistics (CAL), where Deborah Short worked as director of language education and academic development, created two videotapes with teachers trained in the SIOP® Model and classroom scenarios. A training manual for use at the Institutes was also produced by CAL.

Within a year, the SIOP Institute® LLC was created to offer professional development to teachers and administrators at various sites throughout the country. The SIOP II Institute®, advanced training in the SIOP® Model, and the SIOP Institute® for Administrators were subsequently created to respond to the many requests for additional training by educators who had attended the SIOP I Institute®.

Although many interviewees for this book attended SIOP Institutes®, attendance is not a prerequisite for effectively implementing the SIOP® Model. Receiving training from Institute presenters who have deep knowledge of the SIOP® Model was beneficial to many districts, but others have learned and practiced the model by using the core book (Echevarria, Vogt, & Short, 2002, 2004, 2008) as a guide.

Currently (as of this writing) there are three types of SIOP Institutes® offered (see www.siopinstitute.net for more information):

1. The SIOP I Institute® is a 2 1/2-day intensive training on the model that provides an opportunity for participants to explore the research-based framework of the SIOP® Model for English learners and identify and describe the eight components of the SIOP® Model. In addition, participants develop skills and instructional strategies for introducing the SIOP® Model to teachers, coaches, specialists, administrators, and teacher educators.

2. The SIOP II Institute® is a two-day session intended to be advanced training for individuals who have previously attended a SIOP I Institute®, who have read the core text (Echevarria, Vogt, & Short, 2008), and who have experience implementing the SIOP® Model. At the SIOP II Institute®, participants identify issues, successes, and challenges of SIOP® Model implementation, develop teachniques to help teachers differentiate classroom instruction, identify various coaching methods, discuss ways to assist struggling readers and learners, and practice rating SIOP® Model lessons, justifying and negotiating the SIOP® protocol scores.

3. The SIOP Institute® for Administrators is a two-day session designed for school and district leaders. Administrators are provided an abbreviated overview of the SIOP® Model including its research underpinnings. Implementation issues, such as funding, inservices and workshop schedules, establishing teacher buy-in, and supporting teachers through use of the SIOP® protocol are discussed.

Between 2002 and 2005, interest in the SIOP® Model and the SIOP Institutes® grew much more quickly than the SIOP Institute® LLC could possibly accommodate. Furthermore, we received many requests from school districts throughout the country for follow-up training in the SIOP® Model. Certainly, sustained professional development is something we advocate, as we well know that learning to implement the SIOP® Model consistently and systematically is a process that takes time and ongoing support. Therefore, in 2005, the SIOP Institute® LLC was acquired by Pearson Education, and a new professional development division, Pearson Achievement Solutions, was created to coordinate and manage all of the SIOP Institutes®, a variety of district trainings in the SIOP® Model (see www.siopinstitute.net) and other offerings (see www.pearsonachievement.com). National Faculty, educators with extensive professional development experience with the SIOP® Model, provide most of the training through the SIOP Institutes®.

As the authors of the SIOP® Model, we are now primarily involved in research and writing about the model. Although we developed the format and content of the original SIOP® Institute, and we appreciate Pearson's continuation of these professional development opportunities, we no longer operate or have a financial interest in the SIOP Institute®.

appendix b: reliability and validity study of the SIOP®

The raters were four experts in sheltered instruction (or SDAIE) from three major universities in southern California. Three held doctorates in education while the other was earning a second master's degree (one in education). Their total teaching experience was more than 55 years.

A single-blind design was employed. Three of the videos were judged by the principal investigator to be highly representative of the tenets of SI while the other three were not. The raters observed all six videos (each video was approximately 45 minutes long) and scored the teacher on a 1 (no evidence) to 7 (clearly evident) Likert-type scale on the 31[*] items that comprised the 8 subscales. Preparation, Building Background, Comprehensible Input, Strategies, Interaction, Practice/Application, Lesson Delivery, and Review/Evaluation. Cronbach's Alpha was calculated for all 8 scales. Because an important decision was going to be made about an individual, Alpha's of 90 or higher were deemed acceptable.

All but one subscale (Comprehensible Input; alpha = 0.8727) achieved this a priori level of acceptance. The other subscales ranged from 0.9589 (Preparation) to 0.9138 (Lesson Delivery). A principle component analysis (PCA) with varimax rotation was then performed on the 31 items to assess the instrument's discriminate validity among the subscales. Three factors were extracted accounting for 98.4 percent of the variance as indicated by the eigenvalues of the factors that accounted for variances greater than 1.

A discriminant functional analysis (DFA) using the eight subscales as predictors of membership in two groups (performing or nonperforming SI) was used to measure the instrument's concurrent validity (the Principal Investigator's assessment of the videotapes). One discriminant function was calculated, with a chi-square $(17) = 24.07, p < 0.01$. The univariate tests suggest that the best predictors for distinguishing between SI and non-SI educators are Preparation, Lesson Delivery, Comprehensible Input, Building Background, Strategies, Practice/Application, and Review/Evaluation. Only Interaction failed to discriminate between a SI and non-SI environment. The stability of the classification procedure was checked by a cross-validation run and there was an 81.25 percent correct classification rate. This indicates a high degree of consistency in the classification scheme.

The preliminary findings of the study on the psychometric properties of the SIOP® were that the SIOP® was confirmed to be a highly reliable and valid measure of SI. Further, the findings suggested that the instrument could be modified by attenuating the factor structure from 8 to 3, and Interaction failed to differentiate between SI and non-SI teachers. Based on these findings, we modified the SIOP® to a three-factor structure (Preparation, Instruction, Review/Evaluation) and modified the Interaction items to strengthen their distinction from nonsheltered instruction (e.g., eliminated the item, "Pronunciation and intonation easily understandable"). Further we changed the scoring to 5-point scale, using the range 0 to 4.

Guarino, A. J., Echevarria, J., Short, D., Schick, J. E., Forbes, S., & Rueda, R. (2001). The Sheltered Instruction Observation Protocol. *Journal of Research in Education, 11*, (1), 138–140.

---

[*]*Note:* This study used an earlier version of the SIOP®.

references

August, D., & Shanahan, T. (2006). *Developing literacy in second-language learners*. Mahwah, NJ: Erlbaum.

Bambino, D. (March 2002). Redesigning professional development: Critical friends. *Educational Leadership, 59* (6), pp. 25–27.

Borko, H. (2004). Professional development and teacher learning: Mapping the terrain. *Educational Researcher, 33* (8), 3–15.

Center for Applied Linguistics. (2006). *Academic literacy through sheltered instruction for secondary English language learners.* Phase 2, Year 2 Progress Report to the Rockefeller Foundation.

Costa, A.L., & Garmston, R.J. (2002). *Cognitive coaching: A foundation for renaissance schools.* 2nd ed. Norwood, MA: Christopher-Gordon.

Costa, A.L., & Garmston, R.J. (1994). *Cognitive coaching: A foundation for renaissance schools.* Norwood, MA: Christopher-Gordon.

Cushman, K. (May 1998). *How friends can be critical as schools make essential changes.* Oxon Hill, MD: Coalition of Essential Schools.

Duffy, G.G. (2004). Teachers who improve reading achievement: What research says about what they do and how to develop them. In D.S. Strickland & M.L. Kamil (Eds.), *Improving reaching achievement through professional development* (pp. 3–22) Norwood, MA: Christopher-Gordon.

Echevarria, J., Short, D., & Powers, K. (2006). School reform and standards-based education: An instructional model for English language learners. *Journal of Educational Research 99* (4), 195–211.

Echevarria, J., Vogt, M.E., & Short, D. (2008). *Making content comprehensible for English learners: The SIOP® Model (3rd ed.).* Boston: Allyn & Bacon.

Garet, M.S., Porter, A.C., Desimone, L., Binnan, B.F., & Yoon, K.S. (2001). What makes professional development effective? Results from a national sample of teachers. *American Educational Research Journal, 38,* 915–945.

Goldenberg, C. (2006). Improving achievement for English-learners: What research tells us, *Education Week,* July 26, 2006.

Goldenberg, C. (2004). *Successful school change.* New York: Teachers College Press.

Harris, T.L., & Hodges, R.E. (Eds.), (1995). *The literacy dictionary: The vocabulary of reading and writing.* Newark, DE: International Reading Association.

Hasbrouck, J., & Denton, C. (2005). *The reading coach: A how-to manual for success.* Longmont, CO: Sopris West.

Hawley, W.D., & Valli, L. (1999). The essentials of effective professional development: A new consensus. In L. Darling-Hammond & G. Sykes (Eds.), *Teaching as the learning profession* (pp. 127–150). San Francisco: Jossey-Bass.

Hiebert, J., & Stigler, J. (2000). A proposal for improving classroom teaching: Lessons from the TIMSS Video Study. *Elementary School Journal, 101* (1), 3–20.

Hillyard, L. (2007). Observing SIOP® teaching: The conferencing and observation cycle, part 2. In A. Sherris, T. Bauder, and L. Hillyard, *An insider's guide to SIOP® coaching* (pp. 49–57). Washington, DC: Center for Applied Linguistics.

International Reading Association. (2006). *Standards for middle and high school literacy coaches.* Newark, DE: IRA.

Joyce, B., & Showers, B. (1996). Staff development as a comprehensive service organization. *Journal of Staff Development,* 17, 2–6.

Klingner, J., Ahwee, S., Pilonieta, P. & Menendez, R. (2003). Barriers and facilitators in scaling up research-based practices. *Exceptional Children, 69,* 411–429.

Lewis, C. (2002). *Lesson study: A handbook of teacher-led instructional change.* Philadelphia, PA: Research for Better Schools.

Lindholm-Leary, K., & Borsato, G. (2006). Academic achievement. In F. Genesee, K. Lindholm-Leary, W. Saunders, D. Christian, *Educating English language learners: A synthesis of research evidence* (pp. 176–222). New York: Cambridge University Press.

National Commission on Teaching and America's Future (NCTAF). (1996). *What matters most: Teaching for America's future.* New York: Columbia University, Teachers College.

National Institute of Child Health and Human Development. (2000). *Report of the National Reading Panel. Teaching children to read: An evidence-based assessment of the scientific research literature on reading and its implications for reading instruction* (NIH Publication No. 00-4769). Washington, DC: U.S. Government Printing Office.

National Staff Development Council. (2001). *NSDC standards for staff development.* Retrieved January 18, 2007, from www.nsdc.org/standards/index.cfm

Pacific Resources for Education and Learning. (2005). *A focus on professional development.* Honolulu, Hawaii: PREL.

Pajak, E. (2003). *Honoring diverse teaching styles: A guide for supervisors.* Alexandria, VA: Association for Supervision and Curriculum Development.

RAND Reading Study Group. (2002). *Reading for understanding: Toward an R&D program on reading comprehension.* Santa Monica, CA: RAND Corporation.

Short, D., & Bauder, T. (2006, May). *Research on SIOP® professional development: Year 1 findings.* Paper presented at the NJTESOL/BE Conference.

Short, D., & Echevarria, J. (1999). *The sheltered instruction observation protocol: A tool for teacher-researcher collaboration and professional development.* Educational Practice Report No. 3. Santa Cruz, CA & Washington, DC: CREDE.

Short, D., Vogt, M.E., & Echevarria, J. (2008). *The SIOP® Model for administrators.* Boston, MA: Pearson/Allyn & Bacon.

Stein, M., Smith, M., & Silver, E. (1999). The development of professional developers: Learning to assist teachers in new settings in new ways. *Harvard Educational Review, 69* (3), pp. 237–269.

Stigler, J., & Hiebert, J. (1999). *The teaching gap: Best ideas from the world's teachers for improving education in the classroom.* New York, NY: The Free Press.

Tharp, R., Estrada, P., Dalton, S., & Yamauchi, L. (2000). *Teaching transformed: Achieving excellence, fairness, inclusion and harmony.* Boulder, CO: Westview Press.

Toll, C.A. (2005). *The literacy coach's survival guide: Essential questions and practical answers.* Newark, DE: International Reading Association.

Vogt, M.E. (1989). *A study of the congruence between preservice teachers' and cooperating teachers' attitudes and practices toward high and low achievers.* Unpublished doctoral dissertation, University of California, Berkeley, CA.

Vogt, M.E., & Echevarria, J. (2008). *99 ideas and activities for teaching English learners with the SIOP® Model.* Boston: Allyn & Bacon.

Vogt, M.E., & Shearer, J. (2007). *Reading specialists and literacy coaches in the real world* (2nd ed.). Boston: Allyn & Bacon.

Weiner, C. (2001). *Preparing for success: Meeting the language and learning needs of young children from poverty homes.* Youngtown, AZ: ECL Publications.

index